MW00781394

A
NARRATIVE
OF
Colonel ETHAN ALLEN's
CAPTIVITY,

From the Time of his being taken by the Britiſh, near Montreal, on
the 25th Day of September, in the Year 1775, to the Time of his
Exchange, on the 6th Day of May, 1778:

CONTAINING,

His VOYAGES and TRAVELS,

With the moſt remarkable Occurrences reſpecting himſelf, and many
other Continental Priſoners of different Ranks and Characters,
which fell under his Obſervation, in the Courſe of the ſame;
particularly the Deſtruction of the Priſoners at New York, by
General Sir William Howe, in the Years 1776 and 1777.

Interſperſed with ſome POLITICAL OBSERVATIONS.

Written by himſelf, and now publiſhed for the Information of the
Curious in all Nations.—*Price Ten Paper Dollars.*

When God from Chaos gave this World TO BE,
Man then he form'd, and form'd him TO BE FREE.
American Independence, a Poem, by FRENEAU.

PHILADELPHIA:
PRINTED AND SOLD BY ROBERT BELL, IN THIRD STREET.
M, DCC, LXXIX.

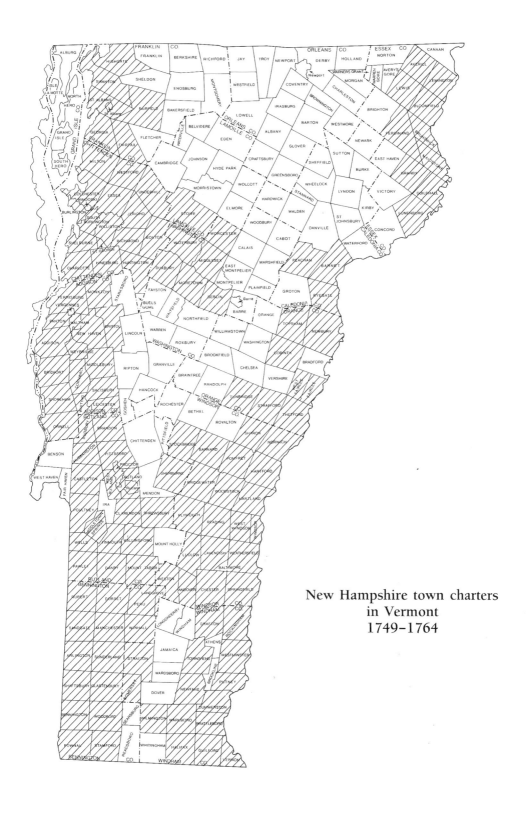

New Hampshire town charters
in Vermont
1749–1764

INVENTING
ETHAN ALLEN

INVENTING
ETHAN ALLEN

JOHN J. DUFFY AND
H. NICHOLAS MULLER III

University Press of New England
{ Hanover & London }

University Press of New England

www.upne.com

© 2014 University Press of New England

All rights reserved

Manufactured in the United States of America

Designed by Eric M. Brooks

Typeset in Monticello by Passumpsic Publishing

University Press of New England is a member of
the Green Press Initiative. The paper used in this book meets
their minimum requirement for recycled paper.

Endpapers: Title pages courtesy of Special Collections, Bailey Howe
Library, UVM. Maps courtesy of Kevin J. Graffagnino.

Frontispiece courtesy Fort Ticonderoga Museum.

Library of Congress Cataloging-in-Publication Data

Duffy, John J.

Inventing Ethan Allen / John J. Duffy and H. Nicholas Muller III.

pages   cm

Includes bibliographical references and index.

ISBN 978–1–61168–553–4 (cloth : alk. paper) —
ISBN 978–1–61168–554–1 (pbk. : alk. paper) —
ISBN 978–1–61168–555–8 (ebook)

1. Allen, Ethan, 1738–1789. 2. Soldiers — United States — Biography.
3. United States — History — Revolution, 1775–1783 — Biography. 4. Vermont —
History — Revolution, 1775–1783. I. Muller, H. Nicholas, III. II. Title.

E207.A4D84   2014

974.3'03092 — dc23   [B]   2013043807

5 4 3 2 1

Samuel B. Hand

{1931–2012}

Our dear friend and amiable colleague

Frequent co-author and co-editor

Dean of Vermont Historians

CONTENTS

ACKNOWLEDGMENTS

Around Christmas 2010 Nick Muller finished a rough draft of an article on Ethan Allen's death and the events that immediately followed. Earlier, writing a piece that appeared in *Vermont History* in 2007 asserting that no evidence points to Ethan Allen uttering what has become his famous "The gods of the hills are not the gods of the valleys," he had noticed anomalies, contradictions, and exaggerations surrounding Allen's death. His son, Brook, marked it up, and Nick sent the improved version to John Duffy for his opinion. They had previously co-authored several journal articles and a book. From his researching and assembling the Allen family correspondence that appeared in the two-volume *Ethan Allen and His Kin: Correspondence, 1772–1819* (1998), John had become the best sounding board for work on Allen. John responded quickly, suggesting the draft article should become a chapter in a larger exploration of the many questions surrounding Ethan Allen's life, the epic story that emerged, and the creation of a Vermont hero. John and Nick met in Plattsburgh, more or less conveniently between their respective residences in Isle La Motte, Vermont, and Essex, New York, discussed the project, and produced a chapter outline. That outline changed over time, sometimes in response to colleagues who read and commented on early drafts.

We have a deep gratitude to good people who in various ways nudged, helped, and encouraged the completion of this book. Many had become friends and colleagues of ours over the years as we thought and wrote about Vermont's history. Others who share our mutual interest we came to know in the course of writing this book. To all of them, we say, "thank you very much" for their help and encouragement.

Michael Sherman, editor of *Vermont History* and co-author of *Freedom and Unity*, helped sow the seed for the book over the past two decades by publishing our essays and reviews. Several of our colleagues who read the early drafts contributed to the improvements in the original chapter outline. J. Kevin Graffagnino, director of the William L. Clements Library at the University of Michigan, applied his sharp critical sense and red pen to improve the manuscript. His own research and publication provided answers for many questions about

Vermont's past. Ralph H. Orth, Marshall M. True, Connell Gallagher, and James R. LaForest read all or portions of the early drafts, made organizational suggestions, and proffered caveats, especially about retaining focus on the creation of an icon and not the debunking of a hero.

Other friends and colleagues brought their special knowledge to bear. Gregory Sanford, emeritus Vermont state archivist, and Paul Carnahan, librarian, Vermont Historical Society, helped us search for a spy who reported Allen's intentions to ally with the British to his spymaster in Quebec, a figure known only by the code name "Telemachus." A positive identification of "Telemachus" would have emphasized Allen's seriousness in the Haldimand Negotiations beyond his admirers' excuses about a separate peace with Britain. We did not locate it. Paul Carnahan also helped in other ways, providing photographic images to illustrate the text and rosters of early members of the Vermont Historical and Antiquarian Society. At Special Collections, Bailey-Howe Library, the University of Vermont, Jeff Marshall, Chris Burns, Prudence Doherty, Ingrid Bower, Nadia Smith, and Silvia Bugbee provided a welcoming environment for us, retrieving obscure manuscripts and suggesting additional documents we found useful. Special Collections at UVM also helped with the illustrations.

Others lent their particular expertise. Eugene A. Coyle of Oxford University shared his ardent research into the Irish aspects of the Crean Brush story, Ira Allen's international arms purchases and related political schemes, and Ethan Allen's Irish benefactors at Cobh Harbor in early 1776.

David Bennett of Ottawa, Ontario, and Montgomery, Vermont, pursued and shared with us his lively interest in Ethan Allen's Canadian connections. UVM Professor Harvey A. Whitfield opened his research and conveyed his insights into the place of slavery in early Vermont history. Former U.S. Attorney Gary Shattuck, Esq., shared his extensive research and knowledge of late eighteenth- and early nineteenth-century Vermont legal and court records in the Vermont State Archives.

We thank Mark Bushnell of the *Barre-Montpelier Times-Argus* and the *Rutland Herald* and Tim Johnson of the *Burlington Free Press* for their continuing interest in the story of Ethan Allen. Thank you as well to John Devino and The Ethan Allen Homestead Trust for an invitation to present a draft chapter of this book with a friendly and interested audience. Thanks also to the Vermont Genealogical Society for its invitation to present a draft chapter at their Annual Meeting in 2012.

We found many folks willing to assist in the issue of the look-alike versions of the Larkin Meade statue of Ethan Allen in the National Statuary Hall Collection in the U.S. Capitol. Ellen McCullough-Lovell, former director of the Vermont Arts Council and now president of Marlboro College, shared her interest in the statues of Ethan Allen and led us to others with similar interests, including David Schütz, curator of the Vermont State House. John Dumville, state historic sites operations chief, provided important information on the statue of Allen at the Vermont State House and guided us to staff at the Bennington Battle Monument for information about the statue of Seth Warner there. Tyler Resch at the Bennington Museum directed us to Richard B. Smith of the Manchester Historical Society for information about the look-alike Green Mountain Boy statue in Manchester and the history of that memorial. John Huling, Bennington photographer, musician, and seventh-generation Vermonter, provided photographs of the statues in Manchester and Bennington to compare with the Ethan Allen statue in the U.S. Capitol. Thank you all.

Gene Sessions, emeritus professor of history at Norwich University, and Danielle Rougeau in Special Collections, Middlebury College Library, researched the earliest Ph.D.s who taught American history at their institutions. Christopher Fox, Anthony D. Pell Curator of Collections at Fort Ticonderoga, made archival material available and assisted with the illustrations.

Thank you University Press of New England Director Michael Burton and Editor-in-Chief Phyllis Deutsch for accepting the manuscript and entering into production with alacrity. Their decision to intersperse the illustrations where they illustrate the text has pleased us greatly.

After roughly two years of writing the book and often paying attention to it rather than other matters, we wish to thank Carol Muller for patiently reading drafts, making comments, and cleaning up writing problems on material that did not especially enthrall her, and Barbara Duffy for her enduring patience with yet another book project.

We are grateful to the named institutions and individuals for their permission to publish in this book copies of images credited to their collections.

JJD & HNMIII

PROLOGUE

Ethan Allen, even after more than two centuries, remains the most remembered figure in Vermont's past as evidenced by the continuing and frequent use of his name and stylized image. No other Vermonter, not even Calvin Coolidge, has achieved such cachet in Vermont. How did he acquire and retain that iconic status? How does the memory of Ethan Allen coincide with the reality of his life as well as the much repeated supplemental legends and myths composed long after his death? How and why did those who lived after him shape and reshape memories of him? Why do recollections of him live on synonymously with the "story of Vermont" and the creation of an independent state, and why do they persist? Why do some Vermonters assign to Allen their own cherished and idealized values, and why do they think he continues to embody them?[1]

How did Allen achieve his rank as a military leader, when his formal experience amounted to only two weeks marching as a volunteer in a Connecticut militia unit and his capture of a crumbling, undermanned, and somnolent fort at Ticonderoga at the head of the "antient mobb," as he and brother Ira later called the eighty-three farmers who followed him? He led successful bloodless excursions against recalcitrant settlers in southeastern towns who refused to recognize Vermont. But he also committed calamitous blunders — in early June 1775 British regulars routed Allen at St. John and the fiasco before Montreal three months later resulted in his imprisonment. How did a man who seriously entertained allying Vermont with the British Empire in negotiations with Governor General Frederick Haldimand in Quebec become a hero of the American Revolution?

Memory demands a starting point, a platform, on which succeeding generations build and shape that memory or diminish it. What forms the platform that underlies recollections of Allen? What constitutes the clear facts retrievable from public and private records, scrubbed of the contrivances, myths, legends, and fictions that came to describe much of his life? Understanding the platform requires an exhibition of the facts, of course, but it also demands an examination of how Ethan Allen began constructing his own image by his actions and inventions, as if inviting the future to have its way with the basic persona he sought to create.

Divining that evolving process begins with the facts, often difficult to sort out when dealing with the famous. Understanding the past and the memory of Ethan Allen requires unraveling an intricate web of memories, myths, and history. The approach this book takes follows a well-trodden path from the eighteenth into the twenty-first century through textual and other representations of Allen, focusing on historical, biographical, autobiographical, fictional, and other accounts, as well as monuments produced to honor his memory. These recollections of Allen have often relied on fallible memories and selective or skewed evidence, but they have led to Allen's place today in Vermont's collective memory.

Maurice Halbachs introduced the concept of "collective memory" in 1925. He explained that functioning collective memory requires frameworks that "people living in society use to determine and retrieve their recollections."[2] A social frame is an implicit or explicit structure of shared concerns, values, experiences, and narratives. Individuals incorporate the family, the neighborhood, the peer group, the nation, and the culture into their identity by calling the group or collective "we." "The step from individual to collective memory does not afford an easy analogy," Aleida Assman and others have admitted.[3] Without the individual's neurological system, institutions and larger social groups, such as states, nations, governments, or business firms, do not "have" a memory and must "make" one with "such memorial signs as symbols or logos, texts, images, rites, ceremonies, places and monuments." Groups and institutions thus "construct" an identity from the contents of such a memory.[4]

Collective memory is mediated by the group or institution sorting out the relevant and useful from the nonuseful, nonconforming, or irrelevant memories found in material media and identifying those symbols and practices that will be grafted to the individual hearts and minds of the group. An effective implant depends on the effectiveness of public education (Assman calls it political pedagogy) and patriotic or ethnic fervor. Allen figured large in Vermont's school curricula by the 1870s.[5]

Many writers have been drawn to the story of Ethan Allen the hero by his own effective literary self-creation in *A Narrative of Colonel*

Ethan Allen's Captivity Containing His Voyages & Travels etc. . . . , in which he presented himself as a public servant of the common good acting without self-interested purposes, the version of him that prompted this study.[6] Yet soon after his death in 1789 and into the 1830s, despite the best efforts of his brother Ira to enhance the record of his heroic contribution to the welfare of Vermont and the early American republic, Ethan Allen occupied a somewhat shadowy place in public memory. The exigencies of time had their way with Allen and cleared the field for others to finish the work he began in his own lifetime with his captivity narrative, his own account of nearly three years as a British prisoner. By the 1840s, a half-century after his death, Allen had been transfigured in recollections and revisions of the past that recalled a hero who could serve contemporary ideological purposes in the mid-nineteenth century. Those later recollections have had their way with, and sometimes simply ignored or invented, the past. Those who wrote about the Vermont icon through the nineteenth and twentieth centuries turned the content of their recollections into mythology and then attempted to state that mythology as fact to support various purposes of a later time. The historian Patrick J. Geary reminded us not to ignore the purpose of remembering, for in a broad sense all memory is political, as it is "memory for something." Not always trustworthy, human memory gets shaped by a variety of factors that may alter the past. Even the best reputations can fall victim to time's erosion or rise in contrived memory.[7]

Barry Schwartz, who has examined the creation and fading of national memories of the American presidents George Washington and Abraham Lincoln, reported in 2001 that admiration for these two traditional heroes had significantly declined. Surveys of the public's evaluation of the three most popular presidents indicated that admiration for Washington had fallen from 47 percent in 1956 to 28 percent by 2001. Abraham Lincoln's prestige fell from 62 percent to 43 percent in the same period, and Franklin Roosevelt's ratings dropped from 64 to 25 percent.[8]

Despite declines in popular affection for national leaders, George Washington continues to hold a significant place in the American collective memory. Modern reprints of Parson Weems's 1800 *History of the Life and Death, Virtues and Exploits of General George Washington* still appeal to readers drawn to Weems's version of young George piously confessing, axe in hand beside a felled tree, to his father, "I cannot tell a lie Father, I cut down the cherry tree." Weems's version of a truthful young Washington continues to appear on informational websites to assist children celebrating Presidents' Day, though usually noting that young Washington's confession is a legend. Professional historians have debunked Weems's anecdote of the truthful Washington and the cherry tree, as well as Henry Brueckner's 1866 painting of the adult general praying for guidance in the snow at Valley Forge. Yet the painting remains an American favorite.

Readers continue to purchase professionally written, usually reliable popular biographies of Washington, John Adams, and other founding fathers, despite reports of declining admiration for George Washington, suggesting that many Americans still need political heroes and exemplars of ideal values. The historian Robin Einhorn recently remarked on an interesting aspect of a trend in ranking popular approval of presidents, observing that a long, well-written biography elevated John Adams, the second president of the United States and a difficult founding father to like at any time, to hero status.[9] The favorable reception of the historical biographer Ron Chernow's recent treatment of Washington's life, a book praised by both newspaper and academic reviewers, also marks such a trend.[10]

This book aims in part to debunk accounts of Ethan Allen that carry a strong tincture of Weems's work on Washington and to present him as an important, complex figure more in the manner of Chernow's Washington. This study plumbs the impetus and the reasons for the Weemsian portrait of Allen, and seeks to uncover the real Ethan Allen.

This study directly and indirectly explores the nature of history, recognizing that participants see events through their own lens and maintaining that they often deliberately attempt to shape the story. This book asserts that the narrative Ethan Allen wrote of his captivity and his introduction to his "philosophical tract," *Reason the Only Oracle of Man*, and Ira Allen's incomplete autobiography and history of Vermont unabashedly sought to present themselves as they wished others to regard them. The brothers distorted the record, as they deemed advantageous. Those who would write the history of the Allens and of Vermont came with their own vantage points, biases, and questions. It comes as no surprise that the authors who penned biographies of Ethan Allen with the subtitles such as *Frontier Rebel*, *A Hero of the Revolution*, or *The Robin Hood of Vermont* presented a Green Mountain leader who revolted against authority, took from the powerful and gave to the less fortunate, and played a leading role in achieving Vermont's and America's independence. Asking the question often dictates the answer.

Reverend Samuel Williams's pioneering history of Vermont asked the question of how in a new setting Vermont established a new polity. He portrayed the natural and civil conditions three years after it achieved statehood in 1791, and though possibly tainted by giving Ira Allen some editorial access to the text, Williams's book muted the importance of Ethan Allen, failing even to mention his death. Subsequent historians of Vermont generally followed Williams until the 1830s, when they posed different questions about Vermont's past. Circumstances in Vermont had changed, and in that uncertain environment they sought the presumed certainty of purpose of the state's founders in general and Ethan Allen in particular. They sculpted Allen into the heroic beacon that lighted the course of a defiant new state that achieved its own successful revolution within the larger Revolution. For a full half-century Allen's biographers and historians concerned with Vermont built on and embellished that theme to such an extent that it became accepted as reality. Even when professional historians posing a new set of questions brought the study of early Vermont into the context of the trends in American historiography, they did not find much traction.

Ethan Allen of Vermont, the "Hero of Ticonderoga," has continued to hold an unchallenged place in cultural memory into the twenty-first century for his role in seizing a British fort for the revolutionary cause in 1775. Biographers honored him among the second rank of heroes remembered for their roles in the American War for Independence. But his cachet in Vermont promotes him far beyond his meager military success. In Vermont, the public recalls no other figure from the state's formative years with more affection. They have largely forgotten most of the founding fathers. Some biographers insist that Allen was mainly responsible for the independence and founding of the Green Mountain State. Yet today many respondents to a survey seeking to assess his standing in national memory also might first think of Ethan Allen as the brand name for a global corporation that manufactures "American colonial-style" furniture. They may be rightly confused about the real Ethan Allen when they see his name on old milk bottles and shabby motels on a highway he never built or rode over, on a bowling alley or a Lake Champlain tour boat. Consumerism has enlisted and embraced Ethan Allen.

What forces cause memory to magnify lives and to create super-heroes? How do they serve a purpose in addressing the needs of later generations? The Ethan Allen whose stylized stone image in full military regalia graces the National Statuary Hall Collection in the U.S. Capitol and also stands atop a monument in a Burlington cemetery has become in Vermont, and beyond to a lesser extent, an easily recognized symbol. His contemporaries probably would not have recognized these representations, however, as no image of Allen created during his lifetime exists. But those in later generations, who never saw him, easily recognized graphic images of the victor at Ticonderoga in a Continental Army uniform he never wore, brandishing a sword at a hapless British officer. Both image and memory of Ethan Allen now serve as powerful correlatives of what these later generations regard as the best of Vermont values and actions. And Vermonters affix the created notion of his image and deeds on products and ideas they hope to imbue with traditional values. Long before the twentieth century Allen had come to represent what Vermonters wanted their founders to stand for and what they hoped to emulate. When in the 1920s historians began to question the reality of the stylized, romantic hero, despite the documentary evidence they presented, the larger-than-life Allen remained in the popular mind and ultimately emerged triumphant in the books of scholars in the late twentieth and early twenty-first centuries.

Many could ask today, who was Ethan Allen, what made him widely memorable, and why is the real Ethan Allen not easily remembered? The basic, verifiable facts of the story of Ethan Allen, not the myths, legends, or fictions, are retrievable from public and private records, a process made difficult because they are often incomplete and on occasion deliberately misleading. Reports of his demise in 1789 demonstrate the difficulty of following the confounded record of his death produced by his survivors' impulse at the time to embellish the facts. Some evidence suggests he had anticipated that event, but accounts of it from his contemporaries and later writers into the twenty-first century omit, ignore, and exaggerate the few facts surrounding Allen's death. The confusion over Allen's last days, beginning with the trip to cousin Ebenezer's in South Hero on February 11, 1789, provides a fitting context to begin exploring the events and meaning of his life and the ways in which two centuries of Vermonters have shaped his legacy.

We must therefor admit that if our souls have a future existence,
we must then have a consciousness, not only of our identity
or being, but also of our demeanour in this life.

{ ETHAN ALLEN, *Reason the Only Oracle of Man* }

CHAPTER I

CONFUSED ACCOUNTS OF ETHAN ALLEN'S DEATH

Later Accounts Compound the Story

The simple, if unexpected, and inevitable act of dying demonstrates a pattern that surrounds much of Ethan Allen's half-century of life. He could not attempt to give shape to the event and write his own account as he had with his capture of Fort Ticonderoga and his nearly three years in captivity. The accounts remained to others, often with their own purposes. The two remaining brothers of the six Allen boys, Ira at home looking after arrangements and the family business and Levi in England attempting to foster trade from Vermont through Canada, treated Ethan's passing with a surprising degree of restraint for a man who would become the symbol of Vermont. The few contemporary accounts contained inconsistencies. Ira's fuller account, written a few years after the fact, added even more confusion. As the subsequent years passed, the accounts began to gather the tales through which biographers and storytellers attempted to define a hero. When the most famous figure in Vermont left the temporal world, his reputation did not. The story of the death of Ethan Allen contains elements that make it difficult to describe his life, however important, with certainty.

"To all the Survivors of the Allen family. If any," Levi Allen addressed a letter on August 2, 1789, to his wife Nancy and his youngest brother Ira. Hurt, angry, and an ocean away in London, Levi complained bitterly about not receiving news of his brother Ethan's death. "The expense of a letter," he upbraided them, "would be one Shilling Stg." Though "the public papers announce the death of E____ A____," he had received "no confirmation" from them. He could not respond to "being asked every day whether my Brother is really dead" because the wrong answer would make him look "redicalous," harming his credibility and the tender business relationships he had courted in England. If "detected in a falsehood," he would have to admit he had "no official Acct.—which at once shews I have no letters to my Eternal disgrace." Petulantly, Levi declared to his wife and brother that since he must regard them as dead, he would not write again until he learned otherwise. After venting his spleen, he quickly turned to the business of expanding trade between Vermont and England and promoting a canal around the Richelieu River rapids that encumbered Champlain Valley traffic to the St. Lawrence River, to the merchants of Quebec, and across the Atlantic to England.[1]

Ira had in fact sent a perfunctory, emotionless account of Ethan's death to Levi on June 5. The letter, written from Ira's home in Colchester nearly four months after the event, must have taken some time to reach an Atlantic port, probably Quebec or Boston, and make the voyage to England. Levi never mentioned receiving it, but despite his threat he did resume writing letters to Nancy and to Ira. Like his brother, after relating the news about Ethan, Ira quickly reverted to business matters.[2] Ethan's brothers reacted to his death as a matter of fact without much apparent emotion, with no speculation on the future of his soul, and certainly not with the fanfare of the outlandish tales that punctuated the accounts of his demise by later biographers, historians, and novelists. Ira's 1798 *The Natural and Political History of the State of Vermont* neglects to mention Ethan's passing.

It had taken Ira nearly four months to get around to writing a short paragraph to Levi confirming their brother's death. Had Ira written in more detail, the many discrepancies in subsequent stories of Ethan's last hours might not have developed. Inconsistencies and lacunae plague the understanding of almost every facet of Ethan Allen's life, beginning with variations on the date of his birth. In the more than two centuries after his death, both fictional and scholarly interpretations of Allen display a changing array of accounts, suppositions, explications,

ETHAN ALLEN'S HOMESTEAD.
Ethan Allen retired from public life to this Burlington house, residing here
with his wife and children from 1787 to 1789. Restored and with much of its
surrounding woods and fields preserved, it serves to interpret frontier life in
early Vermont and Allen's retirement from public life. *Photograph by John J. Duffy.*

rationales, images, and conclusions. Contemporary accounts of Allen's
death exhibit the same irregular pattern.

DEATH RELINQUISHES THE STORY TO OTHERS

Ethan Allen died at his Burlington farm on the bank of the Winooski
River. On February 23, 1789, Anthony Haswell's *Vermont Gazette*, published in Bennington about 120 miles to the south, carried a front-
page notice of "the death of General ETHAN ALLEN, who expired in
an epileptic fit, on Tuesday last." That notice places the date of death
incorrectly on February 17. Ira, ascribing the cause of death to "a fit
of Arperplaxey," wrote from his home in Colchester to Levi that "on
the evening of the 11th of February [I] arrived at this Place after Part-

IRA ALLEN (1751–1814).
Ethan Allen's youngest brother and
business partner from 1773 to 1784,
Ira played a leading role in the founding of Vermont and the Haldimand
Negotiations. *Courtesy of Special Collections, Bailey Howe Library, UVM.*

ing with you . . . when I was surprised with the solemn news of the
Death of Genl Allen." This contradicts the assertion by Allen's most recent biographer that Ira and his wife Jerusha attended Ethan's death.
Ira's fragmented letter may have carelessly misstated the date of Allen's
death, but it does come close to confirming Thursday, February 12, as
the day on which Ethan Allen took his last breath. Other accounts variously place Allen's death on the thirteenth and, definitely in error, as
late as the sixteenth and seventeenth.[3]

Living on his farm with his young and pregnant wife Fanny, their
two children, and three daughters from his first marriage, Ethan had
no opportunity to discuss "Philosophy" and talked instead "of Bullocks, we glory in the gad. We mind Earthly things," he concluded.[4]
The poor growing seasons of 1787 and 1788 in northwestern Vermont
had created severe shortages of all grains. Traveling through Colchester, Burlington, and surrounding towns in the spring of 1789, Reverend Nathan Perkins noted, "The seasons have been for two years back
very unfavorable. A famine is now felt in this land." He went on to report, "it is supposed by ye most judicious & knowing that more than
1–4 part of ye people will have neither bread nor meat for 8 weeks — and
some will starve."[5] In March 1789 Governor Chittenden called a special
session of the Vermont Council, a body with members elected at-large
statewide to serve as an upper house of the legislature and informal

governor's cabinet, to meet in Fairhaven and consider measures to re-
lieve "the distressed situation of the inhabitants of the State for want of
Grain." The Council proposed "an Embargo be laid to prevent the Ex-
portation of wheat & other Bread corn."[6] On February 11, 1789, Allen
and his farmhand Newport, one of the three African Americans who
worked for him on the farm and in his house, set out for South Hero
over the ice to fetch a load of hay to feed his "Bullocks." His cousin and
distinguished Revolutionary War veteran Ebenezer Allen had plenty of
hay and invited Ethan to come to the island to get some.

The events of the night of February 11–12 at Ebenezer Allen's house
have become the stuff of legend. Cousin Ebenezer, a former Green
Mountain Boy who had taken part in the capture of Fort Ticonderoga
and later distinguished himself as a Vermont militia officer at the Battle of Bennington and other actions against the British, hosted local
men, many of them settlers on land in the Champlain islands they had
bought from Ethan, to visit with his famous cousin. Descriptions of the
evening vary—a quiet evening with Ethan and some friends; a convivial reunion of men drinking and sharing tales of fights against Yorkers
and the British; an improbably lurid event of the sort often attributed
to meetings of Hellfire Clubs in the eighteenth century. One highly
imaginative account claims the throng told stories through the night in
drunken outbursts of wild revelry. As if quoting from a house menu of
early American alcoholic drinks, rather than reporting an eyewitness
account, this version tells us they "guzzled nobly of punch, of flip, and
downed the inevitable stonewalls [a mixture of whiskey or rum and
cider]." The noble guzzlers had to "put Ethan to bed," and the drinking
continued until the inebriated "bottle men lay on the floor in front of
the big fireplace."[7] Others draped themselves "on the table, on benches.
Some actually found beds." Before daylight "the house was aroused by
a new roaring and thumping loud enough to raise the deepest drink-
ers," as Ethan prepared to leave with his sled loaded with hay.[8] Another
author claimed that the men gathered at Ebenezer's hearth, "tossing
the flowing bowl, reliving in these piping times the splendor of more
spacious years. None spoke oftener, laughed louder, drank deeper than
he who had been chief hero to those old adventures."[9] Some of the
accounts have Ethan "so drunk that he had to be loaded on the hay-
rack the following morning to return to Burlington."[10] For years Ethan

Allen had flaunted his garrulous and bibulous ways, sometimes even feigning drunkenness to gain an advantage over an opponent, and the reputation stayed with him in the descriptions of his last hours.[11] Allen himself employed the "flowing bowl" image in his *Narrative of Colonel Ethan Allen's Captivity Containing His Voyages & Travels etc. . . .* (1779) in a benevolent characterization of the drunken mob that descended on Ticonderoga the day after its capture and again on the first anniversary party at Bennington celebrating his release from British captivity. The "flowing bowl" promoted "rural felicity, sweetened with friendship, glowed in each countenance" as they drank "loyal healths."[12] A commonplace literary figure of seventeenth-century pastoral poetry, by the eighteenth century the flowing bowl image signified the theme of mutability, an appropriate coda for Ethan's personal tale of a captivity that ends in freedom.[13]

The *Burlington Free Press* in 1858 and again in 1943 reprinted a seventy-year-old recollection by another of Allen's farm laborers of what he learned from Newport, the black sled driver Allen's biographers described as a freed slave. According to this report, which could reflect a septuagenarian's failing memory, "The mulatto said that he [Ethan] was taken with a fit just as they entered the mouth of the Onion [Winooski] River. He said, 'It seems as if the trees are very thick here'—the last words he spoke. He then fell over back and struggled so the mulatto man had to hold him. He became still and remained so" until they arrived at the farm, where the driver carried Allen into the house in an "insensible state." The record remains silent on the duration of the ten-mile trip from South Hero to Allen's farm with a team of oxen pulling a sled load of hay, or at what time Newport carried Allen into the house. The *Burlington Free Press*'s twentieth-century writer filled in some blanks in the "eyewitness" account of Allen's death by reading the new widow's mind 154 years after the event. This account recalls without source Frances Allen running into another room, "supposing him [Ethan] intoxicated." Allen never regained consciousness, and after several bleedings he took his last breath on February 12. Ira and Fanny had the body removed to Ira's house upstream and across the Winooski River in Colchester, where they apparently planned the funeral service for February 16, 1789.[14]

Oddly, because they disclaim the authenticity of their tales, some biographers recall the "insensate" hero loudly defying Christianity in his final moments. In one a minister tells Ethan, "The angels are waiting for you General Allen," which provoked him out of a coma, and he angrily sat up and bellowed, "They are, are they? Well, Goddam 'em, let 'em wait."[15] Others tell a different story in which Allen finally recants his sinful life and his publication of his anticlerical *Reason the Only Oracle of Man*. Another depicts him requesting a "local minister" to provide "Communion with Christ." This tale, probably made up much later by those who wanted the Hero of Ticonderoga and the leader of the Green Mountain Boys to exemplify their own pious views, also has no factual basis. They are both impossible anecdotes, for Burlington had no church or minister in 1789. The earliest "settled" minister, a Congregationalist, came to Burlington in 1810. Before that "the privileges of public worship were but rarely enjoyed, even by the few who desired them, from the occasional itinerant missionaries and other transient preachers of various sorts." A Methodist clergyman first visited Burlington in 1799, and Baptists and Episcopal clergy did not come before the second quarter of the nineteenth century.[16] Reverend Nathan Perkins, during his 1789 travels, visited the local ministry in every town in which he found one. He mentions none in Burlington, Colchester, "Shelburn," or Jericho. He scornfully noted, "Colchester & Burlington all deists & proper heathen. About one quarter of ye inhabitants & almost all ye men of learning deists in ye State. People pay little regard to ye Sabbath, hunt & fish on that day frequently."[17] Another and probably firsthand account has Allen at home and "insensible until he died," despite repeated attempts to revive him by bleedings administered by Steven Law, a "tooth puller."[18] The *Vermont Gazette*'s death notice reported that he "expired in an epileptic fit." Most accounts accept Ira's diagnosis that his brother died of "Arpoplaxey" or "Arperplaxey," in modern terminology a stroke.[19]

THE HERO LAID TO UNCERTAIN REST

If Ethan Allen could not die without controversy, he also could not escape conflicting accounts of his funeral. Ira wrote to Levi that on February 16 their brother's "Remains was Interred with the Honors of War, his Military friends attended from Burlington & Parts adjacent."

Ira reported that "the Procession was truly solemn & numerous." The procession probably "Passed over Colchester-bridge . . . About sixty feet from ye ground on two high rocks on each bank, where all ye waters of ye onion river are compressed into a narrow space of 40 feet" to reach the cemetery in Burlington at the crest of a hill overlooking the river, "within the sound of its cascades."[20] The Winooski River was in sound and sight of the grave. In 1789 Burlington residents knew the cemetery as only "the burying yard." By 1873, when a statue of Ethan Allen was erected there, "the burying yard" had become known as Green Mount Cemetery. In the twenty-first century it is officially Greenmount Cemetery.[21]

In June 1795 Ira sent a sketch of Ethan's life to Reverend Samuel Williams, whose *Natural and Civil History of Vermont*, the first history of the state, had appeared the year before. Ira recalled Ethan's "Direction to me" that "in case I survived & attended his funeral not to have any Prayers or Sermons." The purpose of the sketch remains unclear, but in this version of the event the "Military & other friends attended his funeral from Different Parts of the State. The pallbearers included Govr. Chittenden Maj^r Genr. Enos [and] Maj^r. Gen^r. Safford." The throng attending the service consisted of a "Large Circle of his Acquantance."[22] At the time Roger Enos, Ira Allen's father-in-law, resided in Hartland across Vermont on the Connecticut River and Samuel Safford lived in Bennington far to the south. To reach Bennington the news of Allen's death had to travel 120 miles during the short days in the depth of a Vermont winter over difficult roads. Three months later Reverend Perkins described the few miles from Burlington to Shelburne as "wilderness on ye Lake Champlain — next to no rode — mud up to my horse's belly — roots thick as they could be."[23] If Samuel Safford came from Bennington to take part in the funeral and help carry the casket, he would have had less than 4 days to learn about Allen's death and the funeral plans and to travel 120 miles.

Ira Allen's 1795 letter to Reverend Samuel Williams probably provided the basis for one generally reliable biographer to assert, "Ethan's body was laid out in Ira's house, facing the river, in Colchester. A great company of people came from Bennington to see the face of their hero for the last time."[24] More recently, a biographer asserted that the entourage included ten thousand people, a number equal to one-eighth of the total Vermont population and one-fourth of everyone who then resided west of the Green Mountains. The military friends "from Burlington & Parts adjacent" had expanded into "a great company" that had traveled from Bennington. The account goes on to provide details of the procession led by Major Goodrich of Vergennes as marshal. "Muffled drums and the coffin with drawn swords laid across it" followed the marshal. With "fresh snow on the ground," but the sun shining, "once every minute, the Major gave the command to halt and a cannon was fired." At the gravesite "the coffin was opened" and "everyone present manifest a wish to render his burial honourable as his character had ever been respectable." After interment "six platoons" discharged three volleys with their muskets and the procession quick-stepped back to Ira's house.[25]

MIXED EULOGIES

The news of Allen's passing met a mixed reception. It did not always evoke the same mournful and laudatory sentiments of the loss of a friend and hero given in the descriptions of the funeral, many of which came well after the fact. The first printed account in Haswell's *Vermont Gazette* praised Allen's "patriotism and strong attachment which ever appeared uniform in the breast of this *Great Man* . . . worthy of his exalted character. The public," the notice continued, "have to lament the loss of a man who has rendered them great service, both in council and in arms." Tempering the encomiums, Haswell continued (without having seen them) to describe the family "deluged in tears for the loss of their best friend," tears tempered with "the consolation of being left with a handsome fortune." With Ethan Allen, the story would often turn on money.[26]

While friends lamented, others probably rejoiced. Jacob Bayley, a member of the Council, had once referred to Allen and his associates as "all of the Fiends of Hell Combined." He would not have wasted tears.[27] Nor did an anonymous critic reacting to *Reason* in crude verse mind Ethan's death. The first and last stanzas of doggerel reprinted from a Connecticut newspaper by the *Vermont Gazette* on August 14, 1786, panned Allen with biting humor:

> Allen escaped from British jails,
> His tusks broke by biting nails,
> Decend from Hyperborean skies,
> To tell the world, THE BIBLE LIES.
> Behold him more, ye staunch divines!
> His tall head busting through the pines;
> At front he seems like wall and brass,
> And brays tremendous like an ass,
> One hand is clenched to batter noses,
> While t'other scrawls 'gainst Paul and Moses.

Writing from England in *A Descriptive Sketch of the Present State of Vermont* (1797), John A. Graham, an educated Vermont lawyer hostile to Ethan and Ira Allen, remembered Ethan as "a man of extraordinary character," who "possessed great talents, but deficient in education." Despite his condescension, Graham lauded Allen as "an intrepid soldier, and an able General," as well as a man of "the strictest sense of honour, integrity, and uprightness." But Graham found nothing to redeem "*Allen's Theology*, or *Oracles of Reason*," a publication in which Allen had taken great pride. For the composition of this book, Allen apparently retrieved the bulk of a manuscript on Deism from the widow of his old mentor Thomas Young and added perhaps as much as the final third to produce a 477-page polemic with a title cribbed from seventeenth-century English Deist Charles Blount's *Oracles of Reason*. Graham concluded that Allen's "vanity defeated itself," for the tract "was so *repugnant to Reason* (the oracles of which he would fain have been thought to deliver), that few would so much as read a Work so gross and monstrous; and at the very outset it sunk into the oblivion and contempt it merited."[28]

Reason had more buoyancy than Graham thought, bouncing on the tortured waves stirred up by a rambling, verbose attack on orthodoxy rather than floating calmly on carefully argued and convincing philosophy or theology. New England's clergy certainly did not think it destined for oblivion, and they gave it more attention than its argument deserved. Allen had predicted "that the clergy, and their devotees, will proclaim war with me, in the name of the Lord."[29] With Allen now in no place to defend himself, they formed their own chorus of voices condemning him as one of the "Fiends of Hell." They saw his death as validating their own theology and as divine retribution for Allen's temerity in publishing the lengthy, muddled book. Reverend Perkins, visiting Ethan's gravesite three months after the interment, commented with a mixture of disgust and faintly disguised relish, that he "stopped & looked at his grave with a pious horror." Perkins labeled Allen "an awful Infidel, one of ye wickedest men ever walked this guilty globe."[30] In Newark, New Jersey, the Episcopal Reverend Uriah Ogden told his congregation that "Allen was an ignorant and profane Deist, who died with a mind replete with horror and despair." In New Haven on February 28, Yale College President Ezra Stiles, echoing the clerical talking points, noted in his diary, "Died in Vermont the profane and impious Deist Gen Ethan Allen . . . and in Hell he lifts up his eyes, being in Torments."[31]

Timothy Dwight, grandson of Congregational divine Jonathan Edwards and one of the Connecticut or Hartford Wits, succeeded Stiles as president of Yale in 1795. Religiously and politically conservative, Dwight began traveling each fall in the 1790s. He recorded his impressions, published posthumously in 1821–22 in four volumes as *Travels in New England and New York*. Traveling north through the Valley of Vermont from Bennington to Vergennes, Dwight commented on Ethan. He called Allen's conversation "voluble, blunt, coarse, and profane." Dwight considered Allen "a pigmy in the field of literary contention, demonstrated by Oracles of Reason." When Allen's book "came out, I read as much of it as I could summon patience to read. Decent nonsense may possibly amuse an idle hour, but brutal nonsense can only be read as an infliction of penal justice." Dwight in a later letter called Allen a "freak." He unsparingly reviewed *Reason*, probably having read more of it than he had let on. "The style was crude and vulgar, and the sentiments were coarser than the style. The arguments were flimsy and unmeaning, and the conclusions were fastened upon premises by mere force."[32] Yale, which in his teens Allen had hoped to attend, did not approve.

MONUMENTAL ERRORS

Well after the funeral the Allen family marked the grave with a marble slab inscribed "The Corporeal Part of Ethan Allen Rests beneath This Stone, the 12th day of Feb. 1789, Aged 50 Years. His spirit tried the Mercies of His God, in Whom Alone He believed and Strongly Trusted." At some time in the following decades Allen's corporeal remains ceased to lie under the marker. The historian Charles Jellison was amused by the biographer Stewart H. Holbrook's "entertainingly told" version of the wandering gravestone. Was the stone marker moved, or was it misplaced in that vague "sometime after the funeral," which could have been any number of years? Or was the first gravestone planted in the wrong place at the start? In 1849 Benson Lossing visited the site in preparation for his *Pictorial Field Book of the American Revolution Or Illustrations By Pen and Pencil, Of the History, Biography, Scenery, Relics, and Traditions of the War for Independence*, which published Lossing's rendering of the marble stone.[33]

Erection of a monument symbolizing the stature of a man who had decades after his passing emerged as a revered founding father and personification of the state waited until the middle of the nineteenth century. In 1855 the Vermont legislature appropriated $2,500 to mark Ethan's gravesite. The new monument would provide a more fitting tribute to the man many had come to regard as the central figure in the creation and maintenance of the State of Vermont. Three years later, the state erected a "column of granite, forty-two feet in height and four and a half feet in diameter at its base, with a pedestal six feet square in which are inserted four plates of white marble."[34] In the process of preparing to install the column, the monument committee failed to discover human remains at the site. Two elderly people then living in Essex, Henry Collins, age eighty-five, and Hilda Lawrence, age seventy-seven, claimed to have attended the funeral at the ages of fourteen and six. But they could not pinpoint the burial site, and agreed only that Allen rested near the site for the memorial. The missing body caused the monument committee to hedge the inscription on the west-facing plate of white marble to read, "Vermont to ETHAN ALLEN, born in Litchfield, Ct 10th Jan O.S. 1737, died in Burlington VT 12th Feb 1789 and buried *near* the site of this monument," but by employing the Julian calendar for his birth and the Gregorian calendar for his death, they also made him appear a year older than the first gravestone had recorded.

The absence of Allen's body set off a storm of claims about his actual burial site and speculative theories of the disappearance of the remains both spiritual and temporal. Ezra Stiles, Timothy Dwight, and Reverends Ogden and Perkins would no doubt have believed Allen's soul and corpse traveled to Hell in divine retribution for the heretical *Reason* and other blasphemies. Other rumors held that Allen believed in the transmigration of souls and that he had told friends that he expected to live on reincarnated as a white stallion.[35] Similar folkloric claims had him buried in Ira's barn, under his home beside the Winooski River, or in Bennington, Westminster, Arlington, Sunderland, or Windsor. A creative academic story had medical students exhume the general to provide a cadaver for dissection, though the first medical study in Burlington did not commence until more than a decade after his death, by which time the remains would have decayed beyond usefulness.[36]

Confusions surrounding Allen's burial continued into the mid-nineteenth century. The Vermont General Assembly in 1855 had also commissioned a statue of Allen as part of the new memorial. After interruptions by the Civil War and insufficient donations to a public subscription for funds, in 1873 the Boston sculptor Peter Stephenson produced a model from Larkin Mead's heroic statue of Allen then standing on the Vermont State House porch. Stephenson's version of the Allen statue was cut in Italy and mounted atop the granite column set at the gravesite fifteen years before. The dedication scheduled for the Fourth of July reignited some of the speculation about the whereabouts of Allen's remains. A crowd of four hundred heard the oratory of Lucius E. Chittenden, the grandson of Vermont's first governor Thomas Chittenden, transform and elevate Allen in the world from his immediate posthumous status as a hard-drinking farmer cursed by clergy to a model for inducing a new world order by spreading a Vermont version of life, liberty, and the pursuit of happiness across the globe.[37]

The issue of the *Vermont Gazette* that first announced Allen's death in 1789 inaugurated the use of the late general as a metaphor for Vermont in the same first-page column without graphic division to introduce a new topic. As if all of a piece with the death announcement, a fictional *"anecdote of an Old Gentleman belonging to the State of Vermont,"* told a hoary tale set appropriately for Ethan in a tavern. Enjoying the proprietor's spirits, a clever old Vermonter outwitted a pestering pack of young New York dandies by challenging their courage and endurance against him in a tooth extraction contest. Participants would submit to the total extraction of their teeth or pay £5 to the contestant who fully met that challenge. Playing his opening gambit, the old Vermonter surrendered his only tooth to the tooth puller. Well tricked by "one old veteran rake from Vermont," the sixteen dandies understood "they were outgeneraled and, rather than part with their teeth settled a truce with the old hero; paid him five pounds each; [and] paid the landlord his bill for the wine &c." Without prompting, the *Gazette*'s readers would understand the tale as an allegory of how Ethan Allen, a courageous and clever old Yankee, had played a central role in seeking and securing Vermont's future as an independent state against the pretensions of New York's pampered aristocrats. In a Dickensian interpretation of Allen's death as a "far better thing" than he had ever done before, one biographer asserts that Ethan Allen's passing helped smooth the path to Vermont statehood.[38]

Ethan Allen died in an undocumented manner, and the precise details remain uncertain to this day. The conversion of the memory of his life into a legend to explain and promote Vermont in Ethan's image gained strength with each passing generation, who employed it to buttress their own needs and visions. The late "gentleman" who died having surrendered his last tooth to defeat New York now belonged "to the State of Vermont." This exploration of the accounts of Allen's death and its immediate consequences foreshadows how his "future existence," how he will be remembered, will not necessarily rest on a reliable "consciousness" of his identity or his "demeanor in this life."

*Ethan Allen's education "furnished him with a mere
smattering of knowledge, but his mind was naturally haughty,
restless and enterprising."*

{ TIMOTHY DWIGHT, *Travels in New England and New York* }

CHAPTER II

SEEKING THE MAIN CHANCE

Limited Education, Failed Ventures, and the
Promise of the New Hampshire Grants

To characterize Ethan Allen's roots and origin as a preparation for his adult heroics, biographers have consistently mixed a bit of Frederick Jackson Turner's frontier theory of the ever-advancing edge of settlement with the legends of later settlers, like Daniel Boone, who packed up and headed out whenever they spied a new neighbor's chimney smoke on the horizon. In those versions of his upbringing, the Allen family's place in the westward movement of New England's population over their first hundred years reduces to this formula: "[they] raised families and moved. Four generations averaged ten children each and lived in eight different places. Restless, energetic, hopeful, they followed the frontier persistently." The large families and changing places of residence ring true for many eighteenth- and nineteenth-century emigrants to the American colonies of the British Empire and to Canada, Australia, and South Africa.[1]

At birth Ethan and his siblings became part of a large, extended family that had begun with Samuel Allen coming to Massachusetts from England in 1640 and moving west to Windsor, Connecticut, where he established a productive farm and built a large home. Each generation of his descendants would move to new lands and towns in the Connecticut River Valley and to the west. They generally prospered, earned respectable status, and lived in substantial homes. They counted a number of clergy among the clan, and some held civil offices at the town level. In 1740, three years after Ethan's birth, his parents left their farm in Litchfield, Connecticut, and moved ten miles west to a newly granted, unsettled tract in Cornwall. Ethan's father Joseph and his uncle Daniel laid out the road to the new town where Joseph served as the first town moderator. In 1742 only three residents of Cornwall owned a larger "rateable estate." Ethan came from solid middle-class stock.[2]

SETTLING FOR WEALTH

But Ethan Allen's biographers' explanation of his family's motives to move depends on a mythic metaphor in which the Allens spent their years "moving restlessly from here to there, as if drawn by some secret compulsion to a point just beyond the next horizon where the battle might be joined once more with the wilderness." A hint of Darwinian struggle adds some pathos to the story. More likely, families seeking to maintain their standard of living moved because of the ineluctable facts of the frontier economy of subsistence farming, soil exhaustion, and difficult access to markets, as well as the maintenance of necessarily large families to supply the required labor, rather than an innate impulse to tame new land. Also, as sons and daughters matured and married, they would have to seek new lands.

The thin and stony soil of farm acreage in the older settlements quickly wore out. Despite the long known importance of fertilization, "the supply of manure was often inadequate." Without enough manure "by the middle of the eighteenth century, much land, of only moderate fertility in the first place, particularly in areas distant from the shore and herring rivers [where seaweed and fish provided fertilizer], had been cropped." Ethan's father Joseph Allen owned eighteen cows, at least two of them probably milk cows for domestic consumption. Once calves were weaned, the oldest brood stock could be slaughtered to feed the family or driven to Albany or Hartford markets by an able son. Yearlings, market beef, and a few milk cows produced insufficient manure to improve crop yields. Soil depletion from cultivating wheat and corn combined with large families "posed a fundamental threat to family life" because of "too many sons and not enough land." Thus farmers and their sons "were anxious to find new land."[3]

Even with a life expectancy of less than fifty years for those who survived youth, the Allen men, like most of their neighbors, tended to delay marriage until they could provide for a family. To acquire new land to settle, start a family, and farm, their options were limited. Those without their own money might inherit the farm or house and care for their parents in return for possession of their property. With money and good credit they might buy a separate farm. Or they moved on to find cheap wild land. Men generally married between their mid-twenties and early thirties. Ethan wed at age twenty-four, two of his brothers married at twenty-two, another at twenty-five, and one at thirty-four. Zimri died unmarried at age twenty-seven. In 1750 an estate appraiser in Concord, Massachusetts, warned against dividing a family farm, as it would "make but one Settlement without Spoiling the Whole."[4] The Allens moved to find enough fertile land to protect and improve their status in life, not to satisfy a primordial urge to tame the wilderness.

In eighteenth-century New England the acquisition of land became a primary means not only to maintain family status by providing farms for the next generation, but also to improve a family's estate and advance its standing. The ascendancy of leading families often rested on owning land. By 1800 only 10 percent of a town's population owned 40 percent of the land and provided most of the civic leadership.[5] Earlier, colonial authorities often considered land acquisition a privilege of office to be taken in preferred locations for little if any cost. Others, for a small investment, joined informal associations of speculative investors to become investor-proprietors of newly chartered towns, mostly without intentions of settling it themselves.[6] In 1779, for example, Ethan Allen and Samuel Herrick, both with prominent military reputations in Vermont at the time, with 360 associated investors, including brother Ira and cousin Ebenezer Allen, petitioned and received from the State of Vermont a grant of the two largest islands in Lake Champlain, later named the Two Heroes, at a cost in fees of £10,000.[7] Very few of the grantees took up residence there; most of them sold their rights for negotiable bills of credit to pay off other debts. Ethan and Ira Allen increased their shares in the Two Heroes grant through buying rights from fellow proprietors. Land speculation by investor-proprietors and their agents (land salesmen known as "landjobbers," who could also be investors in the secondary land market) was a primary factor in the financial growth of eighteenth-century New England. Levi Allen made that point in a 1792 letter to John Simcoe, Upper Canada's first governor general, to support his petition for Crown grants to several townships. Addressing Simcoe with a view to improving his own land business, Levi observes on "Peopling a new Province" that "All extensive settlements in America, have been made by a set of successive enterprising men (known in America by the appalation of Landjobers)."[8] The functions of government could also be supported by the state selling land. During the Revolutionary War, for example, the newly independent states, including Vermont, levied no taxes, but supported government by confiscating and selling Loyalists' lands and property.

New Hampshire Governor John Wentworth, in the immortal argot of tulip bubbles, Florida swampland rushes, and the prospects for any issue of "bundled securitized investment instruments," offered for the usual fees a grant of land to a friend, promising that while "no revenue could be expected from the investment for ten years, there would be an annual increase in value to ten per cent of the cost." Overall Wentworth estimated a return of 15 percent on all expenditures in fifteen years beyond the "rising value of the land."[9] Ethan Allen and his brothers early on learned the methods of buying and selling from their father, who in 1753 had joined with other Connecticut men speculating in the Wyoming Valley lands of Pennsylvania. They became fluent in the dialect of the land business, fully understanding that opportunity lay in buying land "cheap as they can and selling dear."[10]

Ethan Allen's early formative years in Cornwall, as his father created a productive farm on newly settled land, survive only as clues in letters and documents prepared decades after the fact or event and almost always written for other purposes. They sometimes appear much later in biographies as general suppositions about creating a farm or in the early history of Cornwall, and often as tenuous interpolations based on few solid facts. Ira, thirteen years younger, who wrote the most about Ethan, did not observe much of his oldest brother's formative years.

Ethan Allen's brief formal education began when he was about sixteen years old. Displays of his argumentative skills might have signaled potential that would benefit from formal schooling, including a degree from Yale that would enhance his opportunities for financial and social advancement, so his father sent Ethan to Salisbury to "Prepare for

College" under the tutelage of a cousin, Reverend Jonathan Lee. A 1742 graduate of Yale, Lee was "an animated and popular preacher" who "exerted important influence in Connecticut churches." The religious cross currents that followed Jonathan Edwards's revivalism and stimulated the "Great Awakening" split the Congregational establishment into factions of "Old Lights" and "New Lights" over the older core doctrine of predetermined sanctification. New Light congregations required a dynamic preaching style. Lee subscribed to New Light views, delivering impassioned, extemporaneous sermons and insisting that salvation was more important than training.[11] Preparatory studies for Yale could have included introductions to selected classical Greek and Latin texts in English, certainly excerpts from Homer and Euclid, perhaps some Aristotle, Pindar, and Plato, and the Latin works of Juvenal, Cicero, and Virgil, all excerpts in English translations. But Lee's New Light affinity for experimental religion, as opposed to scholarship or training, would not assure a rigorous course of study. Nor would the abbreviated single term have allowed for in-depth study in any of those texts or subjects. Ethan's later political writing and harangues sometimes deploy misphrased quotations from the English Bible and also suggest a minimal familiarity with John Locke's theory of property rights and a few rhymed platitudes of the English poet Alexander Pope. By the 1770s he was fluent in the rhetorical commonplaces of New England's legal and political polemics. His college preparation lasted probably only six months under Reverend Lee, ending abruptly with Joseph Allen's death in April 1755. Later Ira recalled that "the Circumstances of the Family were such that he Proseed no further in his Studies."[12] Ethan returned to Cornwall as the eldest male of the Allen family with the responsibility of managing the farm. Though he did not have the advantages bestowed by a formal education like Thomas Jefferson and James Madison or his Vermont contemporaries Stephen R. Bradley, Isaac Tichenor, and Nathaniel Chipman, Allen grew up in a literate environment and his father apparently thought he had intellectual promise.

Ethan learned at the side of his father who "was of the Church of England," a dissenting position in Connecticut where Congregationalists and Presbyterians constituted the established church. As a youth Allen read at home from the Bible, and probably from Plutarch's *Lives*. He

most likely heard sermons constructed on biblical lessons. Throughout his life Allen sprinkled his personal correspondence with biblical
allusions; they also appear frequently in his published polemics, especially his anti–New York tracts during the land title disputes of the
early 1770s and later during efforts to gain the Continental Congress's
recognition of Vermont's independence. Biblical phrases and images in
Allen's arguments or threats did not persuade his opponents in New
York or their Yorker supporters in southeastern Vermont. When he
threatened to crush an insurgency of diehard Tories in Guilford in 1782
with death and devastation, his biblical reference probably had far less
persuasive effect than the Vermont militia force of one hundred armed
men he had led over the mountains to the Tory and Yorker stronghold.
He threatened to turn them loose on the town, unless the folks of Guilford swore an oath of loyalty to Vermont. They complied.

As a youth, Ethan Allen observed and learned the elements of wrestling a productive farm from previously uncultivated land. His father
probably taught him how to use a firearm and how to hunt, though he
claimed in a letter to Canadian Indian tribes that he had learned to hunt
and fight from Indians. In his *Autobiography*, his youngest brother Ira
provides accounts of Ethan's prowess as a hunter. His most recent biographer several times asserts Ethan's familiarity with the ways of the
woods and "skill at hunting" honed in particular by the Mohawk Indians.[13] Every account of Allen's early life implies or asserts that he
did not think life on the farm offered enough stimulation or opportunity for rising in provincial society. In August 1757 the nineteen-year-
old youth and head of household left the farm to his brothers' care and
joined seventy-two other men with Captain Lyman's company in Colonel Ebenezer Marsh's Litchfield County militia regiment to respond to
the French and Indian threat against Fort William Henry at the head
of Lake George. By the time the company reached the upper Hudson River, retreating British and provincial troops related the French
victory and subsequent massacre at the fort. The Litchfield regiment
turned around and returned to Connecticut. After two weeks in service
spent mostly marching and bivouacking, his only formal military experience, Ethan returned to his Cornwall farm.

In 1760 the Allens sold the family farm. Heman became a store-
keeper, but Ethan tried to find his fortune in a succession of somewhat

impetuous and speculative ventures in enterprises that had already seen better days. In 1761 he married Mary Brownson, and they lived in Salisbury near his brother Heman's store. The newly married Allen worked casting iron kettles for making potash in a partnership that dissolved into brawling dispute and litigation over sharing limited profits. Digging in an old played-out mine near Roxbury failed to produce silver. In 1765 Allen joined a second partnership with his wife's brothers Abraham and Israel Brownson in another extractive venture near Northampton, Massachusetts. Like his previous partnership, the lead mine, where he also hoped to find silver, proved unproductive. The partnership collapsed in a dispute over wages Allen expected, this time with animosity between him and his brothers-in-law. His brawling nature and sharp, profane tongue also caused local magistrates to warn him out of town.

Ethan and Mary moved to Sheffield, Massachusetts, in 1765, and that fall he made his first trek north into the Green Mountains in pursuit of his next commercial venture, hunting deer for their hides. Like the nearly exhausted lead mine, the New England deer herd had already begun its decline to near exhaustion.[14] Many of his Litchfield County neighbors and even a cousin, Remember Baker, had migrated there, as the land granted by the Province of New Hampshire was very inexpensive because of the dubious titles. For three winters Allen traveled into the New Hampshire Grants. He found the scenery pleasing, and he knew many of the settlers. The deer hide venture returned less than he expected, however, perhaps even less than mining for lead. But the demand for cheap land in the Grants, from both downcountry investors and speculators and migrating settlers from middle and southern New England and the Hudson River Valley offered Allen opportunities that he could not ignore. He gave up chasing deer to seek his fortune buying and selling land.

BUYING AND DEFENDING
THE NEW HAMPSHIRE GRANTS:
THE GREEN MOUNTAIN BOYS

Eighteen years after his father's death in 1757, Ethan Allen would become a prominent figure at an important early point in the northern theater of the American War for Independence from Britain. His initial education for war consisted of two weeks on a roughly 150-mile march into New York and back to Cornwall.[15] Later, from 1771 to 1775, he led agrarian insurgents among the New Hampshire Grants settlers in a campaign of terror, violence, and general harassment against settlers with conflicting New York titles, as well as New York surveyors and officers who sought to impose their provincial authority on the Grants. Without combat training or experience, Ethan Allen nonetheless joined the movement for American independence in 1775 by leading a mob of eighty-three men in a night attack on the British fort at Ticonderoga. The fort's twenty-three "serviceable" defenders asleep in the fort offered no opposition. Allen's overpowering four-to-one advantage gave him and his men an easy success on his first real military adventure.

Until the late 1760s, a simmering controversy over the legality of New Hampshire Governor Benning Wentworth's land grants in the territory west of the Connecticut River and north of Massachusetts had largely occupied the attention of colonial governors, other high-ranking officials, and their London agents. They articulated their arguments, claims, and counterclaims in letters and lengthy legal representations and petitions to the king, the Privy Council, the Board of Trade, and other authorities in London. An Order in Council in 1764 made it clear that New York owned and had governmental authority in the disputed territory, but it did not definitively resolve the issue of the validity of actions taken before 1764, including all of Wentworth's New Hampshire grants. Nor did it settle the titles of settlers already on the land and of those who continued to carve farms out of the territory and who argued that their plain act of occupying the land validated their titles.

Expanding the controversy from the provincial capitals in 1767, a group of Massachusetts's proprietors holding New Hampshire grants sent Samuel Robinson, a prominent Bennington settler and landowner, to London to present their case. The rhetoric of Robinson's appeal to the Crown, though unsuccessful, represented his associates as struggling settlers working to secure a living on farms in the face of unjust and rapacious New York authority and landjobbers. Robinson's presentation to the Crown failed to mention nonresident speculative investors with large interests in the New Hampshire Grants or his own and other settlers' substantial investments in land speculation, a rhetorical and counterfactual omission Ethan Allen later employed in his pamphlet war with New York. Robinson managed to enlist the aid of Connecticut's London agent to secure an Order in Council from the Board of Trade in July 1767 that sternly warned New York to cease issuing grants in the disputed territory and to stop vexing settlers.[16]

New York's forbearance lasted about two years. Then, in the face of continuing settlement based on New Hampshire titles and the lure of self-enrichment, the New York authorities resumed making grants. Between 1767 and 1771 people streaming north into the New Hampshire Grants began settlement of twelve new towns. In the entire area that became Vermont, the population increased in those 4 years by 95 percent, from 3,926 to 7,664, with 2,888 living on the west side of the Green Mountains.[17] New York speculators and provincial government, by 1771 the hated Yorkers, thought they had to act before the growth limited their options. They interpreted the 1767 Order in Council as applying only to the governor at the time of the order. Succeeding New York governors issued grants and proclaimed their colony's authority.

The controversy heated to a boil in 1769 when a group of Bennington settlers threatened a New York surveying team and drove them back to Albany. New York titleholders responded by suing for writs of eviction in the New York Supreme Court against nine settlers in Bennington and Shaftsbury. A group of Connecticut investors recognized the suit as a test case that threatened their investments in New Hampshire land titles. They held several meetings to organize a defense in Sharon and Canaan, Connecticut, familiar country to Ethan Allen, who by then had also begun speculating in unimproved land. The investors hired Allen as their agent, and he went to Portsmouth, New Hampshire, to collect documents in support of their claims. He met with Governor John Wentworth and, apparently confident of New Hampshire titleholders prevailing, during the trip purchased additional New Hampshire titles for tracts in Poultney and Castleton. From Portsmouth he traveled to New Haven and engaged Jared Ingersoll, a leading Connecticut attorney and the colony's former London agent, to assist with the defense.[18] Together Ingersoll and Allen traveled to Albany for the trials. In Albany they also engaged local counsel.[19] The New York court heard the Ejectment Trials on June 28, 1770. Attorney General John Tabor

JAMES DUANE.
Grandson of an Irish immigrant
and raised in the powerful Livingston family, Duane became a successful New York lawyer with extensive
landholdings west of Albany and in
the disputed New Hampshire Grants.
James Duane represented New York
in the Continental Congress from
1774 to 1784 and was the first post-
Independence mayor of New York
City and the first judge of the Fed-
eral District Court in New York.
Source: Katharine B. Baxter, A Godchild
of George Washington, p. 63.

Kempe and James Duane represented the New York claimants. Both
owned considerable holdings in the disputed territory. Two of the pre-
siding judges, including Duane's brother-in-law Robert Livingston,
also held New York titles to significant acreage in the contested land.
Duane owned large tracts of New York grants, some of them conflicting with New Hampshire grants, and thus had a great deal of interest in the outcome of the trials.[20] By affirming the validity of a New
York title that antedated the New Hampshire title, the court set aside
the first case. It then found for the New York titleholders in the following cases by summarily pronouncing New Hampshire titles invalid
and inadmissible. Ingersoll declared his client's case "prejudged" and
went back to Connecticut. The court decided every case in favor of
the Yorker plaintiffs. Ethan, according to Ira Allen's account published
twenty-eight years after the fact, retired to a tavern where Duane and
Kempe and another associate sought him out. They threatened force
against the New Hampshire settlers and offered Allen and "other men
of influence on the New Hampshire Grants, some large tracts of land to
secure peace and harmony." Some later versions of the meeting include
Duane and Kempe providing Allen with money and a horse. Their
threat, according to Ira, elicited Ethan's enigmatic retort, "The gods of
the valleys are not the gods of the hills." When the Yorkers asked for

clarification, Ethan told them that the meaning of the comment would become clear if they would accompany him to Bennington.[21]

According to Ira Allen's account of Ethan's experience in Albany and the meeting with his New York adversaries after the day in court, Ethan's return to Bennington and report of the proceedings in New York prompted the immediate formation of the Green Mountain Boys. Many years later Jared Sparks, a well-known Harvard faculty member, and Zadock Thompson of Burlington, recognized as the authority on Vermont's history, published the account; they made Ira's account the standard version in Vermont historical lore.[22] Novelists and historians embellished the story beginning in the mid-nineteenth century. In those later versions, Allen warned Kempe and Duane to regard the hills as different from the valleys, turned down their blandishments, and immediately left Albany. Back in Bennington, he made the case for resistance to New York at a meeting in Stephen Fay's Catamount Tavern presided over by Reverend Jedidiah Dewey. Much later still, in the twentieth century, academic and popular biographers related the incident in the Albany tavern in a variety of ways. One suggests that Allen posited an indefinite response to the bribe as a ploy to "offer a chance to keep the Yorkers guessing."[23] Another concluded that Ethan took the bribe and later lied about it.[24] The most recent biographer, who transposes Ira's sequence of "valleys" and "hills," states correctly that "no record of what Allen was thinking exists," but that he did accept some money and he "never gave it back." In this version Ira's account moves the sequence of events directly and without qualification from the Albany tavern to the Bennington meeting and the formation of the Green Mountain Boys with Ethan at its head.[25] Writing three years after the Ejectment Trials, Duane said that he and two associates met with Allen the morning after the trial, not the previous evening specified in Ira's account. According to Duane, Allen declared "he had been deceived, that he was now perfectly convinced of the right of New York, and that Governor Wentworth, who he censured with great Freedom and Bitterness, had been alone to blame." Allen lamented that "the people who claimed under New Hampshire, should continue under their delusion" without an "impartial Representation of the Merits of the Dispute." Allen "voluntarily undertook" to provide that representation to the New Hampshire claimants, and he "performed a journey to Bennington at the Expense of some of the New York Proprietors to advise his Friends to come to an immediate Agreement" with the Yorkers.

Duane initially thought that Allen had succeeded in this mission. Allen returned to Albany and related that at the meeting in the Catamount Tavern, Parson Dewey "advocated the Cause for New Hampshire, and he [Allen] for New York." Allen indicated "that everything would be Adjusted," and Duane found "no reason to Doubt, but that thus far he acted with Sincerity."[26] Biographers and others aver that Allen slyly twisted the meaning of "Adjusted" to allow Duane to interpret it as coming to a settlement with the New Hampshire claimants instead of the resistance by the Green Mountain Boys.[27] Allen himself never addressed the possibility of his wavering loyalty to New Hampshire titleholders. By his silence on the issue he retained control of his own narrative of the event. Much later, Allen's silence on this issue also helped generations of Vermonters in constructing a hero, as they chose to ignore the real possibility of Allen striking a bargain with Duane.

Duane, a shifty lawyer known as "Swivel Eyes" by his opponents and who could distort truth as proficiently as Allen, might nevertheless have related an accurate account. On February 27, 1771, Ebenezer Cole, who had settled in Shaftsbury in 1764 and who attended the Ejectment Trials in Albany, discussed them and their aftermath in a sworn deposition. Cole recalled "that many of the claimants under New Hampshire in consequence of these Trials proposed settling their Dispute with the New York Proprietors." Echoing Duane's account, he swore that "Many of the leading People" holding New Hampshire titles "went to some of the Proprietors under New York, then in Albany, owned their [Yorkers] title to be good, confessed their moderation, and declared they could only blame the Government of New Hampshire" for the problem. He thought only the delay in issuing "writs of possession" changed their minds and as a result "they had confederated to support each other by Force of Arms."[28] Another deponent from Shaftsbury, John Munro, a Yorker justice of the peace, swore that for some time after the trials "he found the claimants under New Hampshire in his neighborhood fond of coming to a settlement" with the Yorkers, but after "repeated encouragements" from Governor Wentworth of New Hampshire "to hold their Lands [titles]" until they were "defeated in England" by the

Crown, they had mounted opposition to New York authority.[29] The settlers on the Grants hoped for relief from England that never came.

Immediately after the trials and Allen's suggestion that he had "adjusted" the issue, the Yorkers worked to formulate a "Treaty" that would "defer" the consequences of the trials and establish reasonable terms for the defendants and others to come to an accommodation with New York. But the "People of Bennington were become deaf to Reason and Persuasion." Duane blamed the failure to reach an accommodation on the "fickle and enterprising" Allen, who had "changed his Sentiments, and once more professed himself a zealous Advocate for the New Hampshire Claims."[30]

By 1771 settlers had risen against New York's impositions in several west-side towns, gathered under the leadership of "captains" Seth Warner, Robert Cochran, and Remember Baker. After New York's governor threatened to drive them back into the Green Mountains and they called themselves the Green Mountain Boys, Ethan Allen stepped up to lead them all with a crude and mixed strategy designed to keep New York from invalidating New Hampshire titles in which Allen and others had staked their future. On the ground they would resist New York efforts to assert authority or make accommodations to New Hampshire titleholders. They would also mount a campaign of printed words to elevate the dispute to the philosophy of property and landholding and of public policy. Ready to muster on short notice, they would terrorize and drive off New York settlers and officials through rough tactics of threats with firearms, swords, clubs, and other weapons; burning houses and barns; hocking and killing livestock; destroying mills; random beatings; separating women and children from their men; and physical punishments handed out by hastily convened kangaroo courts. They would also use this approach to keep settlers on the Grants from seeking an accommodation with New York. Allen and the mob that followed him terrorized their Yorker neighbors as well as New York's agents with shouted threats, loud profanity, and defiant exclamations against the New York government. At the same time, Allen also produced a measured, well-articulated public discourse, frequently published in Connecticut and New Hampshire newspapers, with New York Governor Tryon. Allen argued the validity of the New Hampshire titles on legal and moral grounds, and he cast the dispute as pitting virtuous, hard-working yeoman settlers against rapacious, uncaring, authoritarian New York officials. His melodramatic recitation of the settlers' situation on the Grants depicted "Women lamenting over their Children, and they crying; Men pierced to the Heart with the most pungent Grief and Affection of them, and bitter Indignation at the approaching Tyrany of New York."[31] His polemic required Allen to remain silent on the Green Mountain Boys' terror campaign against the Yorker settlers that produced similar anguish and pain.

After the Ejectment Trials and the failure of the attempt to create an accommodation with the New Hampshire titleholders, the Yorkers quickly moved from a policy of accommodation to force. In late September 1770, three months after the trials, Albany County Sheriff Henry Ten Eyck and a surveying party backed by three hundred unarmed men arrived at James Breakenridge's farm on the Bennington-Shaftsbury border. A band of armed townsmen forced Ten Eyck and the posse back to New York. For the following four years, until the issues of the American rebellion against British authority moved from protest and violence to armed clashes, the Yorkers' attempts to stake their claim and begin settlements on the west side of the Green Mountains triggered violent reactions that kept the region in constant tumult.

In November 1770 Yorker authorities seized Silas Robinson, son of Samuel Robinson, a founder of Bennington who had died three years before on his mission in London to seek support for the New Hampshire claimants. They carried Silas off to jail in Albany. A few weeks later they seized Moses Robinson, Silas's brother and a close associate of Ethan Allen. This time "A great Number of Persons settlers thereabout . . . with their Faces blacked, and otherwise being disguised," assaulted the Yorker posse and freed Robinson.[32] The Green Mountain Boys employed disguise on more than one occasion. Yorker settler Samuel Gardenier left his wife and children to confront about one hundred "Rioters," "some of whom disfigured with Black; others with wigs and Horse tails, and Women's caps and other Disguises, and armed with Guns, Swords, Pistols, and clubs." They burned his fences and haystacks, and "scattered and rolled it [hay] thro' the Mud and Filth about the field, and Flung" away the portion of the fence that they had not burned. Had he not fled, Gardenier thought he "would be gelded and whipped . . . and tied to a Tree with a Gag in his Mouth" and left to starve. Terrified, Gardenier and other victims of the Green Mountain Boys abandoned their farms.[33]

What New York deemed riotous behavior continued to escalate. When a Yorker deputy sheriff came to serve a writ of possession, Isaiah Carpenter, who had a verdict go against him at the Ejectment Trials, greeted him with two associates wielding guns, "one of them loaded with powder & Bullets, and the other with Powder and kidney beans," and the threat "to blow out the brains of any person who should attempt to take possession." Allen's violent mixture of profanity and quick fists first displayed in business disputes at Salisbury and Northampton in the mid-1760s burst forth again in January 1772 against Benjamin Buck, who "called at the House of Capt Stephen Fay in Bennington Tavern keeper for some refreshment for himself and Horse." Buck stumbled into a meeting that included Samuel Robinson, "Ethan Allen," and "Robert Cockrun" as they considered a proclamation from the governor of New York they thought James Duane had drafted. They asked Buck what he thought of the New York position. When Buck allowed that he thought it would prevail, Allen approached him from the rear, struck him three times, and "said you are a Damn Bastard" of Yorker Justice of the Peace Munro. Allen then snarled that "we shall make hell of His House [Munro's] and [in] turn burn him in it, and every son of a bitch that will take his part." Allen went on to mock New York's capacity to assert its authority. "If they shall ever come [into the Grants] again, we shall Drive them two hundred miles and send them to hell." After reading the governor's name on the proclamation, Allen added, "So your name is Tryon, tri on and be Damn he shall have his match if he comes here."[34] In a deposition sworn a day later than Buck's, Jonathan Wheate recalled that one of Allen's associates declared the proclamation "a Damn thing" that "the Governor may stick it in his ARS."[35]

As the story of the Green Mountain Boys' resistance to the Yorkers and Ethan Allen's physical prowess became legend in its telling and retelling, he became the "Robin Hood of Vermont," for whom "the use of violence was relatively rare, and when it did occur, was with fists, whips and clubs, rather than more lethal weapons." In the conflict with Yorkers "he neither killed nor seriously injured anyone. . . . It is no mean tribute to his leadership that for several years when tempers ran high Ethan and his small contingent of farmer-soldiers managed to frustrate Yorkers' designs upon the Grants without firing a single shot at anyone. For the most part he relied on bluster, and he blustered exceedingly well."[36]

While leading the "antient mobb," Ethan continued to buy and sell land and invest more heavily in New Hampshire titles to land on the Grants. In 1772, he, his brothers Ira and Heman, and cousin Remember Baker established the Onion River Land Company, a venture to organize their growing business of buying and selling New Hampshire titles to vast tracts in the Winooski River Valley. With his fortune tied to establishing the validity of New Hampshire titles, Allen could give no quarter to New York nor allow any others to pursue it. But his continued rants against leading Yorkers did not prevent his dealing with them. After the Ejectment Trials, he managed civil discourse with Kempe and Duane. Until Tryon declared him an outlaw in 1772, Allen visited Philip Skene, a retired army officer with extensive landholdings who had developed an estate of nearly 30,000 acres with a large stone manor house and docks and boats at the head of navigation on Lake Champlain. Skene's more than two hundred tenants and a group of slaves he had bought in the West Indies grew crops and operated mines and mills. A New York justice of the peace, Skene warned Allen that he should leave the Grants to avoid arrest. Allen responded with a letter at once defiant and obsequious. He brazenly said he would not quit the Grants, as "they are Not Allowed to hang any man before they ketched him." But in the same letter, Allen thanked Skene for "Your Generous & Sotiable Treatment to me when at Your house." He continued, "Tho Your Station in Life is Honourable and Commands Submition from Those of Inferior rank, Yet it is Your Personal Merit that Demands Esteam. Ever Since my Small Acquaintance with You I have Retained the Most honourable Sentiments Toward You." Allen asked forbearance for his "Disorderly and Riotous" ways as "the law of Self preservation Urges me to Defend my Property." Allen, who apparently aspired to Skene's status along with his friendship, confessed that he never "had ground to Distrust Your friendship . . . I Do Not Esteam You Merely Because You are Colo Scane but Because You act the Honourable part of a man [who] is Either famous or Infamous in Proportion as Either Brave or Mean." Allen hoped that Skene would not hold his defiance of New York against him. After discussions with Allen,

Amos Bird of Castleton, and several other New Hampshire Grants settlers, Skene left New York for England in 1773 seeking a Crown grant
and governorship of a new province carved out of the vast mountainous
region of New York. It would encompass the New Hampshire Grants,
extending north to the Quebec line, west almost to Lake Ontario, and
south toward a south boundary on the Mohawk River.[37]

About the same time Governor Tryon published a letter in the *Connecticut Courant* that tendered free passage to New York with "full Security and Protection" to any, other than Allen and the other leaders
of the mob, to lay their case before New York authorities. "With the
Concurrence and Advice of his Majesty's Council," Tryon offered the
opportunity to discuss ways to come to an accommodation. A group
in Bennington responded by denouncing the activities of the Green
Mountain Boys and accepting Tryon's offer of a truce. In response,
Allen and the Green Mountain Boys took actions that made it impossible for Tryon to treat with the New Hampshire claimants.[38] From this
time until the American Revolution eclipsed their resistance to New
York, the Green Mountain Boys accelerated their activities, becoming
more brazenly destructive to property and more threatening to anyone
they thought supported the Yorker cause.

Perhaps the most notorious of the Green Mountain Boys' depredations smashed Tryon's proffered truce when they destroyed the settlement that Colonel John Reid had begun on his military patent along
Otter Creek. Reid had imported Scots settlers; erected a mill, houses,
and barns; and purchased "Milch Cows" and other provisions for his
tenants. The tenants had produced "Indian Corn, Wheat and garden
Stuff" along with hay when Allen and Baker and about one hundred
men showed up armed with "Guns, swords, and Pistols." They destroyed the gristmill and burned five houses, two "Corn Shades," and
hay. Their horses trampled the crops still in the fields. The "Ring-
leader" announced "his name was ETHAN ALLEN Captain of the Mob
and his authority was his arms pointing to his Gun, that he and his
Companions were a Lawless Mob, there Law being Mob Law." He
threatened "that if any of Colo Reids settlers offr'd hereafter to Build
any house & keep possession, the Green Mountain Boys as they called
themselves they would burn their houses and whip them to the Bargain." Baker raised his hand, displaying "where his Thumb had been

cut off" when Yorkers led by Justice Munro had attacked him and his family in a failed attempt to whisk him to jail in Albany, and called it his "Commission."[39] The deadly antics laced with "the most opprobrious language"; beatings with a gun, a bullwhip, or a beech limb; and property destruction continued. Allen invented a "*Judgement Seat*" from which "Ethan Allen and Seth Warner, Remember Baker and Robert Cochran" harangued the "Mobb" and passed judgments as a mock court on the Yorkers and their government.[40]

Contrary to later traditions, the mob did not always spare women and children. Many victims of their activities complained that their wives and children suffered from the loss of clothing, food, and shelter and that the Green Mountain Boys left them with no place to go. Late in 1773, a gang used an axe to "split down the outward door . . . and also the door of the Room" where Anna Button lay in her bed. "With many curses" they insisted on knowing where her husband had gone. They threatened to reduce the house to ashes before they left, and "they searched the House with Fire brands" made "with parts of the doors . . . which they carried about burning for Tapers."[41]

The cumulative outrage provoked by these activities drove New York Governor William Tryon, who came to New York with a reputation for severity toward any who challenged his authority, to issue a proclamation in March 1774 based on a new law he had promoted and the General Assembly adopted. The New York law, effectively a riot act written by Assemblyman Crean Brush from New York's recently established Cumberland County east of the Green Mountains, declared a felony any gathering of three or more "riotously and tumultuously assembled" in Albany and Charlotte Counties, the affected area of the Grants. Officers of the law could kill a rioter in the act of apprehension without penalty. The law also convicted the Bennington rioters without a trial. Tryon proclaimed Allen and his outlaw associates guilty, putting a price on their heads of £100 for Allen and Baker and £50 for the others. He hoped that cutting off the head of the snake would kill it. At the same time he also sought help and renewed his plea for British military support to employ force to quiet the Grants.[42]

When news of New York's action, dubbed "The Bloody Law," reached him in Bennington, Allen immediately responded with a letter addressed to the people on the Grants. He promised that the Green

Mountain Boys would defend themselves, and they would "inflict *immediate death*" on anyone who tried to capture them. He then turned the letter into a firm defense of the New Hampshire claimants based on "the nature and energy of the *English* constitution," asserting that their "bitter and merciless enemies, who, to obtain our property, have inhumanly, barbarously, and maliciously, under the specious and hypocritical pretence of legal authority, and veneration for order and government, laid a snare to our lives."[43]

While the Allen-led mob wrought mayhem on the Grants, Ethan began to compile a long defense of his activities and the merits of the New Hampshire titles. Published in 1774 at Hartford, Connecticut, as *A Brief Narrative*, Allen's work exhibited a persona quite different from the loud, profane, marauding ruffian who led his mob to scorch the Grants. Even his Bennington neighbors, probably including Parson Dewey, had publicly decried the violence and "riotous, tumultuous and disorderly" behavior, including "firing on those People, and wounding innocent Women and Children" by the "Friends of Mr. Remember Baker." They wrote to curry Tryon's favor, but they also reflected their own growing impatience with the constant disruption of their community.[44] Tryon had also received petitions from settlers on the east side of the Green Mountains unhappy with the west-side tumult across the mountains and asking that he restore order.

Allen's *Brief Narrative* skillfully pieced together a collection of relevant documents, including an extract from Charles II's grant of the Province of New York and later British documents, the exchanges of correspondence between Governor Tryon and leaders of the Grants, and writings of the Green Mountain Boys — that is, Ethan Allen — "as they were published in sundry public News-Papers." Depositions relating to the dispute were interlaced with Allen's briskly argued defense of the Grants activities against New York. Point by point he countered the New York arguments based on the letter of the law in royal proclamations and orders, provincial law, and court decisions like the Ejectment Trials. Though he argued specifics and interpretations of law, Allen based his appeal on a higher law of natural rights. He "replaced Blackstone with Locke"; the latter's name he may have heard nearly two decades before from Reverend Lee and probably had explained to him later in his conversations with Thomas Young.[45] He also demonstrated considerable rhetorical skill in composing a powerful populist appeal.

As the Green Mountain Boys swore, scorched, and flogged their way across the western Grants, Allen had collected an archive of historical and legal information and had devoted hours at assembling his *Narrative*. The Allen brothers' archival bent, their proclivity to write and retain letters and documents, and their frequent use of the public press made them a major source of information about the Grants and the early years of Vermont. To an important extent that habit allowed the Allens a measure of control over the subsequent story of early Vermont.

Allen's arguments in his *Narrative* demonstrated reflection, a grasp of the issues, and an ability to write, and affected a reasonable composure that contrasted sharply with his actions in the field at the head of a mob of Green Mountain Boys. He made reference to the Bloody Law, other attempts to push settlers off of the Grants, and the earlier tenant riots in the patronial manors of the Hudson River Valley that many of the Green Mountain Boys had experienced personally as examples of New York malfeasant governance.[46] "By Legerdemain, Bribery, Deceptions of one Sort or other," he wrote, "they have extended their Domain and Fraud." New York encroached on New Hampshire, made "Tenants groan," and shed "innocent Blood."[47]

Instead, he argued, "LAWS and Society-compacts, were made to protect and secure the Subject in their peaceable Possessions and Properties, and not to subvert them. No Person or Community of Persons can be supposed to be under any particular Compact or Law, except it presupposeth, the Law will protect such Person or Community of Persons in his or their Properties." Otherwise, Allen continued, a person "would by Law be bound to be an accessory to his own Ruin and Destruction, which is inconsistant with the Law of Self-preservation, but this Law being natural as well as eternal, can never be abrogated by the Law of Men."[48]

Allen, like many British American colonials, knew the arguments and rhetoric that fueled the gathering American revolutionary movement. In the *Brief Narrative*, he professes loyalty to the British Crown, but invokes the precedence of a higher natural law that ought to constrain both the Crown and its New York agents. Those who suffered at the hands of tyrannical government had the right, indeed the moral imperative, to resist its impositions. Natural law justified defying New York by means well beyond rational legal argument. Historians Darlene Shapiro and Barbara Arneil have noted how Ethan Allen incorporated the framework of Locke's theory of property in his defense of the New Hampshire Grants settlers with a new twist on Locke's theory of government.[49] In Allen's argument, but not in Locke's theory, organized government is not the servant of the landholding proprietors in general, but specifically the laborers who work the soil and support the world of mankind; "the farmers [in reality] uphold the state." Allen thus added a strong populist strain to his defense of the Grants settlers, one strong enough to overshadow his simultaneous proprietary aggrandizing across the Grants.

Appearing as partisan advocate for the New Hampshire grantees in this dispute, Allen depended on the sanctions of natural law to protect their life, liberty, and property, but excused or brushed off as trivial the Green Mountain Boys' terror tactics to cleanse the region of Yorker grantees and hold allegiance of Grants' settlers. He is similarly silent on his own interests. His *Narrative* makes no allusion to his own expanding personal motives in establishing the validity of the titles in his and his partners' growing portfolio of tracts under New Hampshire title. In his *Narrative* Allen presents himself as a rational champion of the natural rights of the settlers on the Grants, a case hard to make for those like him who had speculated in New Hampshire titles during and after the dispute over their validity had begun. He had not been a farmer since 1761, when he sold the family farm in Cornwall.

Which Ethan Allen roamed the Grants perpetrating violent acts and at the same time filled the *Connecticut Courant* with reasoned political and philosophic arguments presented with brisk verve in language and a style that would appeal to the public he sought to influence? Which was the real Ethan Allen: the brawler, the backwoods philosopher, the polemicist, the publicist, the propagandist, the prevaricator, the man in dogged pursuit of a fortune as a self-serving landjobber (a scurrilous epitaph he reserved for Yorkers in the land business), or an aspiring and mannered gentleman? The evidence suggests that, driven by the pursuit of fortune and fame, he donned all of those guises individually or in combination as it suited him, selecting and changing them as he thought one or the other would help him seize the main chance.

I would Not for my Right arm act without or Contrary to Orders.

{ ETHAN ALLEN to Jonathan Trumbull, July 12, 1775,
The Great Adventure Against Ticonderoga }

CHAPTER III

CHASING FAME AND GLORY

Success at Ticonderoga, Blundering at
St. John, and Defeat at Montreal

On May 10, 1775, Ethan Allen, along with Benedict Arnold of Connecticut and James Easton and John Brown of Massachusetts, led a band of eighty-three New Hampshire Grants farmers as well as Connecticut and Massachusetts volunteers across Lake Champlain to seize control of the British fort at Ticonderoga on the western shore of Lake Champlain. They surprised the sleeping garrison by attacking at dawn's first light.

Allen recounted the raid and seizure of Ticonderoga in the opening pages of *A Narrative of Colonel Ethan Allen's Captivity Containing His Voyages & Travels etc. . . . .* (1779). The story of that victory in the earliest stages of the American War for Independence became the signal event for which he has been remembered. Like so many of the events in Ethan Allen's life, controversy, contradictions, and hard feelings attended the capture of Fort Ticonderoga. Recollections of other participants in the event have both supported and contradicted his version of seizing the decaying fort. Allen's account, written four years after the event in his *Narrative*, emphasized his tactical diligence in deploying a rear guard and blocking routes for possible alarms reaching the fort before him, as well as the presence of 230 Green Mountain Boys and others that messengers had alerted to gather on the lakeshore across from the old fort. He vaguely acknowledged a near-failure in logistics. "With utmost difficulty . . . I procured boats to cross the lake," but owing to the lack of foresight to gather sufficient boats, only eighty-three of the massed attackers were transported to the western shore.

Allen ratcheted up his narrative's dramatic tension in the final moments before the raiders entered the fort. Suggesting some uncertainty about a successful raid, he delivered an emboldening harangue (a speech reported only by Allen in his *Narrative*) to go forward with "a desperate attempt, (which none but the bravest of men dare undertake). I do not urge it on any contrary to his will." None of the other militia leaders who accompanied the attackers—John Brown, James Easton, and Benedict Arnold—reported Allen's oration.[1] Ticonderoga had seen heavy fighting during the French and Indian War and by 1775 it had become a ruined shell of its former self. A year earlier British army engineer Captain John Montresor, whose illegitimate daughter Frances would marry Ethan Allen in 1784, reported the useless conditions of Ticonderoga and Crown Point, recommending their demolition and replacement by a single new fort built at Crown Point.[2]

John Brown of Pittsfield, Massachusetts, went as a spy to Montreal and Ticonderoga during February 1775. Peleg Sunderland, one of Allen's subalterns in the Green Mountain Boys, served as his guide. Brown reported the fort's crumbling stone walls and a feeble garrison with few able men to repel attacks. Equally significant, he wrote to Samuel Adams in Boston that "the Fort at Tyconderoga must be seised as soon as possible should hostilities be committed by the Kings Troops. The people on N Hampshire Grants have ingaged to do this businees, and in my opinion they are the most proper Persons for this Jobb."[3] In March 1775 British Lieutenant Jocelyn Feltham had led a reinforcement of only twenty soldiers of the 26th Regiment from Montreal to Ticonderoga. Later in June, as a prisoner in Connecticut, he reported that on the night of the American attack, only twenty-three of thirty-five rank-and-file soldiers were deemed "serviceable"; the remainder were "old," "lame," or "worn out."[4] The eighty-three raiders outnumbered the twenty-three "serviceable" defenders almost four-to-one.

Allen's men aroused the sleeping British, disarmed them, and took control of the old fort, with gunfire limited to a musket misfire by a drowsy guard at the gate. Allen batted him on the head with the side of a cutlass or shortsword and proceeded into the parade ground and up the steps to the officer's quarters. Allen's "do or die" harangue fit for "the bravest of men" implied an equally brave leader, the very figure he displayed when Lieutenant Feltham, the fort's second officer, asked for Allen's authority to seize control of the fort. Allen wrote in his *Narrative* that he replied, "The Great Jehovah and the Continental Congress." Several other versions of Allen's reply to the British officer's demand have been attributed to him — "come out of there you damned old rat" or "come out you sons of British whores" — and they more realistically echo the scurrilous terror rages he shouted during his anti-Yorker attacks in the years leading up to Ticonderoga. The *Narrative*'s text, written in Bennington in 1779, exhibits the rhetorical balance of a calculated composition produced later than the actual event.

The Green Mountain Boys ran into the fort at dawn and quickly took control of the dumbfounded garrison. Later that morning, however, when they found the fort's rum supply, any military order still present quickly dissolved. In a few hours, the victorious Americans, accompanied by others who came to gawk or plunder, had degraded into an uncontrollable mob of four hundred more or less drunken men. Allen failed or simply neglected to control or remove any of the reveling mob from the fort. In his subsequent account of that first day possessing the fort, he lightly sketched an idyllic scene: the sun rising over "Ticonderoga and its dependencies smiled on its conquerors, who tossed about the flowing bowl, and wished success to Congress, and the liberty and freedom of America."[5]

Tossing the "flowing bowl" led to random gunfire, however, some of it celebrating the victory, while "friendly fire" warned off Benedict Arnold as he attempted to bring order to the wild scene. Arnold had a Massachusetts commission to seize Ticonderoga. When Arnold arrived on the Grants claiming command of the gathering force, however, Allen's men rejected him. Only after Allen invited Arnold to march into the fort by his side with James Easton and John Brown, who had also brought militia from Massachusetts, would Allen's followers move against the fort. As the mob's drunken antics turned to chaos by midday on May 10, Arnold demanded order and discipline, but Allen's men ignored him. His tolerance of the rum's effects on the mob led Arnold to demand that the command of Ticonderoga revert to him so he could disperse the mob and restore public, if not military, order. Allen refused and turned for support to Edward Mott, the Connecticut chairman of the so-called Committee of War that accompanied Allen to Ticonderoga. Mott immediately provided a postdated Connecticut commission for Allen's command authority.[6]

As undisputed commander of Ticonderoga between May 11 and June 9, Allen wrote post-victory reports and other communications to the Continental Congress and the new revolutionary governments of Connecticut, Massachusetts, and New York, assessing the effects of the raid on the old fort and proposing strategies for driving the British from Lake Champlain, reducing Montreal and Quebec, and capturing Canada. His tone affects the battle-hardened after-dinner confidence of a veteran strategist holding forth to subalterns over a tablecloth map he had finger-sketched in red wine. The letter on May 11 to Massachusetts gives credit to John Brown, James Easton, and "forty-six" Massachusetts volunteers for their roles at Ticonderoga. In a letter of the same date to New York's Committee of Safety, Allen only once notes Arnold's presence at his side when they entered the fort. Four years later, Allen's *Narrative* recounts the capture of Ticonderoga as the result of his leadership and the efforts of the Green Mountain Boys; he mentions no other participants.[7]

FIASCO AT ST. JOHN

On May 16, Arnold and twenty men of his Connecticut militia company took command of an armed schooner that Samuel Herrick and a small force had seized at Skenesboro. Renaming the vessel *Liberty*, they headed down the lake to the British outpost in St. John on the Sorel (Richelieu) River, seeking to capture the armed sloop moored there before the British could turn it against the Americans. Allen, still flushed with the glory of an unopposed victory, at first remained on land watching his chief competitor for fame and glory sail north far ahead of him in the only armed boat at Ticonderoga. Allen rashly reacted by launching an ill conceived and poorly executed sortie to Canada with volunteers in three row galleys to seize the same armed sloop that Arnold sought. The size of Allen's force has been variously reported from twenty to one hundred men; some accounts include Seth Warner, others give only a number without mentioning him.[8] Once again, muddled logistics marked Allen's leadership. He had earlier provided insufficient

BENEDICT ARNOLD.
Arnold joined Ethan Allen in the attack on Fort Ticonderoga, which Allen ignored in his reports, and shortly thereafter captured an armed British sloop in St. John. During the American invasion of Quebec he led a regiment from Boston across Maine to Quebec, where he was wounded in the attack that killed Richard Montgomery. He went on to play a critical role in the American victory at Saratoga before defecting to the British. *Fort Ticonderoga Museum.*

boats for the night attack on Ticonderoga. In spite of sufficient bateaux this time, he nonetheless failed to provide food and rum for the volunteers who accompanied him.

Two days after setting out and approaching the lake's outlet about eighty miles from Ticonderoga, Allen's party met Arnold and his raiders sailing back to Ticonderoga on the captured British boat with Skene's schooner in tow. Arnold's warning not to pursue his "mad scheme" and his report of two hundred regulars and Indians advancing on St. John failed to deter Allen. He led his men downstream until they collapsed with fatigue on the riverbank at dark, failing to post guards. At dawn British musketry and a field gun firing from across the river surprised and routed the Americans. In their hasty retreat they left three men behind. The British eventually captured one and two others had to find their own way back to Ticonderoga.

On his return to Ticonderoga, Allen told Noah Lee, commander at Skenesboro, that the Green Mountain Boys' gunfire "at 100 rodds," or 556 yards, dispersed the British regulars' firing line of muskets and grape shot, clearly improbable for firelocks with maximum effectiveness of about 60 to 70 yards. Grape shot from the British field gun, probably a 3-pounder "grasshopper," could be lethal up to 300 yards. The river's width between Île aux Noix and Fort St. John varies from 220 yards to more than 400 yards at Fort St. John. Still excited by his first engagement with a hostile force, an obviously confused Allen reported inaccurately to Noah Lee at Skenesboro that two of his men had been captured and none killed, though in fact he had left three behind. The remainder of the letter orders Lee to send all the men he can spare to Crown Point for a raid down the lake to seize the earthworks and buildings of the British post on Île aux Noix. Allen's second raid never took place. Almost four months later General Philip Schuyler led the Continental Congress's Northern Army invasion of Canada and in September established his headquarters at Île aux Noix.

Four years later in the *Narrative of Colonel Allen's Captivity*, Allen mentioned he met a successful Arnold entering the lake from the river, who invited Allen to dine with him on the captured British boat. Neither Arnold's warning him off his "mad scheme" nor the approaching British reinforcements appear in this later version. Closing the scene with Allen and Arnold exchanging after-dinner toasts to Congress, the next few paragraphs coolly resume with the confident tone of a victor discussing the tactical and strategic value of the Americans now controlling the lake. The debacle on the riverbank finds no place in the *Narrative*.[9]

FAILURE AT MONTREAL

In the weeks after the success of Ticonderoga, Allen effectively began to compose fragments of his personal story in reports he wrote from Ticonderoga to revolutionary councils in New York and Connecticut and to the Continental Congress in Philadelphia. With perfect bravado, his letters displayed his unbounded self-confidence as a military analyst and leader. In prophetical exhortations to the New York Congress, Allen echoed the prophet Isaiah. America, he predicted, "might rise on eagles' wings, and mount up to glory, freedom, and immortal honour, if she did but know and exert her strength. Fame is now hovering over her head." Prophetic enthusiasm charges his martial vision with a deadly wager: "I will lay my life on it, that with fifteen hundred men and a proper train of artillery, I will take Montreal." In the coming months, however, additional hindrances emerged in Allen's pursuit of fame and glory, including another engagement with the enemy that dissolved into a second graceless debacle and his capture before the walls of Montreal. When the moment for that vision's fulfillment appeared in late September, Allen was lucky to be taken alive by British regulars and Indians who once again rebuffed him and routed his feeble band.[10]

Still at Ticonderoga in June confidently expecting to lead the invasion of Canada, Allen appealed to the revolutionary New York Provincial Congress to support and endorse his command. Early in his June 2 letter to that body, Allen boldly affirmed New York's claim to jurisdiction on the New Hampshire Grants. Ostensibly seeking praise and approval for the Green Mountain Boys he led against Ticonderoga, he calls them "the subjects of your Government, viz: the *New Hampshire* settlers, [and they] are justly entitled to a large share" of praise, as they made up a large part of the attack. This was a cheeky gambit from an outlaw who still had a reward on his head in New York for violently opposing the previous royal government and only a year earlier had published a lengthy tract opposing New York authority on the Grants. He arrives at his conclusion and the real purpose in writing the New York Congress: "Lastly, with submission, I would propose to your Honours to raise a small regiment of *Rangers*, which I could easily do, and that mostly in the Counties of *Albany* and *Charlotte*, provided your Honours should think it expedient to grant commissions, and thus regulate and put the same under pay. Probably your Honours may think this an impertinent proposal; it is truly the first favour I ever asked of the Government [of New York], and if it be granted, I shall be zealously ambitious to conduct for the best good of my Country and the honour of the Government." No reply to Allen survives.

In late June the Continental Congress authorized an invasion of Quebec, and a month later Allen and Seth Warner convinced the Congress in Philadelphia to commission a Green Mountain regiment. The New York Provincial Congress agreed to pay for the troops as a unit of its own militia, a response perhaps partly based on Allen repeating his promise of June 2 to settle the land controversy after the war. But any reaction from New York's leaders to Allen's earlier promise to negotiate a settlement of the New Hampshire Grants controversy with New York — "an adjustment," he called it — remains unclear. James Duane and other large land owners, however, probably recalled with special

GENERAL RICHARD MONTGOMERY. A seasoned veteran of the British Army, Montgomery succeeded General Philip Schuyler to command the 1775 American invasion of Quebec, captured St. John and Montreal, and became the first general officer of the American army killed in battle at Quebec on New Year's eve 1775. *Courtesy of Special Collections, Bailey Howe Library, UVM.*

skepticism Allen's 1770 promise of an impending "Adjustment" satisfactory to New York after the Ejectment Trials invalidated New Hampshire titles. Within a year of that event Allen and "the Bennington mob" had begun to cleanse the New Hampshire Grants of New York titleholders and officials. And between 1772 and early 1775, with the Green Mountain Boys active in most of the towns on the west side of the Grants, Allen and his brothers in the Onion River Land Company aggressively bought and sold New Hampshire titles, acquiring more than 65,000 acres in the northwestern townships of the Grants by the summer of 1775.[11] Even a little imagination in New York could conjure up a reignited land title dispute after the war with Ethan Allen leading a "small regiment of *Rangers*": veteran Green Mountaineers, battle-hardened obstacles to a postwar resolution of the New Hampshire Grants dispute, "zealously" led by the famous and glorious Hero of Ticonderoga and subsequent victorious battles in the wider war they anticipated.[12]

Congress approved the invasion of Canada but appointed Philip Schuyler, a veteran of the French and Indian War and one of the Hudson Valley's great landholders, to organize and lead the Northern Army against the British in Canada. Schuyler's second-in-command, Richard Montgomery, a former officer of the British army, had also earned extensive combat experience with the 17th Regiment of Foot in the French and Indian War. He fought in Havana against the Spanish; against the French at Ticonderoga, Montreal, and Martinique; and against the Wyandots in Pontiac's War.[13]

Without a Continental commission, Allen nonetheless fully expected to command the new Green Mountain rangers in the expedition against Canada. Delegates from Committees of Safety "in the several Townships on the New Hampshire Grants West of the Range of Green Mountains" convened at Cephas Kent's public house in Dorset on July 27, 1775, to select officers for the new regiment. Allen's reputation for leading an armed mob to terrorize and cleanse the Grants of Yorker sheriffs and settlers and his bungled adventures as a military leader apparently earned him few votes at the Dorset convention. The drunken mob and chaos after taking Ticonderoga, as well as the subsequent debacle at St. John, further underlined his shortcomings in the business of war. Allen's overblown self-confidence in his capacity to lead, his ignorance of military tactics, and his pretentions to strategic expertise produced an overwhelming majority of votes by the delegates to elect Seth Warner lieutenant colonel of the regiment by a count of forty-one to five.[14]

Still seeking an opportunity to join the invasion of Canada, Allen condemned the "old farmers" who rejected him and offered his services to New York. General Schuyler overcame his reservations and found a place for Allen on his staff as a civilian observer. Allen later claimed in the *Narrative* that "the general requested me to attend them in the expedition; I had no commission from Congress, yet they engaged me, that I should be considered as an officer the same as though I had a commission; and should, as occasion might require, command certain detachments of the army." Knowing Allen's reputation for heedless enthusiasm, however, Schuyler first extracted his promise not to start his own personal war when the American army set off for Canada in August.[15] The Dorset convention had also ordered green woolen uniforms for the Green Mountain rangers from the commissary in Albany. Without a commission and troops to lead or a uniform to display his military intentions, Allen went to war in mufti dressed as a hunter *à la mode canadien.*[16]

Once in Canada, with the army at Île-aux-Noix in September, Schuyler sent Allen into the hostile countryside on a special mission with John Brown, the lawyer from Massachusetts who had gone as a spy to Montreal and Ticonderoga in March before joining Allen's raid on May 10. They carried Schuyler's proclamation soliciting Indian and other Canadian support to the Chambly lawyer James Livingston, a

Canadian-born relative of the New York Livingstons, who actively supported the American cause. Montgomery assumed command of the invasion army when rheumatism immobilized Schuyler. On his return to Montgomery's encampment outside St. John, Allen assisted in the excavation of siege trenches around the fort. Later in the month Montgomery dispatched him on a more dangerous mission closer to Montreal to collect new recruits and gather intelligence.

At this point in his life, Allen badly needed another success like the capture of Ticonderoga for fame and glory to lift him high again. His failure to control his followers' drunken chaos tarnished that brief shining moment. Then came the indecorous dispute with Arnold over commanding the occupation of the fort and the worse folly of his attempt to beat Arnold to the armed sloop at St. John, in all a depressing display of incompetence capped in late July by his fellow settlers roundly rejecting him for leadership.

On September 20, still a free-ranging adjunct to General Montgomery's staff without commission, command, or uniform — risking hanging as a spy if caught so close to Montreal dressed as a hunter — Allen reported successfully recruiting 250 Canadian volunteers under arms, but failed to mention that Livingston had originally recruited and now supported them at a campsite near his home in Chambly. Fully aware that eagle wings rarely lift muddy sappers or itinerant recruiters to the pantheon of heroes, Allen told Montgomery that other unnamed officers on the recruiting tour advised him to return to the siege as a combatant. Allen urged Montgomery to press the attack on St. John for the good results it would bring: "You may rely on it that I shall join you in about three days with five hundred or more Canadian volunteers. I could raise one or two thousand in a weeks time . . . The glory of a victory . . . will crown all our fatigues, risks and labours; to fail of victory will be an eternal disgrace, but to obtain it will elevate us on the wings of fame."[17] Ethan Allen was back in the hunt, but as events developed, he nearly lost the wager "to lay his life on" pursuing fame and glory.

On September 25, instead of returning to fight with the army at St. John as he promised Montgomery, Allen led eighty Canadian volunteers and thirty American rangers to cross the St. Lawrence and attack Montreal. Allen's version of this event in his *Narrative* reported that early during the day of September 24, marching to the American camp at St. John, with his personal "guard" of only eighty, not five hundred, Canadian volunteers who had joined him somewhere along the way, he met John Brown, also out to recruit Canadians. Brown, according to Allen, enlisted him in a scheme to attack Montreal with their small forces. They were to cross the river about nine miles distant from each other. Allen succeeded in crossing the St. Lawrence, anticipating a signal from Brown that he had also crossed the river. Brown never crossed, the signal never came, and Brown never joined Allen to attack the town at dawn. The alarm was soon raised in Montreal as Allen's group was seen advancing from the riverbank. Guy Carleton sent out three hundred counterattacking British regulars, English and French militia, and loyal Mohawk warriors. Recognizing the dangers of his position, Allen sent out flank guards who prudently ran away after the first British volley. He surrendered after the ineffectual return fire of his few remaining riflemen and was taken prisoner with thirty-eight Canadians and Americans who had stayed with him during the engagement. In his first full-blown battle with a strong hostile force, Ethan Allen met an inglorious defeat and became a prisoner.

In his *Narrative*, written four years after the ignominious event, Allen presented his account of the engagement and his capture as a warrior's set piece dramatizing the end of his brief career as a combatant, but with a famous precedent in American colonial history. He graphically rendered his final, nearly fatal moments after surrendering his sword to a Loyalist in the swamp outside the walled town. In a nimble dance much like English adventurer Captain John Smith's in a Virginia swamp in 1607, when he used one of his Indian pursuers as a body shield, Allen wards off a Mohawk's coup de grace by shielding himself with the Loyalist who had just accepted his sword, Peter Johnson, the sixteen-year-old son of Sir William Johnson and his Mohawk wife Molly Brant.[18] "I handed him my sword, and in half a minute after, a savage, part of whose head was shaved, being almost naked, and painted, with feathers intermixed with the hair of the other side of his head, came running to me with an incredible swiftness; he seemed to advance with more than mortal speed; . . . his hellish visage was beyond all description; snakes' eyes appear innocent in comparison of his; his features distorted; malice, death, murder, and the wrath of devils and damned spirits, are the emblems of his countenance; and, in less

than twelve foot of me, presented his firelock. . . . I twitched the officer
to whom I gave my sword between me and the savage, . . . keeping the
officer in such a position that his danger was my defence; but, in less
than a half a minute, I was attacked by just such, another imp of hell . . .
I made the officer fly around with incredible velocity, for a few seconds
of time, . . . a *Canadian*, who had lost one eye, as appeared afterwards,
taking my part against the savages; and . . . an *Irishman* came to my
assistance with a fixed bayonet, and drove away the fiends, swearing by
Jesus he would kill them."[19]

An accomplished storyteller, Allen captured readers with this
action-filled moment early in an account that relied on the familiar for-
mulas of popular fiction, particularly the widely read Indian captivity
narratives. He opened his story with a confession of faith to establish
his sincerity and veracity: "Ever since I arrived to a state of manhood,
and acquainted myself with the general history of mankind, I have felt
a sincere passion for liberty. The history of nations doomed to perpet-
ual slavery, in consequence of yielding up to tyrants their natural born
liberties, I read with a sort of philosophical horror."[20] In the course
of the *Narrative*, Allen offsets craven Loyalists, devilish Indians, and
brutal British captors—the tyrants who had taken his "natural born
liberties"—against generous Irish aid and other friendly encounters—
including a kindly refugee Loyalist woman in Halifax he knew from
Connecticut and several gentleman officers of the British navy who
mistakenly honored Allen's claim to equal status as an officer and a
gentleman, a class privilege Allen insisted on exercising, even though
he held no commission at the time. The climactic moment of Allen's
version of his failed attack on Montreal launched him and his story out
of a squalid conclusion to an ill-conceived fiasco into company with famous and glorious heroes of the past.

The incident happens quickly and is told succinctly for its best effect. Allen's vignette of the Indian attackers and his dance to evade
death passes the "exciting story" test. A question remains, however:
Does it pass a veracity test? Well, maybe a captive "twitching" around
his captor "with incredible velocity" to delay paying off a wager on his
life is minimally plausible. However measured, the riveting incident
saves the hero for another day to tell the story of his ordeals as a prisoner of the British.

THE STORY FORMS IN CAPTIVITY

Allen's post-victory reports from Ticonderoga had displayed an over-reaching confidence. But they were written from vivid memory of the event almost immediately after the action a few days earlier. The errors and confusions in reporting them are impeachable, but still within range of the probable. On the other hand, claiming his riflemen's return fire at St. John dispersed the enemy's firing line at a range of three hundred-plus yards must be counted as pure fiction, perhaps attributable to the rush of excitement in his first battle experience—the first time he was directly fired on by an opposing force—but just as likely a conscious addition to the record of his bravery.

Written from a distance of four years after his capture, however, Allen's *Narrative* advantages its author against a veracity test. A story so significant to its author must have been told time and again to reach its most effective form, which could then differ from the original event by exclusion or inclusion of other significant moments or incidents. The drunken chaos and looting at Ticonderoga and Benedict Arnold's presence and opposition to the wild disorder that day, for example, do not find their way into the *Narrative*, raising confirmable suspicions that other exclusions or fabricated inclusions are part of Allen's story.[21] He complains in his report to the Continental Congress on May 29, 1775: "Provided I had but five hundred men with me at Saint Johns when we took the King's Sloop"—omitting Benedict Arnold's success in that incident—"I would have advanced to Montreal."[22]

On parole in New York City and on Long Island in 1777, Allen had a captive audience of fellow prisoners to listen to his war stories. The "famous Col. Ethan Allen was always welcome at our house," John Adlum recalled in his memoirs. A well-educated young subaltern on parole in British-occupied New York, Adlum lived with other paroled officers in Liberty House, the former Patriot headquarters. On dinner visits to his fellow parolees in late 1776, Allen charmed his audience with a "history &c of his voyage to England &c" that kept them awake late into the night.[23] Less taken by Allen's stories, Jabez Fitch, a young lieutenant from Connecticut sent with Allen and other prisoners to Long Island in 1777, tired of Allen's nightly repetitions of "taking Ticonderoga and also many other adventures." Instead, he enjoyed spending an evening

privately with Allen discussing the journal Fitch was writing for publication after the war (perhaps a prompt for Allen to publish his own
text in 1779). He flinched at Allen's scoffing treatment of the biblical
story of Noah and the Flood—according to Allen, the Vermont mountain known as Camels Rump (Victorian propriety later changed it to
Hump) would have given Noah a better view of the flood than Mount
Ararat.[24]

Another parolee, Pennsylvanian Alexander Graydon, wrote about
Allen only long after the war, when he recalled first seeing him stroll-
ing through New York City to the Battery in quasi-regimental dress.
On the voyage back to America from a British prison in January 1776,
the warship carrying Allen and fellow prisoners stayed briefly at Cobh
in Ireland. Irish sympathizers with the American cause collected donations of food, wine, and clothing for the winter sea journey Allen and
his men would undergo on the HMS *Sole Bay*. Allen requested Captain
Symonds of the *Sole Bay* "the privelege of his tailor to make me a suit of
cloaths bestowed on me in Ireland, which he generously granted." The
ship's sail master, Sergeant Gilligen, Allen's friendly Irish bunk mate,
apparently also had the cutting and sewing skills of a tailor to produce
a good suit from the bolt of blue Irish wool given to Allen. To top off
the outfit, he also had from his donors a tricorn beaver hat trimmed
military style with gold braid.[25] Recalling his first meeting with Allen,
Graydon found him "a man of Honour and Sound Casuist," and "I have
seldom met with a man, possessing, in my opinion, a stronger mind, or
whose mode of expression was more vehement and oratorical."[26]

Probably none of Allen's audiences, perhaps not even Ethan Allen
himself, either as a prisoner of war or after his release, realized how
those compulsive repetitions of his great adventure at Ticonderoga
shaped and kept vivid in his mind the substance of a narrative he would
compose after he returned to Vermont. Nearly ten years after his final
combat experience, Allen told readers about his note-taking methods
while preparing to write in the preface to his final book, *Reason the Only
Oracle of Man*. Recollections of significant ideas or moments, memories, unless reduced to writing, he said, fall defenseless against the on-
slaught of time.[27] Beginning in newspaper articles defending the rights
of New Hampshire Grants settlers in 1772 and culminating in 1774 with
a book-length reply to James Duane's pamphlet justifying the outcome

of the Ejectment Trials, Allen honed his skills of argument and rhetoric in a campaign of pamphlets, books, and broadsides waged against New York's efforts to establish jurisdiction over the New Hampshire Grants. New York's leaders read his published writings. John Jay wrote to Gouverneur Morris, "Ethan Allen has commenced author and orator. A phillippic of his against New-York is handed about. There is quaintness, impudence, and art in it."[28] When on parole two years later in New York, however, Allen watched his captors regularly search his personal effects, leaving him to rely on memory fortified by oral repetition — clearly safer than transcription.[29]

Allen's style of reciting his adventures — supremely "vehement and oratorical" in Alexander Graydon's assessment — at times annoyed his auditors by repetitious delivery. Yet the energy and bombast of Allen's personal "war story" helped to preserve, sift, and shape his memories like notes or minutes for the tale he would compose as *A Narrative of Colonel Ethan Allen's Captivity Containing His Voyages & Travels etc.* . . . . He began his story professing his long-held "philosophical horror" of mankind's history "of yielding up to tyrants their natural born liberties." Thus "the bloody attempt at Lexington, to enslave America, thoroughly electrified my mind, and fully determined me to take part with my country." He waited and wished for the call "to signalize myself in its behalf." When revolutionary Patriots from Connecticut secretly recruited him to lead the Green Mountain Boys "to surprise and take the fortress Ticonderoga," the time had come for the aspiring hero to "signalize" himself.[30] Published 1779 in Philadelphia, followed by reprints there and in Boston, Allen's narrative established his public image as a forceful revolutionary hero whose adventures encouraged American readers when the war's success lay in doubt.

Allen's captivity of two years and eight months carried him to Pendennis Castle in England, to Cobh in Ireland, then to Halifax, and finally to parole and prison in New York, where he was exchanged for a British officer on May 6, 1778. Once free, he went immediately to meet General George Washington in Valley Forge. On Allen's departure for Vermont, Washington observed that Allen had an "original something" in him, without further clarifying that "original something."[31]

Subsequent writers and commentators on Ethan Allen have stressed the "original something" in him, freely parsing Washington's ambiguity

PENDENNIS CASTLE, FALMOUTH, ENGLAND.
Held prisoner here for sixteen days around New Year's 1775–76, Ethan Allen awaited a British decision on whether they would hang him as a rebel or return him to America as a prisoner of war. *Courtesy of Special Collections, Bailey Howe Library, UVM.*

in their own versions. Allen's failed attack on Montreal on September 25, 1775, became the clay for biographers in the nineteenth century seeking to shape Ethan Allen into an impeccable hero well suited for the special needs of their own special times. Ira Allen was the first among them, and his version of the Montreal fiasco established the story of that event as a tale of a betrayal by his brother's comrades-in-arms, John Brown and Seth Warner.

Ira's 1798 history of Vermont offers a brief but significantly different version from his older brother's account of the failure at Montreal.[32] Ethan's captivity narrative avoids charging or blaming Brown for the foolish adventure turning sour. He never even mentions Seth Warner in connection with the incident. By 1779, when Allen's narrative appeared, Brown had earned a distinguished record in the war, but was killed the following year in action against Sir John Johnson's Loyalists in the Mohawk Valley. Warner's health had badly deteriorated after the battle for Bennington in 1777, but he continued in command of his regiment in the field until 1781 when, physically exhausted, he moved with his family to Roxbury, Connecticut, his birthplace, where he died in 1784. By 1798 Ethan Allen, Warner, and Brown were long dead and unable to answer or defend themselves. According to Ira's version, Seth Warner as well as Brown attended the meeting with Ethan a few miles outside Longueuil on the south shore of the St. Lawrence on the morning of September 24, 1775. Warner and Brown, in Ira's account, proposed a plan for them and their troops to cross to the island from La Prairie, while Ethan would cross from Longueuil. The two parties would be nine miles distant from each other on the island, and they agreed "upon principles of honour" that if, for any reason, either party could not cross the river, "early notice should be given to the other." Ira claimed that the windy night made the river too dangerous to cross at La Prairie, so Brown and Warner "went quietly to bed" without notifying Ethan. Writing from memory nearly a quarter-century after the fact, with only his word for a tactical agreement among the three planners, Ira delivered a harsh judgment on Brown and Warner: "The conduct of Brown and Warner is hard to be accounted for, on any principles honourable to themselves." This is the earliest claim that Brown and Warner were responsible for Ethan's capture, an assertion that many later accounts would repeat. In effect, Ira had eliminated Brown and especially Warner from competing with Ethan Allen for the pantheon of early Vermont's heroes. They had betrayed their great leader by succumbing to the primitive human need for warmth and sleep.

In 1852 Zadock Thompson delivered the same message in a public lecture on the Allen family of Burlington in which the story of Ethan Allen's capture at Montreal received special attention. According to Thompson, Allen crossed the river as planned and waited on the island of Montreal "with much impatience, for a signal from Brown, that he had passed over and was ready for an advance upon the city, but he waited in vain. Brown, actuated either by cowardice or jealousy, did not pass over."[33] The past is defenseless against time, permitting unsupportable judgments to pass without question.

Ethan Allen returned to Vermont in 1778 with the officer's commission in the Continental Army that had eluded him during his brief four months as a warrior in 1775. Yet he never returned to the war in defense of the new nation's liberty after Congress commissioned him brevet lieutenant colonel. It is not an unfair conjecture to suppose that he had learned between July 1775, when rejected for colonel of the Green Mountain rangers, and his release from a British prison in 1778 that the "fame and glory" he had "zealously" pursued to "signalize" himself in behalf of "my country" was a status quickly won and easily lost. Dangerously elusive, "fame and glory" counted for little — $75 each month for thirty-two months to compensate for the loss of his liberty. And how much would fame and glory support him and his family once Vermont's celebration of his return had passed and the brevet pay ended?

As a prisoner of war in New York Allen played no direct role in establishing the State of Vermont. His patriotic affinity for Vermont was nonetheless real. It was obvious to him and all like-minded Vermonters by 1780 — the real original founding fathers, brother Ira, Governor Chittenden, Matthew Lyon, and others in the group of leaders later known as the Arlington Junto — that the land business and its resultant wealth and a safe future depended totally on the state's viability. For Allen and others who calculated these matters, the fragile State of Vermont had to survive either as an independent state protected by Congress from New York's claims against it or in a protective alliance with the British Crown that would preserve Vermont from both the United States and New York. In either case, the State of Vermont, as it had been since he returned from captivity in 1778 and theatrically took command of the trial that hanged Queen's Ranger David Redding, would be the vehicle for securing his land business, his wealth, and his future.[34]

One story is good until another is told.

{ ETHAN ALLEN to the Canadians, 1775 }

CHAPTER IV

ETHAN ALLEN AND THE HISTORIANS

Discovering a Hero

Though Ethan Allen had not participated in Vermont's declaration of independence, the drafting of its constitution, or the formation of its government, over time he received credit as a prime mover in the state's early years. During his life he had earned sufficient status to receive the attention of historians and later biographers. When some of them examined him, they could see the contradictions, controversies, and fabrications that swirled around him. Others simply accepted and sometimes expanded Allen's tales. He had created them himself in the widely read *Narrative* of his captivity, the preface to *Reason the Only Oracle of Man*, and the spate of published letters and pamphlets in which he argued for his causes and belittled his opponents. Others with whom he interacted added to the complex portrait of an active man through their own activities, official records, reports, and correspondence. The memory of Allen did not disappear with the passage of time. In his case, for reasons largely unrelated to his actions, the story would expand, making him larger in memory than in life.

THE ALLEN INFLUENCE: EARLY ACCOUNTS

The first accounts retold his role as a prominent leader in the New Hampshire Grants resistance to New York authority that led to the establishment of the State of Vermont and depicted the audacious captor of Fort Ticonderoga. By the middle of the nineteenth century, the story had expanded. Historians and other writers had shaped Ethan Allen into an heroic icon whose person embodied Vermont's image of itself. As a prolific polemicist, author of many political tracts and pamphlets, and frequent correspondent, Ethan, along with his brothers Ira and Levi, bequeathed to posterity a large body of material for historians to study and shape their accounts. Ethan and Ira frequently employed broadsides, newspapers, and pamphlets at their own or government expense to expand and win over their audience on the important public and private issues of the moment. That practice and their archival reflex—both Ethan and Levi mention "boxes" containing papers—led to the survival of many of their writings, especially after the late 1770s. Conscious of the importance of public opinion, Allen deliberately, even shamelessly, used his pen to present himself as he wished others to regard him. Those efforts extended the reach of his writing well beyond his lifetime.

Even though Ethan Allen appreciated that "one story is good until another is told," he probably hoped for but could not have foreseen the extent to which, with Ira's help, he contributed to his own posterity, as his published work became a prime source beginning with the earliest historians of Vermont. "As the only early Vermont leaders who published voluminous accounts of their own accomplishments, the Allens dictated to succeeding generations the context in which they and their exploits would be judged." An early twentieth-century biographer thought that because of the "abundant material" that Allen furnished, "few writers have dared to wander far from this hero's estimate of his own services."[1] But the Allens could not control from their graves the way in which historians removed a generation and more would employ the Allen legacy for their own purposes. Ethan could not have anticipated the form and plot in the telling of another story.

The initial historical treatments of Ethan Allen focused on larger issues than his activities. The first history of Vermont, Reverend Samuel Williams's *The Natural and Civil History of Vermont*, appeared in 1794.[2] It exhibited the growing maturity of Americans "as they transformed themselves from transplanted Europeans into Americans." Williams held up Vermonters in settling a wilderness and achieving independence for themselves as the best model of a democratic civilization.

In the eighteenth century a group of men wrote about the land and the flora and fauna in their new North American laboratories of discovery. After the successful Revolution and adoption of the U.S. Constitution, a small knot of American historians moved on to another very striking departure from the Old World, as they attempted to justify and explain the new polity. Williams combined the two strains. He provided details of the setting for an American experiment in which the success of Vermont in asserting its independence and becoming the fourteenth state had no previous model. Williams, whose book preceded most of the other post–national state histories, stands as part of a genre that includes accounts of New Hampshire, New Jersey, North Carolina, and South Carolina, along with John Marshall's multivolume life of George Washington. Williams's *History* became the authority and the source for the generation of Vermont historians who followed.

Williams wrote to celebrate and validate the United States and the new State of Vermont. "Having assumed their rank among the nations of the earth, the states of America now present to the world a new state of society; founded on principles, containing arrangements, and producing effects, not visible in any nation before."[3] He thought that the controversy between New York, New Hampshire, and Vermont "agitated for a while, with violence greatly unfavorable to the peace and safety of the whole union," had gradually abated after the revolution and had turned out quite well. Williams deemed it remarkable that Vermont asserted its independence without a full-scale "civil war."[4] The contending parties, he concluded, displayed the "wisdom and moderation" to prevent an armed clash, virtues the Green Mountain Boys' victims did not report.[5] Williams wrote as a new resident of a confident Vermont, which having achieved recognition as a state equal to the others, rapidly expanded settlement and its population. Its economy and trade flourished, and its wheat crop made it the breadbasket of New England.

Williams's interest in explaining American exceptionalism and his confidence in Vermont's future led him to diminish the tumult that roiled the Grants after the 1770 Ejectment Trials. He acknowledges that in a "scene of violence and opposition to New York, Ethan Allen placed himself at the head of the opposition," but he sees the activities in Vermont as part of the larger movement of the rebelling thirteen colonies.[6] He describes Allen as "bold, enterprising, ambitious, with great confidence in his own abilities," but he also calls Allen "an indifferent writer" whose work nonetheless had great influence on the public. "The cultivated roughness of his own temper and manners, seems to have assisted him" in combating New York's "speculating landjobbers." Williams's evaluation of "cultivated roughness" suggests an understanding of Allen's ability to play to his audience. Williams, making a point that nineteenth-century writers would come to celebrate as a Robin Hood tendency, says of Allen that "though he wrote with asperity, a degree of generosity attended his conduct, and he carefully avoided bloodshed . . . cruelty, or abuse to those who fell in his power."[7] Williams does not mention the Ejectment Trials and Allen's now famous, if fictitious, warning to the Yorker officials that the hills of Bennington had a different set of gods than those of the Hudson River Valley. His history provides a very thin recitation of the activities of the Green Mountain Boys, an appellation he does not use. He also devotes only a single paragraph to Allen's "bravery and success" in taking "Tyconderoga."[8] For Williams, Ethan Allen's life does not embody the story and ideals of Vermont.

Williams devotes much more time to exonerating Ethan and Ira Allen and the rest of their tight coterie in the negotiations with the agents of General Frederick Haldimand, the military governor of Quebec, than discussing the possibilities of a Vermont alliance with the British Empire in the middle of the war. This approach fits his theme of a national union made up of generally harmonious parts. In July 1792 Williams wrote to Ira Allen asking if he could see the papers relating to the Haldimand affair. He would treat the documents with confidentiality, he averred, and would not publish anything without Ira's approval. Allen let Williams see the documents, perhaps appreciating that in this way he could exercise a degree of control over the account of Vermont's origins. After meeting with Allen, Williams wrote, "I have inserted everything that you mentioned to me," promising that his account of the Haldimand affair "now stands in a light that cannot be construed as unfavorable to any person who was concerned in it." His book, he assured Ira, would not provide "an unfavorable view of their proceedings."[9]

Williams's account, which must also be "considered an Allen version," stressed that the eight Vermonters involved in the Haldimand Negotiations, "known to be among the most confirmed friends to the

American cause, had negotiated in the best interest of Vermont and ultimately helped the thirteen colonies secure independence. They had avowed their sentiments, and embraced the cause of their country, from the beginning of the American war." Despite suffering "severely," they "had done everything in their power to defend the independence of the states." The plural "states," rather than the singular "Vermont," reveals Williams's national bias and purpose. "The commissioners from Vermont," Williams explained, "treated the [British] proposals with affability and good humor, and thought they had avoided bringing anything to a decision." Williams devotes more ink to the activities of the "commissioners" who parlayed with the British than to Ethan. In his version, the Vermonters played the British with the skill of sportsmen landing trophy game fish.[10] He and Ira Allen, for different reasons, wished the public to see the negotiations as the "sound judgment" of the patriotic eight who deceived the British and defended Vermont and its frontiers.

Modern historians have largely set aside Williams's treatment and have turned more to Ira Allen's 1798 *The Natural and Political History of the State of Vermont*, which ironically relied on Williams as the source for much of the information that did not relate directly to Ira's and his brother's activities. Because he published his history in London, few copies crossed the Atlantic Ocean, and the earliest historians writing about Vermont may not have seen it. In 1843 Henry Stevens, the preeminent collector of Vermont historical materials, an exercise that Francis Parkman called "grubbing up antiquities," asked his son in New York City to find copies of "Allen['ls History of Vermont and Allen's Olive Branch in two columns," as he had "not been able to procure those works as yet." Despite its scarcity, by the mid-1830s Ira Allen's version had begun to help shape the accounts of Ethan Allen's activities in an increasingly Allen-centric story of early Vermont.[11]

In London in 1798 Ira Allen brought suit in the Admiralty Court against the British captain who had seized Allen's chartered cargo ship *Olive Branch* at sea off the Irish coast and claimed a prize for capturing its cargo of war surplus muskets and cannon. Proclaiming his innocence, Allen argued that he bought 20,000 muskets in France at a cost much lower than in England or the United States as a speculative venture to resell to the American state militias. In reality he embraced an ambitious, almost delusional scheme to wrest Canada from the British.[12] Ira unabashedly wrote his history as part of his plea in the "proceedings of the High Court of Admiralty of England relative to twenty thousand muskets with their bayonets." His aim, he confessed, "has been to lay open the source of contention between Vermont and New York and the reasons which induced the former to repudiate the jurisdiction and claim of the latter." He celebrated that a small number of people "without influence, and in a perilous situation, [of] necessity, the mother of invention, instituted a policy in place of power." To Ira, ironically, "policy" equated to a strategy of cunning and the use of the pen as a weapon that when skillfully applied led to victory and independence rather than resorting to "power" with the force of arms.[13] He and Ethan at the center of activities in this way averted the civil war with New York and the United States that Williams feared. Ira Allen's most recent biographer concluded that his "main subject was the role his family had played in protecting freedom and democracy" and his primary goal was portraying them "in the best possible light."[14] In Ira's account "truth, honor, and selfless dedication to liberty had motivated the family at every turn," and the "Haldimand affair had been a necessary, patriotic strategy to preserve a beleaguered state." All of their opponents "had been greedy Yorkers or dastardly loyalists, or both."[15]

Allen devotes much attention to the Ejectment Trials, and in this telling Ethan's enigmatic response to Yorker lawyers after the trials that they would understand the Grants better if they comprehended that "the gods of the valleys are not gods of the hills" appears for the first time. The stirring challenge would not get resurrected for another thirty-five years.[16] Since then it has become a trope repeated in every account since the 1830s, though authors often reverse the order of "hills" and "valleys." In a certain irony, an utterance Ethan probably never made, along with his dubious claim to have taken Fort Ticonderoga with the authority of "Jehovah and the Continental Congress," have become two of a loquacious man's most famous lines. Ira places the initiation of the resistance and the formation of the Green Mountain Boys at the Bennington meeting that immediately followed the trials. In this version Ethan never considered, much less briefly accepted, a Yorker bribe before organizing the Grants resistance. Ira then devotes nearly one-sixth of his book to the activities of the Green Mountain

Boys, the taking of Fort Ticonderoga, and Ethan's capture at Mon-treal in September 1775, for the first time blaming Massachusetts Major John Brown for the fiasco that bought his brother almost three years in various British prisons. After the British released Allen in May 1778, Ira reports Ethan returned to Vermont "to the great joy of his family and friends," not to a statewide reception and celebration suggested in later accounts.[17] Ira, "certain that the *History* would bolster his sagging reputation on both sides of the Atlantic," did not get the response he wanted. But the book would eventually contribute mightily to the Allen version of the Vermont story that would later prevail, even in the face of twentieth- and twenty-first-century revisionism.[18]

Two other histories of Vermont appeared before Ira Allen's account began to gain traction. In 1831 Nathan Hoskins published *A History of the State of Vermont from Its Discovery and Settlement to the Close of the Year MDCCCXXX.* Hoskins, who relied heavily on Williams's treatment of Vermont's advance to statehood, wrote more to celebrate the "multiple instances of patience, bravery, and patriotism which have honored" the names of the state's ancestors than to explain the existence of a new state within a new and different nation.[19] In casting Allen as a conventional revolutionary hero, Hoskins applied the same mold that Parson Weems used for George Washington: a rural gentleman who treasured his country estate but nonetheless answered his country's call for service. Weems portrayed Washington as "a Christian gentleman" motivated by his religion. Ira Allen, Williams, Hoskins, and others pru-dently left Ethan Allen's Deism unexplored.[20]

This subtle shift to celebrating the American founding fathers rather than the republic they created presaged what would soon become a major thrust. Hoskins wrote in the early years of the developing intel-lectual and cultural movement to recognize and honor American soci-ety and attainments. In five novels published between 1823 and 1841, James Fennimore Cooper's Leatherstocking Tales introduced Natty Bumppo, a frontier hunter-woodsman-warrior who retreats from the advance of civilization in the New York wilderness. William Cullen Bryant's 1821 *Poems* led a trend toward verse with American themes. Thomas Cole began working in New York and the Catskills in the mid-1820s, helping to found the Hudson River School with his romantic landscape paintings, some with historical themes such as his *View of*

Fort Ticonderoga from Gelyna and his depiction of a timber raft on Lake Champlain. Hoskins may not have read or seen their work, but as a literate man, he certainly had felt the influences of a growing ideology to define and express national sentiment, and he conceived of his history of Vermont in that milieu.

As a result, Hoskins, who relied heavily on Williams for his information, did not center his history on Ethan Allen. He did not include the Ejectment Trials or mention the nature of the special gods in Bennington. He did not use the term "Green Mountain Boys" (except in the lowercase to describe the Vermonters who faced the British with Yorker militia across the Walloomsac River during the Revolution), and he confined much of the discussion of the anti–New York antics to the raids on the surveyor Cockburn and Colonel Reid's settlers near the Otter Creek.[21] Hoskins provided a short, straightforward account of Allen's taking Fort Ticonderoga, and he quoted Ethan Allen's *Narrative* that the authority for the attack came from the Continental Congress and Jehovah. But he ignored Allen's failure to command the Green Mountain regiment, and he ascribed Allen's capture in Montreal to "great rashness," not to Brown's deceit.[22]

When Hoskins discussed the Haldimand affair, he slavishly relied on Williams and by extension Ira Allen. Many of Hoskins's sentences find synonyms for Ira and Williams's key words.[23] With his history focused more on the forty years that followed statehood, Hoskins sees Thomas Chittenden, who served as governor for nearly two decades, as a much more important figure than Ethan Allen in the making of Vermont.[24]

Two years later, in 1833, Burlington's Zadock Thompson published his *History of the State of Vermont, from its Earliest Settlement to the Close of the Year 1832,* intended in part for a school audience. He hoped his book would "awaken and perpetuate in the breasts of the young [Vermonters] that spirit of patriotism, independence, and self-denial, which so nobly animated the hearts of their fathers."[25] Thompson eventually came to a more Allen-centric view, and his much larger book, *The History of Vermont, Natural, Civil, and Statistical* (1842), would dominate "Vermont historiography between Samuel Williams' *History* and the Civil War." But in 1833 he closely followed Williams's version of Vermont's past. In 1833 he did not mention the Ejectment Trials, and his narrative leaps directly from Samuel Robinson's partially successful 1767 mission to London to seek relief and recognition for New Hampshire titleholders to Ethan Allen's becoming head of a "military association."[26] Thompson does not employ the term "Green Mountain Boys," nor does he put Ethan Allen at the epicenter of the formation of an independent Vermont. Zadock Thompson's first attempt to chronicle Vermont's past with a muted role for Ethan Allen would soon undergo a radical change.

During the period of transition to the new story of Vermont, Hugh Moore, a Burlington newspaper man, assembled a largely unoriginal *Memoir of Col. Ethan Allen: Containing the Most Interesting Incident Connected with his Private and Public Career.* The vast preponderance of the 252-page book quotes directly from Allen's published tracts and letters, and it reprints in 100 pages almost the entirety of the *Narrative* of his captivity. Apparently feeling the necessity to cleanse his subject's eighteenth-century behavior for the sensibilities of nineteenth-century readers and the developing temperance movement, Moore omitted the final paragraph of the *Narrative* when the celebration of Allen's return to Vermont from his captivity concluded with "the flowing bowl, and rural felicity, sweetened with friendship, glowed in each countenance."[27] Moore could not imagine "what individual, will deny him the tribute of gratitude, or withhold from his memory, that mysterious feeling of veneration which patriotism exacts from the friends of liberty?"[28] Despite references and a quotation from Ira Allen's *History*, which he had probably seen, Moore does not mention the Ejectment Trials, and he confines his coverage of the Haldimand Negotiations to a recitation of their impact on the activities of Congress. Moore, with some editing, allowed a less bibulous Allen to tell his own story and, "so far as possible," he "preserved the language" of a role model and hero "never forgetful of the rights of his fellow men, or the cause of liberty."[29] Moore's use of documents demonstrates the import of Allen's archival habits.

THE TRANSFORMATION OF VERMONT
AND THE STORY OF ETHAN ALLEN

The fact that Moore decided to put together a book on Ethan Allen forecast the movement that would quickly follow. As Hoskins, Thompson, and Moore wrote their books, Vermonters had begun to take note of circumstances in the state very different from the confident times in which Williams wrote. Historians viewing the past from their own vantage point sought answers from it to the important questions of their own time. The first authors to concentrate on Ethan Allen expressed the values of the society in which they lived and worked.

By the second quarter of the nineteenth century, Vermont had undergone significant change, and the response to that change would shape the story and status of Allen. The early histories focused on explaining the confident new polity, statehood, the security of land titles, and Vermont's dramatic population growth as a full member of a new republic. Those historians who followed a generation later composed their accounts in a very different set of circumstances. Treating history as "the common property of a large and significant segment of the population," they told a new story of Vermont.[30] The history of Vermont and the portrait of Ethan Allen became an important context for Vermonters to see, understand, and provide a historical dimension of themselves. Retelling that history carried the dual task of explaining the current set of circumstances and through instruction employing the past to articulate the ways to shape the future they envisioned.

By extolling the past generations that they saw endowed with innate good sense, as egalitarian democrats whose energy led to a robust democracy, unified in beliefs that spawned expansive and economic success, the second wave of historians sought to understand and explain their Vermont, in their view a very different place from the growing, confident prosperous state that had entered the Union in 1791.

Jefferson's Embargo and the Non-Importation Act, the collapse of the Vermont State Bank, the War of 1812, and the postwar flood of British manufactured goods occurred in rapid succession. They disrupted Vermont's economy and changed the nature of Vermont's political life. While some in Vermont prospered during the Embargo, when exports to Canada actually increased and the war stimulated some new industry, it generally had a depressing effect.[31] Southern Vermont farmers and small manufacturers lost the export market through Atlantic ports.[32] After the war, the British flooded the American market with textiles, iron products, and other manufactured goods that with the end of the inflated wartime demand burst the bubble that had lifted parts of the wartime economy.

Vermont generally opposed the Embargo and the war. The elector-
ate reflected the changed circumstances in the hard-fought gubernato-
rial election of 1813, when no candidate received a majority vote. The
election, following the provision in the Vermont Constitution, went to
the legislature for determination. The shrewd lawyer Daniel Chipman,
narrowly elected Speaker by a straight partisan vote, orchestrated the
election of the Federalist Martin Chittenden over the Jeffersonian Republican incumbent Jonas Galusha, who had achieved a narrow plurality in the popular vote but not the majority necessary to avoid legislative
resolution.[33] Siding with those who opposed the war, in 1814 Governor
Chittenden ordered the Vermont militia home from New York across
Lake Champlain as it faced the British thrust south to Plattsburgh. His
effort failed when the militia refused the order. The sharply disputed
election and the disobedience of the militia exposed fissures that divided Vermont's political life and society and a general decline in harmony. While the Vermont militia helped turn back the British, other
Vermonters smuggled into Canada the majority of the beef that fed the
British army.[34] Some Vermonters even went so far as to consider with-
drawing from the Union, a scant two decades after the success of the
long struggle to achieve statehood, although only one delegate and one
observer from Vermont attended the Hartford Convention in Connecticut to consider New England's secession. The gathering died ignomin-
iously with the news of the peace that ended the war, but the episode
illustrated the turmoil and dissatisfaction in Vermont.

The War of 1812 had sharply divided Vermonters, and events during
and following it further exacerbated the stress, leaving many anxious
about the future. In 1813 an epidemic of "spotted fever" swept across
the state, sparing few towns and taking the lives of as many as six
thousand Vermonters.[35] Tuberculosis, commonly called consumption
or the white ague, stalked the entire state. In Pawlet it carried off seventeen young women in a span of two years.[36] In 1832 cholera posed
a threat; people in Burlington could look downhill and see the water-
front shanty "towns" of Irish laborers where the disease took hold. Vermont also suffered an epidemic of "ubiquitous tippling." Two hundred
distilleries turned out hundreds of barrels of whiskey a year, country
stores kept barrels on tap, and taverns sold a multitude of drinks. No
one understood the cause of the diseases, often seen as a form of divine

retribution, and the temperance movement gathered momentum to address the consumption of alcohol.[37]

In 1816 snow and frost occurred somewhere in the state every month
of the year. On June 8 several inches of snow fell "in all parts of the
state," accompanied by "a hard frost" that formed ice on ponds, killed
leaves and young fruit, and severely damaged crops. "The corn, which
was up in many areas, and other vegetables, were killed down to the
ground." It took several days for the snow to melt. After farmers had
replanted, the cold, dry summer that followed prevented most of the
crops from reaching maturity, leading to extreme hardship that some
interpreted as further evidence of divine displeasure.[38]

As people began to leave the state in search of better prospects and
furthering the sense of malaise, Vermonters who remained faced other
profound changes. Destruction of the forest for cropland, the production of pot and pearl ash, and the introduction of close-cropping merino
sheep on vast tracts of pasture beginning in 1810 soon reduced ground-
water holding capacity, hastened runoff, and altered the cycles on rivers
and streams. The consequent exaggerated flooding eroded alluvial soils,
carried off bridges and mill sites, and drowned livestock. A freshet in
1811 destroyed two-thirds of the mills in Rutland and Windsor Counties. Alternately, dry seasons left many mills inoperative. Wheat, Vermont's largest crop and a medium for exchange, began to decline as
the soil wore out. In 1824 the wheat midge, or weevil, for which farmers had no cure, appeared, and in 1826 a plague of grasshoppers, another biblical omen, devastated the crop. The rapid expansion of flocks
of sheep changed the physical face of Vermont and landholding patterns. Many traditional, labor-intensive mixed farming operations gave
way to sheepfolds. Vermonters often equated the changed landscape of
cleared hillsides with decline.[39]

The opening of the Champlain Canal in 1823 made much of western Vermont vulnerable to direct competition from the West, and the
opening of the Erie Canal in 1825 that connected Lake Champlain with
the Great Lakes compounded the commercial challenges. By 1830 Vermont, once the breadbasket of New England, had begun to import
wheat from western New York.[40]

The changes in agriculture, Vermont's largest economic activity,
developed slowly and intensified over time, but economic dislocations

LUDLOW, VERMONT, 1859.
This bird's-eye view of a mid-nineteenth-century Vermont village displays its
surrounding hills denuded by deforestation and over-browsing sheep, conditions that traditionalist Vermonters regarded as a sign of decline. *Courtesy of
Vermont Historical Society.*

created by trade policy, war, financial panics, epidemics, plagues, crop
disease, and climate anomalies lacked the subtlety of gradual change.
So too did the abrupt and disturbing evidence of the sudden slump
in population growth. The Vermont economy could no longer depend
on the steady activity of selling land and supplying goods and services
to people coming into the state. After nearly tripling in the 1780s, the
state's population grew by a robust 45 and 41 percent respectively in
the next two decades. In the 1810s the rate of growth fell to 18 percent,
and in the 1830s it stagnated at a meager 4 percent. As a number of the
largest towns like Burlington, Montpelier, Woodstock, and Rutland
added population, the demographic doldrums became most evident in
rural areas. Vermonters could not help notice that their state grew at a
significantly faster rate than the United States as a whole before 1810,
but after that it lagged. Between 1830 and 1840 Vermont's population growth of 4 percent paled in the face of a national rate of almost

39 percent, a condition that many Vermonters interpreted as yet more evidence of decline.[41]

By 1830 the drastic changes in Vermont had become starkly apparent. Vermonters could not ignore them, but they found little agreement on how best to address them, as they sought explanations, solutions, and palliatives to forces and circumstances that seemed beyond their control. The responses found many expressions. The fire of the religious revivals that swept over western New York and prompted the historian Whitney R. Cross to call it the burned-over district also raged in Vermont. To the horror of much of the settled clergy and orthodox Congregationalists, the revivalist and former circus performer Jedidiah Burchard held heavily attended and protracted meetings in churches across the state. The revivals brought congregations to a fevered pitch. "In the transport of exultation," an observer reported, Burchard "would leap from the pulpit and do acrobatic stunts in front of it and walk among the people on the tops of the backs of the square pews." Burchard and the other revivalists divided Vermonters and challenged the sense of reasoned piety. University of Vermont Professor G. W. Benedict noted, "we are almost at loggerheads here about what is called 'Burchardism.'"[42]

The millennialist William Miller, who convinced adherents that he had calculated the precise date of Jesus' second coming and the end of the world, also found a ready audience. Looking to the New Testament Book of Revelation, Miller preached about the selfishness of rich men who had amassed "unprecedented treasures for themselves through banks, corporations, monopolies, and insurance corporations" that ground down the poor.[43] To prepare for the day in 1843 Miller expected the world would end, some of his Adventist followers disposed of their earthly property and donned ascension robes. They awaited the apocalypse from trees, rooftops, and other heights more easily to join the transport of a spiritual rising that never came. Social experiments like John Humphrey Noyes's perfectionist community in Putney with its "complex marriage" and sexual sharing found adherents and distressed the orthodox. Other religious responses included the Dorrilites, the Mormons, the Pilgrims, and the Swedenborgians. Social movements like temperance, anti-slavery, abolitionism, anti-Masonry, and the support for the *Patriote* rebels in Lower Canada in 1837–38 all tended to go beyond moral suasion and spill into Vermont's political life.

VERMONT CREATES A BEACON

The upper-middle-class, nonfarming elites in Vermont's larger towns sought solutions to what they regarded as moral and economic decay. The trend toward extensive sheep raising changed the landscape and aspect of rural communities, which they found troubling. They nostalgically turned to their past and in a more reserved way than the activist social architects, they looked backward to the times and stories of those heroic individuals who had carved a new country and a new state from the wilderness and escaped the thrall of aristocratic and imperial Yorker overlords. Vermont leaders noted that other states had begun to celebrate heroes. Kentucky, with assistance from the librarian and manuscript collector Lyman Copeland Draper of Wisconsin (who became an honorary member of the Vermont Historical Society), began to celebrate Daniel Boone. Neighboring New Hampshire had John Stark, and the entire nation had George Washington. Vermonters saw that all other New England states had created historical societies, as had five other states. They recognized that in 1838 Harvard College had established the first American chair in history. Vermonters participated in the beginnings of town libraries and lyceums as forums to discuss issues. A group of leaders determined that Vermont could build its own historical base — the story of the Green Mountain State's Golden Age — and build its own pantheon of heroes displaying the virtues and values contemporary Vermont must restore. (See Appendix A, p. 211.)

The interests of Henry Stevens, a founder of the Vermont Historical and Antiquarian Society (hereafter the Vermont Historical Society, though legislation did not officially drop the "Antiquarian," until 1858), "ranged from moral reform and politics, to economic development, to historical collecting, preservation and commemoration."[44] With the written history of Vermont still in its formative stages, Stevens saw an opportunity to construct social and cultural values and revitalize the state through history as a means. He and many of his contemporaries saw history as "the common property of a large and significant segment of the population."[45] In 1838 Stevens, with three associates active

HENRY STEVENS.
A co-founder of the Vermont Historical Society, Stevens gathered the
first large collection of historical documents from Vermont's early years,
and encouraged Jared Sparks to
write a biography of Allen. *Courtesy
of Vermont Historical Society.*

in the growing anti-slavery movement, including George Mansur and
Daniel P. Thompson, a Montpelier lawyer, author, and editor who had
fallen under the sway of revivalist Burchard, secured a legislative charter incorporating the Vermont Historical Society. These three men had
wide-ranging commitments to other reform movements in Vermont and
may have conflated their goals for the Society with those efforts.[46]

The four incorporators—Stevens, Thompson, George B. Mansur,
and Oramel Smith, (who soon dropped out)—consciously sought to
improve Vermont through its history. They thought that the robust
growth in the state's formative years and the bold assertions of its independence held lessons that would help the state deal with what they
deemed as its declining prospects. "They founded the historical society
as part of a broader movement to draw Vermonters together in support
of moral values and spiritual principles that they believed" had once
defined Vermont, asserting the best traits of the state's founders would
help solve contemporary problems.[47] They convened a meeting of the
Society in 1840, with a few associates, at which they named officers.
Stevens assumed the mantle of president, librarian, and cabinet keeper,
while Thompson became recording secretary and Mansur became corresponding secretary. Thompson and Stevens would hold their offices
for the rest of the decade, and Stevens remained president until 1857.

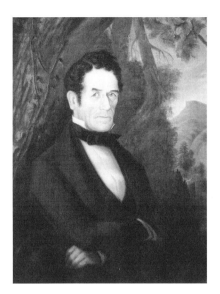

DANIEL P. THOMPSON.
Montpelier judge and co-founder
of the Vermont Historical Society,
Thompson wrote local-color novels
and short fiction based in early Vermont, most famously his widely popular *Green Mountain Boys*. *Portrait
by Thomas Waterman Wood. Courtesy
of Vermont Historical Society.*

They recruited a small and extremely influential group of members
made up mostly of prominent politicians, men of letters, and recognized
community leaders, including some who served on boards of trustees
of the University of Vermont, Middlebury College, and, to a lesser extent, Norwich University. By 1850 the Society's roster had modestly
expanded to form an elite, handpicked coterie of fewer than seventy.

As the president of the Society, Stevens focused "almost exclu-
sively" on "honoring his own state's Revolutionary heroes." Though
not wealthy or regarded as a social or intellectual leader himself, Stevens successfully sought association with such men. As the president
of the Society and an assiduous collector of Vermontiana, he played the
role of the worker bee to the prominent queens of the Vermont hives.
Stevens believed that "history can never be fully, fairly, and accurately
written" without documents and other materials. He also asserted the
importance of history for patriotism: "take away the memory of the
past and what remains, a name and only a name."[48] He set out to sculpt
Ethan Allen as a figure of such stature to inspire and guide Vermont
through the vicissitudes of change he and his cohorts largely regarded
as negative. Stevens searched long for, found, and assembled many of
the papers that the Allens had created. (See Appendixes B and C, pp.
218 and 224).

Stevens corresponded with and lobbied Jared Sparks, a celebrated and prolific writer and editor whose publications included the works of George Washington, Benjamin Franklin, and Gouverneur Morris as well as the diplomatic correspondence of the American Revolution. Sparks held the first American chair of history when he became the McLean Professor of History at Harvard in 1838. He also served as editor and contributed to *The Library of American Biography* (first series, 1834–38), which included Ethan Allen. Stevens wrote to Sparks that in conducting the Haldimand Negotiations Vermonters recognized the "necessity of using deception for the furtherance of Justice and salvation of the Northern Department."[49] Stevens also tried to convince George Bancroft, at work on his important *History of the United States*, asserting that Ethan Allen and not the "Connecticut revolutionary authorities" had first conceived of the assault on Fort Ticonderoga. Norwich University's John Davie Butler would repeat this view in his 1846 presentation at the Society's Annual Meeting. In 1843 Stevens wrote to David Baldwin, a Montpelier insurance executive and treasurer of the Vermont Historical Society, asserting that Vermont needed to "address the current social problems with the same spirit that had once inspired the Green Mountain Boys." "The spirit of Chittenden, the Allens, Warner, Herrick, Robinson, Olin, Baker & Brownson, Tichenor, Smith, Galusha, each is now admonishing us to forsake our follies [and] turn back and walk in their footsteps" and by that example "Incourage industry economy and domestic manufactures."[50] Stevens chose to ignore that his pantheon of Vermont heroes did not all share the same worldview and that some among them had fought each other in the state's rather nasty political life in the 1780s and 1790s. The devout Moses Robinson did not countenance Ethan Allen's lack of church involvement or his published view of reason as the lone source of mankind's wisdom. Isaac Tichenor and others plotted successfully to make Moses Robinson governor, bringing about in 1789 Thomas Chittenden's defeat for reelection, despite his solid electoral plurality to the office he held between 1778 and 1797. Jacob Bayley, a member of the conventions that declared Vermont's independence and wrote and adopted its first constitution and a long-serving member of the Council, the "upper house" of the Vermont legislature, publicly referred to Ira Allen, Chittenden, and their associates as "all the Fiends of hell Combined."[51] Stevens would shape history to fit his purposes to respond to Vermont's difficulties.

After the ballad "The Song of the Vermonters—1779" appeared in Joseph T. Buckingham's *New England Magazine* in 1833, Stevens, who "discovered" it, regarded it as an authentic work dating from the heroic days of Vermont's assertion of independence and the American Revolution. Stirring stanzas from the long poem stressed the plucky early Vermont virtues that Stevens and others read into their cherished past.

> Yet we know no allegiance; we bow to no throne.
> Our ruler is the law and the law is our own.
> Our leaders are our own fellow-men,
> Who can handle the sword, or the scythe, or the pen?
>
> Our wives are all true, and our daughters are fair,
> With their blue eyes of smiles, and their light flowing hair;
> All brisk at their wheels till the dark even-fall,
> Then blithe at the sleigh ride, the husking, the ball.

The "Song" ended with defiance:

> Come York or come Hampshire, come traitors and knaves,
> If you rule o'er our land, ye shall rule o'er our graves;
> Our vow is recorded, our banner unfurled,
> In the name of Vermont we defy all the world.[52]

Stevens resonated to the defiance and the grit of the Vermont founding fathers. He had the song reprinted as a broadside in October 1843, and "the appearance of the ballad in print in Vermont caused considerable excitement and it was pronounced original Vermontiana of 1779."[53] At the third Annual Meeting of the Vermont Historical Society in 1843, Stevens announced his discovery and distributed copies of the broadside, stating "that he believed the ballad to be contemporary with the events of 1779."[54] The *Vermont Chronicle* reported that Stevens led Society members in a singing rendition, though the Society's minutes of the meeting indicate that the members merely recited it. For Stevens the ballad exemplified "the fighting spirit of the Green Mountain Boys."[55]

After John Greenleaf Whittier, the Quaker poet, acknowledged author-ship of the poem in an obscure Massachusetts magazine in 1858, Ste-vens made no further comments on it. Finally, in 1877, Benningtonian Daniel Roberts, preparing to deliver a centennial celebration address, asked Whittier to confirm his previous acknowledgment of his author-ship of the "Song." Whittier called it "a boy's practical joke," saying he had not intended to create such a tempest. Both the *Burlington Free Press* and *The New York Times* reported the saga of "The Song of Ver-monters—1779," with the *Free Press* recommending a chorus of bari-tones to sing the poem to the music of Vincenzo Bellini's 1833 opera *Norma*.[56] Misattributing "The Song of Vermonters" to Ethan Allen underscores the almost desperate attempt to build a history of Vermont as a worthy platform on which to construct ambitions for mid-century Vermont. Stevens and his contemporaries made Ethan Allen the corner-stone of their construction. Other mid-nineteenth-century songwriters honored Ethan Allen, but Stevens never returned to musical remem-brances of him. Abby Maria Hemenway's *Poets and Poetry of Vermont* (1858) included the "Green Mountain Song," "Ethan Allen Song," and "The Grave of Ethan Allen."

In his perceptive study of the development of liberal democracy in Bennington, the historian Robert E. Shalhope understood that the story of Vermont and view of Ethan Allen and other early political and mili-tary leaders had undergone a transformation by the mid-1830s. These new heroes represented "common, ordinary men of true integrity and character." Bennington residents "longing for relief from the unsettling changes of their own day, also identified with these figures from a sim-pler and seemingly more forthright past." Political parties claimed "to be the true heirs of Ethan Allen and the Green Mountain Boys."[57] Shal-hope found it ironic that the Green Mountain Boys, seen as overcom-ing "an eighteenth century aristocratic elite, now helped ease the minds of individuals busily engaged in creating a nineteenth century liberal elite, an elite based more broadly on talent and merit, but an elite none-theless." Shalhope identified Bennington residents David Robinson Jr., Hiland Hall, and John S. Robinson, all among the select members of the Vermont Historical Society, as the three local leaders who "quite innocently viewed themselves as the same sort of resolute democrats as those who . . . forged an independent republic."[58]

JARED SPARKS, 1831.
Harvard's and the nation's first
professor of American history Jared
Sparks's fulsome praises of Ethan
Allen "as a leading Revolutionary fig-
ure and committed democrat" in his
biography of Allen shaped the tem-
plate and set the tone for future biog-
raphers of the Hero of Ticonderoga.
*Portrait by Thomas Sully. Courtesy of the
Reynolda House Museum of American Art,
Winston-Salem, North Carolina.*

THE HERO CONFIRMED

In this new environment, the historians telling the story of Vermont in
response to the perplexing changes the state's leaders experienced made
an abrupt departure in the 1830s. Jared Sparks, followed by Zadock
Thompson's greatly improved and expanded second effort in 1842, initiated both a revised and a fuller account of Vermont's early years. In
these versions Ethan Allen would come to occupy a pedestal that he
had never mounted in his lifetime and a position he has not fully re-
linquished since. The new history diminished Thomas Chittenden,
Ira Allen, Seth Warner, and the rest of the cast, until then generally
credited as the most important midwives to Vermont's declaration and
assertion of independence. Sparks's *Life of Col. Ethan Allen*, the first
treatment of Allen as the embodiment of Vermont in a lengthy list of
books that would follow, appeared in 1834 in a volume containing the
biographies of John Stark and Richard Montgomery. Sparks apparently bought into Stevens's point of view, or at least flattered the collector that he had. "The resolution of the Green Mountain Boys," he wrote
to Stevens, "through all their troubles have hardly an example in history. They are worthy to be lauded and commemorated by their sons"
like Stevens and his colleagues. "The state owes its existence to them

as a state." He then went on to urge Stevens to get on with collecting documents that he could use.[59]

"Among those founders," Sparks asserted, "most conspicuous in laying the foundation upon which the independent state of Vermont has been reared, and indeed the champion of that resolute band of husbandmen . . . was Ethan Allen."[60] Allen, who had eagerly left the farm at the age of nineteen, became a "resolute husbandman" and not an ambitious land baron and speculator. The Ethan who had fled farming as a youth in Connecticut and did not return to it until he settled in the Burlington intervale two years before his passing became an agrarian democrat. For the first time since Ira Allen's *History*, Ethan Allen menacingly warned the Yorkers that "the gods of the valleys are not the gods of the hills."[61] Sparks's publication gave birth to what would become the dominant story of Vermont. After the Ejectment Trials, in a "bold step," and one "promptly taken," upon Allen's return from Albany with the unwelcome news of the failure of the Grants claimants, "the inhabitants of Bennington immediately assembled, and came to the formal determination to unite in resisting all encroachments upon the lands."[62] Long in their graves, Ira and Ethan Allen had gained command of the Vermont story. Though challenged by scholars in the twentieth century, they would not entirely give it up.

Sparks liberally refers to the Green Mountain Boys and has Ethan capture Fort Ticonderoga in the name of Jehovah and the Continental Congress. In Sparks's version, Ethan Allen returns to Vermont from his captivity in 1778 (with no mention of the plundered rum and "flowing bowl" to celebrate the Ticonderoga success or in the conclusion of Ethan's *Narrative*), arriving in Vermont "just in time to buckle on his armor, and enter with renewed vigor into a contest" to maintain Vermont's independence. Sparks asserts that the British overture that resulted in the Haldimand Negotiations, "as artful and positive as it was, made no impression on the patriotism of Ethan Allen." Sparks emphasized the importance of the negotiations to "prevent any further hostilities from Canada" and to put pressure on Congress for recognition.[63] He noted Allen's "roughness of manner, coarseness of language," his character "strongly marked, both by its excellences and defects." He concluded with a character evaluation that presaged subsequent treatments. Ethan "was brave, generous, and frank, true to his friends, true to his country, insistent and unyielding in his purposes, seeking at all times to promote the best interests of mankind, a lover of social harmony, and a determined foe of the artifices of injustice and encroachments of power." Allen "was eccentric and ambitious, but these weaknesses, if such they were, never betrayed him into dishonorable, unworthy, or selfish" conduct.[64] While as a biography rather than a history of Vermont the book would naturally tend to accentuate Allen's role, Sparks had elevated Allen to a new level as a Vermont founder. The leader of the Green Mountain Boys' terrorism had become "a lover of social harmony." Ethan Allen to a large extent became Vermont itself and a worthy symbol of just and innocent agrarian democrats seeking freedom and control of their own destinies. That Jared Sparks would write about Ethan Allen represents a major coup for Stevens. Sparks, the McLean Professor of Ancient and Modern History at Harvard, would serve as the college's seventeenth president in the 1840s. At the time he wrote Allen's biography, he served as the editor of the influential *North American Review*, had gotten well into his work on his twelve-volume *Life and Writings of George Washington*, and had spent time with Alexis de Tocqueville influencing his impressions articulated in *Democracy in America*. A biography carrying Sparks's imprimatur added national gravitas to the story of Ethan. Not surprisingly, other historians, biographers, and novelists confident of their subject would soon expound the same view.

Zadock Thompson's highly influential *History of Vermont, Natural, Civil, and Statistical, In Three Parts, With a new Map of the State, and 200 Engravings* (1842) clearly suggested he had read Ira Allen's *History*, Sparks's biography, and Daniel P. Thompson's popular novel *The Green Mountain Boys* (1839). He had also met with surviving members of the Allen family and others whose families had known Ethan, and he had probably seen some of the Allen material that Henry Stevens had begun to collect.[65] Thompson, who by 1850 had "published enough books to put a copy in every neighborhood in Vermont," "was viewed by Vermonters as the pre-eminent source of the historical knowledge of the state," even for "the most distinguished students of Vermont history." Stevens thought that "Thompson's Vermont . . . is considered a good work so far as it relates to Civil History."[66] Zadock Thompson, an early member of the Vermont Historical Society, stood near the center

ZADOCK THOMPSON.
Burlington educator, an avid
collector of scientific and historical
information in the second quarter
of the nineteenth century, and dean
of Vermont's historians, Thompson
produced several still useful historical compilations about Vermont.
Courtesy of Vermont Historical Society.

of the coterie led by Stevens and Daniel P. Thompson, both founders
and officers of the Society. The historian had written that the "growing
inequalities and distinction threaten the exercise of social virtues and
friendly feelings in Vermont; rank and property is beginning to throw
a chill over those gushing feelings of philanthropy which warmed the
hearts, animated the countenances, and blended the sympathies of earlier inhabitants of our land."[67] Stevens and Daniel P. Thompson, abetted by Zadock Thompson, worked diligently to create a usable past,
ironically by bringing together men of rank Zadock had in part blamed
for eroding Vermont's social fabric. They fervently believed their interpretation, and they apparently had little sense that they might have
served the Allens' storytelling purposes in searching for the meaning
of Vermont in the documents and other material they worked to preserve. The "rendition of the revolutionary mythology," surrounding
Ethan Allen "became a standard for numerous subsequent popular
histories."[68] Nine years after his first bland, derivative 1833 *History*,
Thompson in his 1842 *History of Vermont: Natural, Civil, and Statistical* gave additional attention to the Ejectment Trials.

He included Allen's retort to the Yorker attorneys that if they would
venture to the Grants they would learn the difference between the gods
in the "vallies" and hills, a defiant pronouncement absent from his 1833
work.[69] He devoted sixteen double-column, small-print pages to the an-

tics of the Green Mountain Boys, including an illustration of a Yorker miscreant dangling pathetically under the stuffed mountain lion atop the signpost at the Catamount Tavern in Bennington. Thompson in his new version placed Ethan at the head of the opposition to New York as "a man obviously fitted by nature for the circumstance and exigencies of the times. Bold, ardent, and unyielding, he possessed an unusual degree of vigor, both of body and mind, and an unlimited confidence in his own abilities." Along with his actions, Allen the skillful propagandist also wrote effectively in a manner "well suited to the state of public feeling, [about] the injustice and cruelty of the claims and proceedings of New York."

In the nine years since his 1833 history, Zadock Thompson had apparently experienced an epiphany. His earlier short account of the Haldimand Negotiations, which briefly covered both the first phase ended by the close of fighting in the Revolutionary War at Yorktown in 1781 and the second round begun the following year, became in 1842 a robust, unequivocal defense of the Vermont negotiators and an attack on their unworthy detractors. Thompson held that the "people of Vermont," though stronger than any others in support of American liberty, had "after all their efforts and sacrifices in the common cause . . . the mortification to find themselves denied a just participation in the blessings which they had labored to secure." Congress would neither acknowledge nor defend Vermont. "They could hardly wish to lend their aid for the purpose of bringing the struggle with a foreign enemy to a successful termination, when they perceived, by such an event, they should be subjected to the domination of a more detestable enemy at home," as Zadock Thompson characterized New York. Accordingly, "Vermont wisely consulted her own safety," and Ethan and Ira Allen, Chittenden, the Fays, and others, all with clear consciences, entered into the negotiations with the British.[70]

Thompson in a lengthy note articulated the interpretation of Allen and the Haldimand Negotiations as the clever actions of patriotic, committed apostles of Vermont liberty and independence who "always justified themselves in these proceedings, on the ground of self-preservation," though Thompson ignored the definition of "self-preservation" as the recognition of their New Hampshire titles. They worked "not only to protect Vermont, but [also] the United States, from an invasion by a powerful British army." The act of "concealing the true object of these negotiations" kept Congress anxious and prevented New York "from pressing her claims." In this somewhat upside-down version, the Vermonters concealed the nature of the negotiations not to protect themselves from the stench of treason but to prevent New York and Congress from taking action against them. Thompson went on to impugn the malevolence of those critics who regarded "the continuance of the correspondence and negotiations between the leading men in Vermont and British authorities, after the close of the war" as a form of treason. "There can be no doubt," Thompson asserted, that the Vermonters "were willing that the British authorities should deceive themselves with the expectation that Vermont might yet become a British province, while they themselves entertained no such thought."[71]

Thompson preached to the choir with Vermont readers, but some outsiders did not agree with his sermon. For example, in 1838 William L. Stone claimed in an echo of New York revolutionary authorities and also some members of the 1781 Vermont legislature that the Allens and their colleagues negotiated with a serious intent to rejoin the British Empire. Stone, according to Thompson, had "taken much pain to meddle with the character of those men, who were formerly so great a terror and annoyance to New York land speculators." These detractors "artfully endeavored to revive . . . an impression unfavorable to their reputation for patriotism." In this way Stone had misrepresented the "most indomitable friends of rational liberty, which this, or any other country has produced."[72] Thompson concluded his judgment on what remains a major controversy in Vermont's early history with a clear verdict of not guilty: "[It] is utterly impossible that any unprejudiced person, who is acquainted with the character of these men, and with our early history, should for a single moment doubt their patriotism, or entertain the thought that" Ethan Allen and his associates, "or indeed any of the leading men in Vermont . . . ever seriously contemplated a return of their allegiance to Great Britain."[73] Henry Stevens, fully agreeing with Thompson, also railed against Stone's accusations.[74] Thompson, Stevens, and others could not let the detractors stand unchallenged; they had to protect and defend their hero. The resolute, ringing thunder of Thompson's unqualified words would continue to rumble and echo into the twenty-first century.

After Zadock Thompson, the histories of Vermont and biographies of Ethan Allen in the next six decades all sang in unison and in the same key from an identical hymnal, some with better voice and pitch than others. This new wave that followed Sparks and Zadock Thompson reverently passed on the revised version of the Vermont story and Ethan's role. These new storytellers consciously wrote their version of the Vermont experience to warm "patriotism" and through it "strengthen" Vermont and, by extension, display their own virtue.[75] When Hosea Beckley published *The History of Vermont: with Descriptions, Physical and Topographical* in 1846, he acknowledged his debt to Zadock Thompson.[76] Beckley continued the "eulogistic praise" and reiterated Thompson's version of the Vermont and Allen stories. In 1853, the same year Thompson reissued his 1842 *History*, a professionally written *History of Vermont, from its Earliest Settlement to the Present Time* appeared in the Lippincott series of Cabinet Histories of the states. Pseudonymous authors W. H. Carpenter and T. S. Arthur called Allen "a self-constituted leader in troublous times — rude and overbearing in self-confidence. He was abashed by no consciousness of ignorance, and made boldness in his declaration of opinion serve him in the place of a more refined style."[77] They made Ethan a centerpiece in their arrangement of the state's history. The authors hinted that Vermont may have negotiated seriously with Haldimand's surrogates, but they could not "forebear a smile" at the management of the Haldimand Negotiations.[78] Carpenter and Arthur concluded that "probably nobody in the United States felt more rejoiced at the fall of Cornwallis," which ended the fighting in the Revolutionary War, stopped the first phase of the negotiations, and extricated Allen from an "inexorable embarrassment."[79]

The following year Henry Phinney, who published Bibles, almanacs, and school books in Buffalo, New York, published Henry DePuy's *Ethan Allen and the Green Mountain Heroes of '76*. Previously DePuy had written shallow biographies of famous men of action. His *Ethan Allen*, revised and reissued in 1855 as *The Mountain Hero and His Associates: The Green Mountain Boys of '76*, tells a story that equates Allen and Vermont with the American Revolution. DePuy's effort does nothing to elucidate Vermont's early history; its significance lies in its demonstration of how the efforts of Stevens, Daniel Thompson, and Zadock Thompson had prevailed.

DePuy's book begins with 129 pages of potted colonial history, followed by a 90-page reprint of Allen's captivity *Narrative*. The remaining 220 pages present the story of Ethan Allen from his most active years in the late 1760s until his death in 1789 as the history of Vermont. In his discussion of the "authorities" on which he relied, DePuy profusely thanked and praised Henry Stevens's "indefatigable" success in collecting the papers of the early settlers, "the correspondence of Revolutionary officers," and documents "in the archives of the nation or copies of them." When the Stevens collection is "placed before the public," DePuy asserted, "the world will be satisfied that these early settlers were men of no common mould, and their services will be better understood and more gratefully appreciated than at present."[80] DePuy helped put the Stevens collection before the public. He printed verbatim a long excerpt from Ira Allen's "journal" and more than nine pages of documents concerning the Haldimand Negotiations that Stevens had provided.[81] These documents, according to DePuy, demonstrated "that the odium thus cast upon the names of these men [for the Haldimand Negotiations] is grossly unjust; that they were not only inspired by the purest devotion to the cause of liberty, but their policy actually kept at bay a large hostile army, which otherwise would have been able to march through the northern portion of the United States."[82] He did not document Allen's military failings or the looting and drunken plundering that immediately followed the capture of Ticonderoga, instead asserting that "Colonel Allen exhibited great discretion in his new position."[83]

DePuy relied on the efforts of other members of the nascent Vermont Historical Society besides Henry Stevens. He borrowed heavily from Daniel P. Thompson's fiction, invented dialogue, and repeated the fantastic myths of superhuman strength and accomplishments that had grown up around Allen. He freely "acknowledged" the value of William Slade's *Vermont State Papers*; Daniel Chipman's lives of Seth Warner, Thomas Chittenden, and Nathaniel Chipman; and the major work of Zadock Thompson. DePuy endorsed Thompson's three-part *History of Vermont*, which he characterized as "a large work of six hundred pages of small type" and of "great research" that he thought should "hold a prominent place in the library of every citizen of the state." He also acknowledged the help of other members of the Society. He thanked

George F. Houghton of St. Albans, who had delivered "an eloquent address on the Life of Seth Warner" before the Vermont legislature. He "freely used" material from Hiland Hall's "Historical Readings" published in the Bennington *State Banner* and two addresses by Professor John Davie Butler, who spoke at the Society's Annual Meeting in 1846. DePuy absorbed his mentors' views on Vermont's past, and like them venerated his ancestors. "The American Revolution," he averred, "was no sudden outburst of popular fury. It had its origin in the first landing of the pilgrims." He concluded that "no individual, of equal advantages, and in the station he occupied, contributed more toward establishing the independence of our country, than Ethan Allen." Even with the qualifier of "equal advantages," DePuy overstates Allen's impact on the Revolution, which he sat out for nearly three years of captivity and never fought in after his release.

DePuy, an author outside the clique of the leading Vermonters busily venerating their ancestors, showed respect for their efforts, vindicated their work, and added legitimacy to the story of Ethan and the band of men who they claimed had embraced liberty, fought tyranny, and invented a new country and state. Printed from stereotype plates by Beadle and Company in Buffalo, DePuy's book was frequently reissued into the twentieth century as late as 1970.[84]

Two men named Hall published the best nineteenth-century histories of Vermont. Other than a reverence for serious research and a love of history, they shared little else but their surname in the approach to the formation of Vermont. Benjamin Homer Hall was the lone outlier among those who wrote about Vermont after Sparks's 1834 biography of Ethan Allen. Hall lived in Troy, New York. His grandfather, Lot Hall, had come to Vermont in 1782 after a distinguished naval career in the Revolution. Settling in Westminster, he practiced law, served several terms in the Vermont legislature, sat as a Supreme Court judge, and voted for Washington and John Adams as a presidential elector. His grandson Benjamin had no apparent connection to the Vermont Historical Society and its leaders. Living in New York State, he had no reason to shape his history in reaction to the perception of the problems confronting Vermont in the first half of the nineteenth century. As a Yorker and a descendant of an "east sider" where many holders of New Hampshire titles had made an accommodation with New York, he could appraise the struggle with New York from a vantage point different from most others writing about Vermont. His lengthy *History of Eastern Vermont, From Its Earliest Settlement to the Close of the Eighteenth Century* remains useful.[85] Hall thought the disputes "in which New York, New Hampshire, and Vermont were so long engaged . . . exerted an influence at the time . . . on every town and village and hamlet" in Vermont. But his search for an adequate account of the disputes went "unrewarded." Williams's version of Vermont's history, he thought, was devoted more "to a general account of the condition of the northern frontier of the United States, than to a specific description of the settlement and growth of Vermont." He thought that Ira Allen's account "abounded in inaccuracies, and was only minute in the narration of the affairs with which the author had been connected." Hall complimented Zadock Thompson for "evidences of thorough research and patient investigation," but he found none of the published works adequate. He would write his own account.[86]

Hall's decision to concentrate on the Connecticut River Valley towns led him to documents "which have never been consulted for their historic value." These included materials from the Vermont, New York, New Hampshire, Massachusetts, and the Connecticut Offices of the Secretary of State; the papers of staunch Yorker and Allen nemesis Charles Phelps; and the twenty-three volumes of the George Clinton papers in the New York State Library.[87] Unlike the standard biographical appendixes or chapters common to many nineteenth-century histories, Hall does not include Ethan Allen. With several sketches in the ten- to twelve-page range and the vast majority of three or less, Hall devotes his longest biographical sketch of thirty pages to Crean Brush, a Loyalist lawyer who raised Frances Montresor, Allen's second wife. Brush, who died in 1778 in suspicious circumstances left her one-third of his large estate, including thousands of acres in Vermont, New Hampshire, and New York.[88] Hall does not make Allen the leading actor in his history of eastern Vermont. Three pages in the Brush biographical sketch devoted to his courtship and marriage to Frances Montresor rank among Hall's longest discussions of Allen.[89]

In 1868 Hiland Hall published a thoroughly researched and detailed *History of Vermont: From Its Discovery to Its Admission into the Union in 1791*, generally referred to as the *Early History of Vermont*, the title embossed on the spine.[90] He tellingly dedicated his book to the Vermont Historical Society, which had "elected" him to membership at its first meeting in 1841 and which he served as president from 1859 to 1867. In 1842 he became the first person Henry Stevens had ever enlisted to speak to the Society's Annual Meeting. His long and distinguished résumé, careful research marshaled with the precision of a legal brief, and visibility in Vermont lent a special gravitas to his history and the reputation of Ethan Allen.[91]

Hall began his sketch of Ethan Allen in the biographical section at the end of the book with the comment "so much has been said of Gen. Allen in the body of this work, that little remains to be added, especially as he is widely known to the reading public." Nonetheless, he wrote four pages about Allen, while thirty-five of the other forty-seven biographical sketches amounted to a single paragraph.[92] "Hall researched his book quite carefully," but the premise built on his "firm assumption that Ira Allen's and Samuel Williams' histories were tantamount to unimpeachable primary sources and thus correct in their interpretations" led him to "a spirited defense of the state's early leaders against what he regarded as slanderous imputations by outsiders."[93] The flawed premise tarnished the argument that followed.

Hiland Hall called Allen's warning to the Yorker lawyers about the gods of the hills a "laconic figure of speech," and he denied that Allen briefly worked for them after the Ejectment Trials.[94] What Hall chooses to ignore in the sources suggests his commitment to preserving and building Allen's reputation. He makes no mention of the drunken chaos and looting that accompanied the capture of Fort Ticonderoga, and he devotes only one short paragraph to Allen's vainglorious blunder at St. John after ignoring Arnold's warning.[95] He thought that at the ill-fated attempt to take Montreal in September 1775 Allen commanded skillfully and "fought bravely" before most of his men deserted. John Brown had "failed to perform his part of the undertaking," which helped Hall explain Allen's defeat. After the British take Allen prisoner at Montreal, Hall does not discuss him until his return to Vermont in 1778.[96]

Hall provides a steady, well-documented narrative of the Vermonters' efforts to create a state and to achieve recognition by the Continental Congress and the countervailing forces that New York and New Hampshire brought to bear. He does not make the Haldimand Negotiations a centerpiece, but he does devote a page to refuting William L. Stone — "Mr. Stone" — a highly regarded New York historian Zadock Thompson had contradicted, as one of the "few writers of history who have charged the Vermont leaders with the serious intention of surrendering their state to the British crown."[97] The "leaders were not fools and could never have been guilty of such folly" especially, as he claimed inaccurately with lawyerly logic, because they had purged the state of Tories. The founders "were among the most ardent patriots of the state who during the whole revolutionary period and afterwards, so long as they lived," enjoyed the esteem of Vermonters.[98] They negotiated with the British to protect Vermont from invasion and to pressure Congress for recognition. With the publication of his carefully argued *History*, Hiland Hall, a capable researcher and a distinguished and widely known former governor and Vermont Historical Society president, put the capstone on the veneration of Ethan Allen and the story of Vermont that Jared Sparks had begun three and a half decades before. Few Vermont writers, even if so motivated, would have had the temerity to challenge Hiland Hall.

VERMONT'S NEW HISTORY

Until the 1830s Ethan Allen occupied a major but not dominant role in the creation and independence of Vermont. Other than his brother Ira's idiosyncratic account, Samuel Williams's *The Natural and Civil History of Vermont* and the derivative accounts that followed largely relegated Ethan to the resistance to New York claims, the capture of Fort Ticonderoga, the Haldimand Negotiations, and a few other activities. With Vermont thriving, Williams and the others focused on the success of the state within the new nation. Beginning in 1807 with Jefferson's Embargo through the middle of the nineteenth century Vermont changed. The expansive, confident, exuberant, prosperous, and rapidly growing polity that asserted and achieved its independence and full and equal status as the fourteenth state experienced a reversal. A series of economic dislocations, slowing of population growth, the changing nature of agriculture, and social problems, all perceived but not fully understood, provoked reactions that impacted all aspects of life in Vermont. Millennialism and waves of revivals, perfectionists, and other social architects attracted followers, while temperance, anti-slavery, and anti-Masonry crossed and roiled the state and its social and political life. Vermont leaders interpreted these events as evidence of social, moral, and economic decay, and they responded accordingly.

A major response involved the veneration of the founders of Vermont whose perceived pluck and commitment to principles of freedom and democracy paralleled, if not exceeded, activities in other states and provided Vermonters with a platform for validation of their society and a guide for the future. Ethan Allen emerged as the most important of these figures by a wide margin. He had promoted himself during his lifetime, and his brother Ira added fuel to the flickering flame that in the 1830s burst into a wildfire when a new generation of men pumped oxygen into the combustible mixture. Jared Sparks's 1834 biography, Daniel P. Thompson's fiction, and Zadock Thompson's 1842 history created a hero who blazed to mythic proportions. Henry Stevens amassed the materials from which they could build the foundation for their heroic stories. They erected an intrepid, larger-than-life figure who rose above all others in physical stature and prowess, bold determination, concern, and affection for his neighbors and their independence; an accomplished military leader; an articulate, ardent, and often colorful advocate for democracy; and the scourge of tyrants. Others reiterated the story of Ethan Allen until in 1868 Governor Hiland Hall stamped his august imprimatur on the story and locked it in. That story remained unchallenged for more than a half-century, burnished by derivative accounts. Victorian Vermonters and their acolytes also built an infrastructure to encourage and sustain their story of Vermont and Ethan Allen. They established the Vermont Historical Society and its library, archives, and collections; produced statewide publications like the eight-volume *Records of the Governor and Council* and the *Vermont State Papers*; and participated in and encouraged activities in local history like Abby Maria Hemenway's monumental *Vermont Historical Gazetteer*, a few substantial town histories, and some local historical societies. Joined by others, they also set about establishing an iconography of their hero in literature, statuary, and graphic imagery. By the 1870s public memory of Ethan Allen would contain an array of visual images to complete the story of Ethan Allen symbolizing Vermont's heroic past, and provide a map for what they hoped the state would become.

Fiction resists fact to persist as heritage.

{ DAVID LOWENTHAL }

CHAPTER V

THE MANY GUISES OF THE HERO

Ethan Allen in Fiction, Stone, Uniform, and Popular Imagination

Historians, biographers, and novelists created Vermont's paramount hero in the first half-century after his death and then sustained the image with little compromise even in the face of countervailing evidence. In other media, sculptors, painters, and print makers would reinforce the importance and heroic nature of Ethan Allen. By the second quarter of the nineteenth century Vermont leaders, coping with vast, perplexing, and negative change, invented a virtuous past for Vermont with Allen as its leader. Though specific to Vermont's perceived problems, these treatments coincided with a national movement that revolved around what Michael Kammen has called "a mythos of the American Revolution." Sharing memories of the event helped unify the republic. As the nineteenth century advanced, survivors of the war with active memories contributed to a dominant collective memory that envisioned a citizenry shaped by republican ideals of virtue and sacrifice. Initially, war leaders, most prominently George Washington, provided the exemplary models of virtue. Lesser, but still significant heroes — John Paul Jones, Francis Marion, and Richard Montgomery — came from the ranks below Washington. The methods of late eighteenth-century American biographies reflected the continuing influence of classical antiquity and medieval hagiography. Plutarch's *Lives* became the most popular model, satisfying Henry St. John Bolingbroke's dictum: "History is philosophy teaching by example."[1] The Massachusetts Federalist Jedidiah Morse made a teachable moment of General Richard Montgomery's death in the failed attack on Quebec on December 31, 1775. A Congregational minister and popular geographer in Charlestown, Morse wrote a dual biography for students, a *Life of Washington and also of Brave General Montgomery* (1791). He presented both men as following the Roman model of the farmer-warrior Cincinnatus. A veteran of the French and Indian War, Washington returned to his Virginia plantation, but when called to command the Continental Army left behind the life of a country gentleman to lead the colonies in the war against Britain. Montgomery, also a veteran of the earlier war, emigrated from Ireland to New York's Hudson River Valley to marry into the Hudson River aristocracy and to become a gentleman farmer, and like Cincinnatus, answered the call to join Washington's army. His death in battle pointedly served the purpose of Morse's school book, encouraging young Americans to lead virtuous republican lives of honesty and self-sacrifice.[2]

Ethan Allen had predicted that a victory for Montgomery's army in Canada would bring them fame and glory. As a martyr-hero, Montgomery affirmed that the new nation was worth dying for, but his sacrifice provided no guarantee of enduring fame. Like Allen he would need assistance from others who lived on and kept his memory alive. After more than forty years of persistently lobbying Congress and New York's governors, Montgomery's widow Janet Livingston finally succeeded in bringing his remains from Quebec to a New York City grave in 1818.[3] As it receded into an increasingly distant past in the 1820s and 1830s, the Revolution became a noncontroversial and nonpartisan event. Kammen has further argued that Americans trivialized and "de-radicalized" the War for Independence, as they recalled it for the purposes of historical novels and sentimental biographies.[4] But in the 1840s and 1850s, following the American success in the Mexican War (1846–48), historians and popular writers also fueled a growing militarism in the country with new recollections and biographies of the leaders of the War for Independence.[5]

Ira Allen's history of Vermont, Jared Sparks's biography, and Zadock Thompson's history of Vermont (1842) presented the state's past as a sermon on its creation, an accomplishment they mostly credited to Ethan Allen. According to Ira's disingenuous introduction of his brother — "Ethan Allen, Esq., a proprietor of the New Hampshire grants" (without mentioning the brothers' Onion River Land Company, the largest private land owner in the state) — he was singularly motivated by a disinterested concern for the natural rights of his fellow settlers.[6] These accounts present Allen as the conventional revolutionary hero cast from the same mold that Parson Weems used for George Washington.[7] Ira says that in 1778 he had acquired on behalf of Ethan a 150-acre farm from James Claghorn, commissioner of sales for the Confiscation Court of Bennington County, for the price of £300. Ira's holograph statement of purchase, the only surviving record of that acquisition, notes, "Said land was forfeited by William Marsh, lying on Onion River about 3 miles below the falls on the N.E. side of the town of Burlington/Ira Allen." The tract of land, Ira later wrote, was part of "the country my heart delighted in," the Champlain Valley, where most of their landholdings were located.[8] In 1784 when Ethan and Ira, the surviving partners, distributed their land company's inventory of land titles between them, Loyalist Marsh's land on the Onion River became the first piece of a large tract that would later make up Ethan Allen's 1,400-acre Burlington farm. Allen lived at his retreat from public affairs for less than two years before he died, just long enough to allow subsequent writers to portray him as a simple farmer and champion of his fellow yeomen in their struggle against Yorker aristocrats. Ira took his share in land at the first falls of the Winooski River and other valuable acreage in the Champlain Valley with potential dam sites for water power and navigable connection to Lake Champlain.

THE HERO OF HISTORICAL ROMANCE NOVELS

Nearly fifty years later, however, by the 1840s, the popular success of James Fenimore Cooper's Leatherstocking Tales had stimulated a new generation of regional writers of historical fiction set in the colonial and Revolutionary era. Vermont's Daniel P. Thompson (1795–1868), a founding member of the Vermont Historical Society, resurrected Ethan Allen as the perfect model of imitable virtues to overcome Vermont's moral and social dilemmas. Thompson's frequently reprinted historical romance, *The Green Mountain Boys: A Historical Tale of the Early Settlement of Vermont* (1839), created a new Ethan Allen for the pop-

FREDERIC VAN DE WATER.
A prolific twentieth-century author
of historical fiction set in early New
England and Vermont, Van de Water
frequently drew from the the traditionalist story of Vermont for fictional
versions of Ethan Allen and the
Green Mountain Boys' adventures.
Courtesy of Vermont Historical Society.

ular imagination. His version of Allen lived on through the nineteenth
century in multiple reissues and with various modifications in popular
historical novels, such as Vermonter Rowland Robinson's *The Hero of
Ticonderoga* (1898). It prompted derivative novels well into the twentieth century, including Frederic Van de Water's *Reluctant Rebel* (1948)
and *Catch a Falling Star* (1944).

In 1922 the literary historian Carl Van Doren found that Thompson
"could tell a straight story plainly and rapidly, and he touched action
with rhetoric in just the proportion needed to sell fifty editions of the
book by 1860 and to make it a standard book for boys in the early
twentieth century—by far the most popular romance of the immediate school of Cooper."[9] Also aimed at young readers, a "modernized"
edition of *The Green Mountain Boys* appeared in 2000, and since then
at least eight authors have published biographies of Ethan Allen for
young readers.[10]

The Green Mountain Boys, the most popular novel written in nineteenth-century Vermont, offered generations of readers a condensed
version of events leading up to Ethan Allen and the Green Mountain

Boys defying the Yorkers and taking the old forts at Ticonderoga and Crown Point and then leaps to Seth Warner later leading his Continental Green Mountain regiment in the rear guard battle at Hubbardton in 1777. Presenting Vermont's early history as a fiction allowed Thompson a great deal of authorial freedom. His Ethan Allen is a rugged individualist of the northern frontier and the Robin Hood of the Green Mountains leading a band of "revolutionary outlaws." Though no verifiable portrait or likeness of Allen exist, general reports of his "large frame" have survived. Alexander Graydon, a prisoner in New York with Allen in 1777, recalled him as "a robust, large-framed man, worn down by confinement and hard fare."[11] Thompson's Allen leads the resistance to New York's land claims in the early 1770s as a large, "brawny" figure enhanced with golden locks and dressed in homespun and hob-nailed boots, the outfit of a frontiersman in the later generation of Mike Fink, Davy Crockett, and other folk heroes of the Age of Jackson.[12]

Thompson pads his narrative with several subplots. The novel's principal villain, Jake Sherwood, vaguely resembles Justus Sherwood, an original Green Mountain Boy who turned Queen's Loyal Ranger, spymaster, and chief spokesman for the British in the Haldimand Negotiations. He unsuccessfully pursues the novel's romantic heroine Alma Hendee and her father's wealth. Four additional romantic entanglements expand the tale. The novel concludes with a jocular, though still commanding, Ethan Allen ordering the quadruple nuptials of eight lovers. Charles Warrington, vaguely modeled after Seth Warner, marries Alma. Her long-lost brother, given to the Indians as a child in one of Sherwood's schemes, marries and redeems Jessy Reed, the Tory daughter of a New York land speculator whose Scots tenants Ethan Allen and his men had roughly evicted from Panton. A Green Mountain Boy Pete Jones, a conventional comic Jonathan, marries Alma's maid Ruth; and Neshobee, the Indian friend of the Hendees, marries the ambiguously African American servant girl Zilpha. Each Jack gets his Jill in a heavy-handed comedy ending. Colonel-Commandant Allen's order for the couples to marry assures the continuance of a hierarchical social order.

Thompson's characterization is one-dimensional and banal; the first three characters to appear are named Smith, Jones, and Brown. Rhetoric is overblown and obvious. Dialogue is stilted, excessively formal, and pseudo-literary, doing most of its damage in the story's dramatic crises. The rustic Jones is Monty Pythonesque: "The jolly woodsman turned and bounded down the slope like a young colt, singing out, 'Trol, lol, lol de darly!'"[13] As Old Ethan had duped his Yorker antagonists on the front page of the *Vermont Gazette* in 1789, Allen the tavern trickster prevails again. This time he eludes capture by British regulars with help from the tavern keeper's clever daughter.

A creaky plot avoids important years of real time, echoing earlier warrior tales and anticipating later cowboy stories. First, there's everything before the fight; then the fight; and then everything after the fight. Thompson knows the formula, but he uses the wrong fight — the rear guard action at Hubbardton, from which no real victors emerge — rather than the big shootout, the Bennington battle on the banks of the Walloomsac a few weeks later. He obliquely alludes to the fight at Bennington — the single most important event of the War for Independence to involve the newly organized government of Vermont and Vermonters collectively in its purpose and outcome — only in an aside after the fight. Thus Thompson avoids an explanation to his readers about Allen's foolish failure and capture at Montreal in 1775 and his imprisonment by the British in New York City at the time of the Bennington battle. This silent affront to Vermont's revolutionary past covers the blot on Allen's 'scutcheon.

Neshobee, the "friendly Indian," and the Indian allies of the British army are savages, wild creatures, and demons of the forest. The inscrutable, mysterious Neshobee's only redeeming qualities come from having been taken from his home and family to live with the Hendees. Like Captain Hendee's dog, he has a preternatural sense of intruders approaching the Hendee house, as he dances around the farmyard listening to tree stumps for messages. The dog yelps encouragement as he also senses the intruders, then barks to confirm Neshobee's animal sense of danger. Later, when the story moves to British General John Burgoyne's camp and a war feast for his Mohawk allies, Thompson renders the scene as full of "Hell and thunder! What whooping and yelling there was. One would have thought that all the underworld had been emptied upon the earth, and that the earth was alive with devils!" Whether they serve the British or the colonists, Thompson's Indians are clearly something other than human, suggesting a cognitive

disjunction between his roles as one of Vermont's most prominent ab-
olitionists and a novelist relying on racist clichés for dramatic effect.

As a vehicle for teaching early Vermont history, however, *Green
Mountain Boys* is best understood as a vehicle for myth. The myth
becomes clear when heroines are "fairest in the land" (true of all the
women in this book, including the formidable Ann Story, who hides her
children from Indians and the British by living in a hole in the ground).
The heroes are spectacular but, despite the book's plural title, Ethan
Allen is the dominant hero. *Green Mountain Boys* passes the test for
mythology. While historians, biographers, and others erected Ethan
Allen as an iconic symbol for all that Vermonters had come to cherish
of their past, Daniel Thompson's melodramatic novel did as much as
any other vehicle to make him a popular hero.

Thompson's successful resurrection of Ethan Allen was the first literary treatment of him that attempted to portray his physical dimensions and appearance in some detail, including his clothes and boots.
The novelist Herman Melville, a writer more widely known than Vermont's Judge Thompson in the 1850s, was also drawn to the figure of
Ethan Allen as he appeared in *A Narrative of Colonel Ethan Allen's Captivity* and Thompson's *Green Mountain Boys*. Allen appears briefly in
his short and only historical novel, *Israel Potter, His Fifty Years of Exile*
(1855). With only Allen's *Narrative* and Thompson's novel as sources
for the physical figure of the hero, Melville depends heavily on simile to
portray Ethan Allen. *Israel Potter* recognized and expanded the imaginative power of Allen's popular captivity narrative with its own version
of the imprisoned Hero of Ticonderoga.

In the course of his many adventures Israel Potter, a Revolutionary War veteran and Bunker Hill survivor also taken prisoner by the
British, meets a variety of prominent figures of his time, ranging from
Benjamin Franklin and King George III to John Paul Jones and Ethan
Allen. During the early years of Potter's long exile in Europe, he encounters Allen, iron-bound in Falmouth's Pendennis Castle, and offers
to help free him from the British prison. The novel's narrator observed:
"Among the episodes of the Revolutionary War, none is stranger than
that of Ethan Allen in England; the event and the man being equally uncommon." When Potter comes upon Allen in the prison yard, he seems
a "baited bull in the ring," a "Patagonian" giant, "outlandishly arrayed

in the sorry remains of a half-Indian, half-Canadian sort of dress." His "whole marred aspect was that of some wild beast; but a loyal sort, and unsubdued by the cage." Allen shouts at a crowd of gawkers: "You may well stare at Ethan Ticonderoga Allen, the unconquered soldier, by—! Ha! Three times–three for glorious old Vermont and my Green Mountain Boys! Hurrah! Hurrah! Hurrah! Hurrah!" (Melville set the novel in early 1776; the new state named Vermont came into existence in mid-1777.) Allen combines the strong man Hercules, the jokester Joe Miller, the Perfect Knight Bayard, and the western spirit of Americanism, for "the western spirit is, or will yet be (for no other is or can be) the true American one."[14] The towering image of a rugged giant full of the wild western spirit, who will in a later anecdote weep for babes lost in the woods, dripped with unforgettable melodrama. But what did he *really* look like, curious readers and a parade of biographers and historians have asked. They have concluded: large. But how tall and robust, what shape did his face have, what kind of clothes did he wear, what was the color of his hair? Melville passes over the details of Allen's clothes— "half Indian, half Canadian." Relying on Thompson's version of Allen's hair, Melville reveals its color while Allen flirts with a group of English ladies who have come to see the oddity of a rebel prisoner. Unexpectedly fluent and witty as an English gentleman, Allen manages to kiss one's hand and entice her to clip his "flaxen hair" for a memento. Flirting and titillating, playing Delilah to Allen's Sampson, she sighs, "Ah, this is like clipping tangled tags of gold lace."[15]

ETHAN ALLEN IN A MILITARY UNIFORM

Eventually technological and cultural developments produced imaginative visual imagery of Ethan Allen to answer questions about his form and figure and fully display his celebrity power. New methods of line engraving and steam press printing in the mid-nineteenth century produced graphic figures of Ethan Allen to accompany and expand the literary depictions conceived for his resurrection. Enthusiasm over the Mexican War of the late 1840s stimulated a long dormant militarism in the United States that helped to produce the figure of Ethan Allen in an officer's uniform of the Continental Army, a uniform he never actually wore and an army in which he never served.[16] Uniformed militias had organized across the country by the 1850s, many of them memorializing heroes of the Revolutionary era as their patron heroes. Uniformed militias also provided popular entertainment. They organized and acquired infantry marching skills to perform in competitive military drill exhibitions, marching to their bands' martial music. Vermont's town militia companies were required by law to muster once annually in the pre–Civil War era, but the three-day summer event provided an excuse for merriment and drinking instead of training troops. Disorderly musters and wrong-footed marching prompted wags to characterize their local militia companies as "floodwood." Uniformed militia could also perform police duties, as in 1846 when the Burlington Light Infantry marched to a railway construction site in Richmond to suppress a strike by unpaid construction crews.[17] Uniformed militia companies in other towns, such as the Ransom Guards and the Barlow Grays of St. Albans, conducted combat exercises as the prospects for Civil War heightened. The toothless Yankee trickster Ethan Allen had become old stuff by 1840, and an active, physically impressive military figure in uniform would have had more appeal than even a retired patriarchal veteran, a Cincinnatus. In those circumstances, a visual image of Ethan Allen better suited to the new times began to appear. Most importantly, he had to project an heroic leader for that military role, not simply a brawny common man wearing hobnail boots dressed in buckskin or hard-worn *faux* regimentals.

In fact, Allen and his followers wore no military uniforms when he led the mob of Green Mountain Boys from 1772 to 1775 resisting New York's claims and authority. Allen and the eighty-three farmers who accompanied him across Lake Champlain would have worn their customary homespun shirts, smocks, dusters, and buckskin pants. The small detachment of British troops at Ticonderoga and Crown Point wore the only military uniforms in that region of the world at the time. Allen reported in the narrative of his captivity that on the campaign against Canada, he wore the civilian clothes of a hunter, including a tuque, the Phrygian liberty cap.[18] By September 1775, however, the Green Mountain rangers under Seth Warner, first as a unit of New York militia and later as a regiment in the Continental Army, wore green, red-trimmed woolen uniform coats provided by New York's commissary.[19]

In the 1870s, one hundred years after the capture of Ticonderoga,

ETHAN ALLEN TAKES TICONDEROGA.
This frequently reproduced image by Alonzo Chappel (1859) incorrectly represented Allen and the Green Mountain Boys in Continental Army uniforms.
Source: U.S. National Archives and Records.

the artist John Steeple Davis (1844–1917) produced a frequently reprinted image of that event, representing Allen in the military dress of a Continental Army officer with Benedict Arnold in similar attire. No Green Mountain Boys appear in the scene, but a variant of Davis's picture displays two lines of uniformed Continental troops in the courtyard with muskets and bayonets at the ready confronting surprised British regulars.

Arnold is out of sight. This pictorial representation marks the complete resurrection of Colonel Ethan Allen. Yet the Continental Army did not exist in May 1775. Later, in 1777, as a prisoner on parole in New York City with relative freedom to walk around the town, Allen first appeared in a suit of Irish wool cut and tailored as a business suit, an outfit that with minimal alterations could pass for a military uniform. Alexander Graydon later recalled seeing Allen walking through the city wearing "a suit of blue clothes . . . [and] a gold laced hat that had been presented to him by the gentlemen of Cork enabled him to make a very passable appearance for a rebel colonel."[20] Sometime after his release, he further militarized his costume with a pair of large gold colored epaulettes, which, with the gold-laced Irish tricorn, at least one observer at the Vermont–New York militia standoff over the West Union dispute in 1781, the so-called Walloomsac Siege, found comical.[21] Early in the captivity narrative, Allen described his footwear as a "good pair of shoes." At Cork, his Irish friends also gave him two pairs of new shoes.[22] Thompson and Melville had added feelings, flaxen hair, and bulk to the giant hero, but after Davis's picture of Ethan Allen, whether engraved waving a long sword as he demanded Ticonderoga's capitulation or sculpted in stone to stand on a pedestal, he always wore fine leather boots like George Washington's. Ethan Allen eventually became a military leader in fact as well as story when the Vermont General Assembly commissioned him colonel and then brigadier general to lead the Vermont militia from 1779 to 1781. But after William Hutchins, Simeon Hathaway, and his wife's cousin Timothy Brownson accused him at a session of the General Assembly of treasonous negotiations with the British, he resigned in anger. He eventually resumed command as general of the southern brigade of the Vermont militia.[23]

An incident in New York City during the first months of the Civil War suggests Ethan Allen's currency in nineteenth-century American popular culture. On their way to oppose the Confederacy in May 1861, the 1st Vermont Volunteer Regiment marched down Broadway, led by Brattleboro's Colonel John Wolcott Phelps (1813–85), a West Point graduate and distinguished veteran of the Mexican War. "Tall and of massive form, with an immense army hat and black ostrich plume," Phelps brought cries of "'who is that big Vermont colonel?' The prompt answer was, 'that's old Ethan Allen resurrected.'"[24] Phelps's great-grandfather, Charles Phelps, had vigorously opposed Ethan Allen and the government of Vermont from 1779 to 1789.[25]

Despite the total lack of an authenticated likeness of Ethan Allen, posthumously generated literary and graphic images by authors and artists who had never seen the live Allen were widely available by 1861 and would be reprinted repeatedly into the twenty-first century. Of the eight Allen siblings, only a miniature portrait of Ira, a French passport description of him, and a written description of Zimri survive. Jerusha

Allen directed Ira "to go to the best limner in New york and have your minnature takin and set in sollid gould."[26] A small portrait of Jerusha can be seen in the Wilbur Collection at the University of Vermont and a full body portrait of Ethan's second wife, Frances Montresor Buchanan, at age ten or eleven graces Fort Ticonderoga's collection of colonial and revolutionary portraits. Working in New York during 1770–71, the Boston portraitist John Singleton Copley painted a splendid portrait of John Montresor, Frances's father.

In 1814 Frances's cousin, Henry Rowe Schoolcraft, interviewed her at Lake Dunmore, where she had withdrawn from Burlington and Lake Champlain during the War of 1812. Schoolcraft, who would go on to become an ethnologist of native American life and culture, recalled her many years later: "an erect figure, middle size, with an energetic step, and a marked intellectual physiognomy. Her animated eyes assumed their full expression in speaking of her grandfather Calcraft, 'a loyal Briton . . . whose military services under the Duke of Marlborough she appeared to hold in lively remembrance.'"[27]

In 1773 Constable Nathaniel Buell of Salisbury, Connecticut, posted a reward notice for the second youngest Allen brother Zimri (1748–76), who stood "near six feet high, firm built, goes something stooping, dark hair . . . being arm'd with sword and pistol."[28] The Library of Congress contains several unverifiable images purportedly of Ethan Allen, and from time to time several other equally unverifiable images have been offered for sale by collectors as authentic likenesses of him. The most complete description of his figure as a prisoner in New York is found in Alexander Graydon's memoir: in late 1777 Ethan Allen was "a robust large framed man worn down by confinement and hard fare."[29] In 1858, seventy-five-year-old Burlingtonian Huldah Collins reported to the *Burlington Free Press* that she attended Allen's funeral at age six, had known him as a child, and could recall a generic figure, "a pretty tall man—pretty red faced."[30] Most adults are "pretty tall" to six-year-old children and Vermont then and now receives enough sun and wind for most farmers to acquire red faces. Some readers have tried to connect Huldah Collins's memory of a "pretty red faced" Allen to his excessive alcohol consumption, a diagnosis impossible to confirm or deny.

D. P. Thompson's fictional Allen had replaced the earliest posthumous literary images of him found first in the *Vermont Gazette*'s clever

FRANCES MONTRESOR. Born in 1760, Montresor was the natural daughter of Anna Schoolcraft of Scoharie, New York, and Captain John Montresor of the British Army Corps of Engineers. She grew up in Crean Brush's household, and she married Ethan Allen in 1784. The portrait was painted in 1771. *Fort Ticonderoga Museum.*

old tavern trickster outwitting New York dandies and later in brother Ira's version of Ethan that followed ten years after his death, in which he appears as the thoughtful country gentleman and retired warrior like George Washington. Between his death in 1789 and the mid-1830s, however, the population of Vermont nearly tripled. Generally forgotten even in Vermont by then, Allen regained a place in collective remembrance through historical fiction and biographical sketches that owed much to the self-created hero of his continuously popular captivity narrative and even more to the creative imaginations of writers who found few original and verifiable resources to fill out the character of Ethan Allen for their texts. In the twentieth century, for example, consistent with his generally overblown characterization of Allen, Stewart Holbrook's physical description of him exaggerated Allen's height, presenting a "near gigantic stature, a man to talk to pines."[31] Holbrook offers no sample conversations. And Ethan Allen's actual physical appearance remains unknown, Davis's and other images of him notwithstanding. Ethan Allen was "a large man," and that is the limit of what we know.

Thompson's fictional figure of Ethan Allen underwent changes and evolved in the one hundred years following his resurrection in *The*

JOHN MONTRESOR.
John Singleton Copley painted this
portrait of Frances Montresor's father
in New York, where he was supervis-
ing defense construction during 1771.
Courtesy of Bridgeman Art Library Inter-
national, New York.

Green Mountain Boys. On the eve of television overtaking cinema and
pulp fiction for popular entertainment, Frederic Van de Water's novel
The Reluctant Republic: Vermont, 1724–1791 (1941) replaced Thompson's Jacksonian hero with a military figure graphically indebted to
Steeple Davis's painting and Alonzo Chappell's widely distributed engraving of Allen taking Ticonderoga. Early in the novel, during Allen's leadership of the Green Mountain Boys against New York in the
years before attacking Fort Ticonderoga, he enters a Bennington tavern
full of Yorkers and British officers from the fort. The officers include a
timorous Lieutenant Jocelyn Feltham, who will later in May 1775 trigger Allen's invocation of Jehovah and the Continental Congress as his
authority to seize the fort. Allen's "bulk filled the doorway. His harsh
face shone against the night. He swung his gilt-bound hat aloft in ac-
knowledgement. . . . Epaulettes stressed the vast shoulder breadth of
the green and golden coat. A gorget gleamed below a massive chin.
Scarlet waistcoat and buff breeches further encased the stranger, and
on tall boots immense spurs jingled as he strode forward. Light found
the hilt of a mighty saber and gave it brazen shining."[32] Aiming for a
full celebrity treatment of his hero, Van de Water attired him anachronistically — Allen's Irish friends gave him the gold-trimmed tricorn in
1776; the scarlet waist coat and gorget signify a military man, as do the
boots, a costume fully displayed in Charles Wilson Peale's 1772 portrait

of George Washington in his Virginia militia regimentals; Allen was not a "horse soldier," but the cavalry or dragoon saber seems to have replaced the shorter cutlass the Allens carried during the real time of "the antient mobb," 1772 to early 1775. Van de Water as Allen's uniform designer obviously draws from Davis's black-and-white painting and Chappell's engravings of Allen capturing Ticonderoga, by way of John Pell. Allen in a green and gold coat appeared in the twentieth century in Pell and Van de Water and in the twenty-first century in Randall.[33]

MEMORIAL STATUES OF ETHAN ALLEN

Calculating perhaps that the national interest in the military during and after the Mexican War might offer an opportunity to sell some military statuary, the Massachusetts artist Benjamin Harris Kinney in 1851 carved a now lost wooden statue of the Hero of Ticonderoga swathed in a large cape and brought it to Burlington to exhibit. It failed to draw sufficient viewers to pay his expenses.[34] Nonetheless, a group of prominent Vermonters sought to memorialize Allen with a sculpted full body stone image of their hero. Later in the 1850s and for nearly another one hundred years, stone sculptors of Ethan Allen, without a source image of him for their model, simply ignored the issue of Allen's actual appearance in life. The virtues and characteristics of Ethan Allen would find expression in stone based on the posthumous literary versions of the man. Many leading Vermonters had been critical of the Mexican War, including Congressman George Perkins Marsh, who, in 1848 told the House of Representatives he considered the war with Mexico "in no other light than as a national crime."[35] On the eve of the Civil War, however, a growing interest in Vermont's military past led to the first official efforts by the Vermont General Assembly and Congressman Marsh to memorialize Ethan Allen in stone. Marsh's enthusiastic promotion of this project included a fierce rejection of one version of Ethan Allen's head by the artist Peter Stephenson of Boston.

Stone memorials in themselves have no memory, though they may store or transmit information about the past, or act as social-psychological triggers to recall often very powerful images or emotions.[36] Thus statues as well as literary narratives and imagery lead people to create a past through active remembrances that sometimes help define both personal

ETHAN ALLEN STATUE,
VERMONT STATE HOUSE.
The original 1861 Rutland marble
statue of Ethan Allen by Brattleboro
sculptor Larkin Mead gave way to
this duplicate, less the original heroic
sword, in 1941. *Courtesy of Don Shall.*

and collective identities.[37] In a preview of the memorial battalions of
granite and marble Civil War soldiers erected in cities and towns across
the nation in the 1880s and 1890s, a private committee formed in Vermont in 1855 to raise funds for a monumental statue of Allen to memorialize his unmarked grave. Larkin Mead of Brattleboro completed
the statue, but the committee lacked sufficient funds to pay for it. The
Vermont General Assembly stepped in and paid Mead for the statue of
Allen, but installed it on the porch of the rebuilt State House in Montpelier in 1861 instead of atop the column in Green Mount Cemetery.[38]
After eighty years of exposure to Vermont's freeze-thaw cycles and the
acidic smoke of coal-fired train traffic running nearby, the state replaced
the badly eroded original figure of Allen with a replica of Mead's statue
produced in Montpelier in 1941.

Larkin Mead had left the United States in 1862 to take up residence
in Italy, and his studio in Italy was known in Vermont's marble industry. Many Vermonters believed that his original statue of Ethan Allen
on the State House porch was sculpted from Italian marble. In the
twentieth century for many years the Vermont Marble Company had
offered to replace Mead's marble statue of Ethan Allen with a Vermont

marble figure of him to stand before the capitol of a state widely known for its native marble. Finally, the Vermont Marble Company was called in to remove Mead's weather-damaged original from the State House porch and set it up in one of their workshops, where the sculptor Aristide Piccini replicated it. Unknown at the time, however, the eroded statue of Ethan Allen had not been cut from Italian marble, but from Vermont marble donated to the project by the wealthy banker and marble quarry owner Henry Baxter of Rutland.[39]

George Perkins Marsh and John N. Pomeroy of Burlington, two members of the original committee appointed to oversee the placement of a statue of Allen to mark his grave, continued through the 1860s to lobby for the cause. The sculptor Peter Stephenson of Boston was called on this time to design a model of the statue to be "wrought at Carrara, Italy, by the firm of Cassoni and Isola of Carrara and New York."[40] Stephenson based his model on the statue by Mead then standing at the Vermont State House. In both statues Allen's marble figure holds the pose of the "Hero of Ticonderoga," but the two statues are not identical. The later statue installed in the cemetery in 1873 has Allen poised with his left hand raised in the air signaling victory and his right hand holding a sword. The State House statue has him standing with his right hand raised, allowing a broadside view of him from the State House lawn. Living in Italy and serving as the U.S. minister to the Kingdom of Italy since 1860, Marsh rejected a photograph of the model of Allen's head based on the first Mead statue on the State House porch, calling it "a paltry vulgar expressionless head, and I would rather burn the statue in a lime kiln than see it on the column with such a mug." The second, acceptable head tops off the statue with a generic, youthful face and hair that could have served as well for a statue of Lord Byron. The flowing locks are uncolored marble, but readers of *The Green Mountain Boys* and *Israel Potter* knew those versions of Ethan Allen fashioned him with lacy, golden locks.[41]

On July 4, 1873, a group of Vermont's political and social leaders accompanied by prominent veterans of the Union Army, complete with several military bands and a choir, gathered in Burlington's Green Mount Cemetery before an audience of four hundred for the unveiling of the long-delayed memorial statue of Allen in heroic pose. An Italian studio sculpted Peter Stephenson's reverse image model of Mead's

ETHAN ALLEN'S STATUE,
GREEN MOUNT CEMETERY.
The 1873 statue of Ethan Allen
"near his grave" presents a duplicate
reverse image of Larkin Mead's 1861
State House statue of Ethan Allen
and a more handsome face than the
State House statue that George
Perkins Marsh rejected.
Courtesy of Don Shall.

statue of Allen on the State House porch. Allen appears as a hatless statue atop a plinth and forty-two-foot column near the still unknown actual site of his grave.[42]

A lengthy speech by Lucius E. Chittenden, great-grandson of the state's first governor, detailed the adventures of the "Hero of Ticonderoga."[43] Known for his "fondness for the dramatic as well as a bias for Vermont," Chittenden concluded by invoking an undefined "spirit of Ethan Allen" to help his hearers guard against the evils of the time and recruiting them in a global mission: "Men of Vermont! . . . Yonder shaft and statue, the monument of a soldier's glory, are your instruction. . . . watch with eagle eye the sappers and miners of corruption, approaching with stealthy steps on every side the temple wherein is the treasure of your inheritance." Chittenden admonished the crowd that they had "a mission whose field is the world. Your duty cannot be performed until corruption, tyranny and oppression are driven from the earth—until every human being, created in the image of his Maker is a freeman, in full possession of his natural birthright of life, liberty and the pursuit of happiness." He concluded, "Let Vermonters emulate their [Allen's and his associates'] energy and follow their examples, and there may be yet other Vermonts on the Pacific shores, in the Celestial Empire and Farther India."[44] John N. Pomeroy, the chairman of the

ETHAN ALLEN STATUE,
U.S. CAPITOL, NATIONAL
STATUARY HALL COLLECTION.
The State of Vermont gave this
statue of Ethan Allen by Larkin
Mead to the National Statuary Hall
Collection as an 1876 centennial gift.
*Source: Architect of the United States
Capitol*

event's organizing committee, left unacknowledged the fantastic irony of an imperial Vermont (population 330,000 in 1870) leading a global crusade for a new world order. He politely noted, "The orator was frequently and heartily applauded during the oration and at its close."[45]

That night, fireworks on the university common celebrated the national birthday, concluding with a large representation of Allen's statue and the well-known words of his declaration of authority to seize Ticonderoga in the names of "Great Jehovah and the Continental Congress." The estimated attendance of twelve thousand made up the largest crowd to gather in Burlington since 1809, when an estimated crowd of nearly ten thousand gathered around the gallows in Court House Square (today's City Hall Park) to watch anti-Embargo smuggler Cyrus Dean hang for his leading role in the notorious *Black Snake* incident. Dean and his men murdered three U.S. customs officers at the farm on the Winooski River where Ethan Allen had died twenty years earlier. In 1809 another Ethan Allen had played a minor role in Dean's trial. The younger son of the Hero of Ticonderoga and stepson of Jabez Penniman, the top U.S. customs officer in Vermont, Ethan Voltaire Allen (1789–1855), who later went to West Point and com-

GREEN MOUNTAIN BOY
STATUE, MANCHESTER.
This near duplicate of the Ethan
Allen statue in the congressional
Statuary Hall memorializes war veter-
ans of Manchester who served in the
Revolutionary War, the War of 1812,
the Mexican War, and the Civil War.
Erected in 1905, but unlike the other
statues based on Larkin Mead's orig-
inal in the national capitol, the Green
Mountain Boy presents a youthful
face. *Courtesy of John Huling.*

pleted a career in the army, was excused from jury duty during voir dire
when he declared the smuggler Dean a hero. Heman Allen, Ethan Allen's nephew, attended the trial in his capacity as sheriff of Chittenden
County.[46] For Chairman Pomeroy the large turnout on the university
common in 1873 proved how the people of the State of Vermont "still
hold in undiminished and undying honor, the memory of the Hero of
Ticonderoga."[47] But none knew what he actually looked like, except, of
course, to say he was big.

Without a visual image of Ethan Allen to serve as a model, the several statues that memorialized Ethan Allen in Vermont and the U.S.
Capitol's National Statuary Hall Collection represent him as an idealized hero. At the beginning of his work in 1858 Larkin Mead wrote to
John Pomeroy: "I do not think he should be represented in any particular act—that would not be justice to his whole life of heroic deeds.—
To represent him at the door of Fort Ticonderoga would certainly tell
of one great victory in his life, but it would not tell the whole history
of the man.—The sword is the weapon of a warrior, but Allen's most
powerful weapon was his strong will and determination. I believe his
greatest victories were achieved without bloodshed."[48]

SETH WARNER
STATUE, BENNINGTON.
A Bennington stone cutter in 1910–
11 sculpted this statue from granite.
Except for the face, most features of
the Seth Warner statue closely resem-
ble those of Larkin Mead's figure of
Ethan Allen. *Courtesy of John Huling.*

Other statues of Ethan Allen offer questions rather than prompt memories of him. Three years after the ceremony and installation of the statue of Allen in Burlington's Green Mount Cemetery, Vermont's congressional delegation secured a place in the new statuary hall of the U.S. Capitol for an eight-foot, eight-inch heroic Italian marble statue of Ethan Allen, again by Larkin Mead.

In the last decade of the nineteenth century, the Orvis family of Manchester, Vermont, called for a statue of Ethan Allen to stand in their town, and the citizens of Manchester purchased a duplicate of the statue of Ethan Allen installed in 1873 in the congressional National Statuary Hall Collection to represent a "soldier of the revolution," in 1904 dedicating it to the Green Mountain Boy as a memorial to the town's veterans of the Revolutionary War, the War of 1812, the Mexican War, and the Civil War. Two thousand people attended the dedication of the statue figuring a "Continental soldier of heroic size with drawn sword and determined expression and spirit of our idea of a soldier of that period." It was not the last statue of Ethan Allen renamed for another purpose.[49]

Benningtonians in 1896 had raised a three hundred-plus-foot-tall obelisk to memorialize the American victory over a strong British force on the banks of the Walloomsac River in August 1777, prompting Olin

Scott of Bennington, a wealthy Civil War veteran, in 1910 to commission a granite statue of the heroic figure of Seth Warner, a Benningtonian and commander of the Green Mountain rangers in that battle, for installation at the site of the Bennington Battle Monument. Strangely, and still unexplained, the statues of Seth Warner in Bennington, Ethan Allen in the hall of statuary, and the Green Mountain Boy in Manchester are nearly identical. Allen and Warner were Green Mountain Boys and cousins in life, but their identical images cut in stone fail to tell us what the real Ethan Allen or Seth Warner actually looked like.

One wonders: Has anyone from Bennington ever visited the National Statuary Hall Collection in Washington, seen the statue of Ethan Allen, and said, "Wait, wait, that's really Seth Warner"? Or, when browsing through a biography of Ethan Allen, its dust jacket featuring the Washington statue of Ethan Allen, while the Bennington statue of Seth Warner illustrates the text, did a reader in Manchester familiar with the Green Mountain Boy statue, ever ask, "Will the real Ethan Allen please stand up?"

When the legend becomes fact, print the legend.

{ JOHN FORD, *The Man Who Killed Liberty Valance* }

CHAPTER VI

MAKING IT UP

Anecdotes, Legends, and Other Dubious Tales

Writers who presented Ethan Allen in postures compatible with their views of the Haldimand Negotiations had little doubt about his stance when he harangued fellow Vermonters. He took to the ubiquitous and convenient stump. The same accounts that have him a head taller than most of his audience frequently have him mounting a stump to gain attention. The frontier stump as a convenient rostrum had established a place in popular memory and usage by 1810.[1] Candidates for elective office in both urban and rural districts continue to campaign today with a "stump speech."

But did Ethan Allen really stand on a stump to calm an angry crowd after the Loyalist David Redding was first acquitted of "enemical conduct" in 1778? Did he really encourage greater efforts from searchers for lost children in 1780? Or did those who memorialized him write that into the story?

Historians reciting the Ethan Allen story have reflected both the times they described and the times in which they were writing, as each generation revised history to accord more closely with its own particular values, questions, and preoccupations. Depictions of the American past tell us about the times they represent, but they also reveal something of the times in which they appeared and found their audience. By the mid-twentieth century, the towering figure of a brawling giant full of the frontier spirit, who led the American Revolution to its first victory at Ticonderoga and almost single-handedly secured the political independence of Vermont, had long since found its niche in collective memory and popular culture. But historians and biographers did not provide the sole source for that image of Ethan Allen. The resurrection and near deification of Ethan Allen was also the product of anecdotes, legends, and myths, brief auxiliary versions of the Ethan Allen story; most of them—especially tall-tale versions told at first by anonymous authors—derived from ancient folk tales reworked in the nineteenth century to exhibit some purportedly virtuous or simply amusing facet of Ethan Allen and entertain popular audiences. Occasionally historians employed them and even acknowledged they had woven an anecdote from a "traditional story" into their longer narratives even though no contemporary witness had left a verifiable record. Anecdotes readily perform the ancient role of literature and history—to amuse and teach. Most writers claimed as "authentic" their unsupported reports of amusing moments in the life of Ethan Allen. These tales and colorful anecdotes spread the idea of Ethan Allen to a wide popular audience in various media that would reach men, women, and children.

AN OLD TRICKSTER BECOMES
KIND, RECKLESS, AND A HARDY
RING-TAILED PEELER

Allen himself used anecdotes in composing his captivity narrative, appearing in the text as exempla for some larger point he sought to illustrate. Early in his narrative, he recalls his outrage when his captors lock him in leg irons and manacles. In a fit of defiant anger, he bites off the ten-penny nail that locked the manacles to his wrists, chipping a tooth during his display of strength; Allen claims that "at the same time I swaggered over those who abused me." This event, the earliest of several anecdotes supplementing the Ethan Allen story with a dental theme, exhibits the power of Allen's emotions to trigger heroic actions of physical and moral superiority over his British captors. Dental anecdotes about Allen appeared posthumously, beginning with the *Vermont Gazette*'s 1789 tall tale of "Old Ethan" tricking New York dandies into buying him rum in a tooth-pulling contest.[2]

During the mid-nineteenth century's establishment of the iconic Ethan Allen, the old tales of him heroically eating nails or slyly tricking Yorkers gave way to a frequently repeated tale of Allen's kindness to a woman in painful distress from a rotting tooth. The tale imputes a commendable virtue of generous sympathy and introduces his previously unremarked stoicism. The tale's thin details also suggest the hero serves a minor role as promoter of dental care, as if foretelling his major modern role as flogger of consumer goods and services. In this brief legend, which his modern biographers omit, Ethan, while visiting an unnamed dentist friend, met a frightened woman needing a tooth extraction, but her fear of the pain overwhelmed her. His friendly encouragement failing to persuade her to submit, Allen, according to the tale, said at last, "Madame, I will prove to you that there is nothing to fear." He sat down in the dentist's chair and instructed his friend to remove a tooth while the woman watched. Then Allen turned to her and said, "There, you see. I didn't feel it at all." Reassured, the woman proceeded to her own extraction, while Ethan Allen stood by and suffered in silence.

No time or location is given in this minimalist story. The dental chair might place its origin before the 1850s when chloroform came into use. Allen's visit to a dentist and the repeated use of the title "dentist"—not a barber, surgeon, or "tooth puller," such as Burlington's Steven Law, who also administered several bleedings to a dying Allen in 1789 — suggests the tale's very posthumous composition (the first school for dentists opened in Baltimore in 1840) and a motive to the tale beyond the moral lesson of Allen helping others in a troubled moment. He displays his heroic stoicism by enduring pain. The moral? "Ladies, keep your beauty, bravely rid yourself of rotten teeth [a real concern among nineteenth-century women with high sugar intake], like Ethan Allen."[3] The twentieth-century writer Stewart Holbrook added to the dental anecdotes with one about Allen displaying his outlandish strength by picking up a large bag of salt with his teeth and tossing it over his shoulder.[4]

The Canadian-born Herbert Casson (1869–1951), an apostle of Frederick Taylor's principles of industrial efficiency in the late nineteenth and early twentieth centuries and the author of popular industrial histories, drew on the tale of Ethan Allen and the dentist as an oddly inapt illustration of the necessary character traits of a steel tycoon. A defrocked Methodist minister and writer for Joseph Pulitzer's newspapers, Casson promoted the audacious virtues of American capitalists in numerous books, including *The Romance of Steel: The Story of a Thousand Millionaires* (1907). Ethan Allen appears in his list of heroic ironworkers of the pre-Bessemer era. At his foundry in Salisbury in 1761, Casson claimed, the twenty-three-year-old Allen produced a ton of iron in less than ten hours, an exceptional, if not improbable, feat of strength in the primitive iron foundries of the mid-eighteenth century. Casson goes on to tell the tale of Allen and the dentist to exemplify a valuable character trait that Ethan Allen shared with Captain William "Bill" Jones, a legendary Pennsylvania steelmaker who worked for Andrew Carnegie in the 1870s and 1880s. The similarities are "recklessness and hardihood." Ethan Allen "sat in a dentist's chair and had a good tooth extracted, merely to give encouragement to a timid old lady." Jones "cut his fingernail open as a boy to see what was underneath." While Casson details how Jones's efficient management of the steel gangs led to Carnegie's immense wealth, he fails to mention that Allen's venture in the ironworks at Salisbury, Connecticut, eventually collapsed into a financial dispute with his partners, his violent attack on them, and the loss of his investment.[5]

ANIMAL ANECDOTES: DEER, SNAKES, AND A WHITE STALLION

By the mid-twentieth century, anecdotes of Ethan Allen's dental heroics fell out of favor with his biographers, though tall tales continued to abound. In 1795 Ira told Samuel Williams that Ethan "was fond of hunting most of his youth," and then recounted an anecdote of his prowess as a great deer slayer in Poultney, where he killed five deer in one night: Ethan "ran after Dear and tired them down or tamed them by often firing at them So as to kill them by night."[6] Subsequent anecdotes of Ethan Allen's interactions with animals more commonly employed ancient folk tale motifs than braggart hunting tales. With unlimited literary license, Stewart H. Holbrook's *Ethan Allen* (1940) introduced him as "a swashbuckling, hell-roaring, indomitable man—the one and original old ring-tailed peeler."[7] Holbrook exploits Allen's repeated allusions to the "flowing bowl" by reciting a tall tale based on the myth that if a snake bites a drunken man, the snake will die. Holbrook, who did not know that rattlesnakes do not make multiple strikes,

especially against an immobile object, recounts how Allen once was bit-
ten repeatedly while drunk and unconscious, from which the rattler became cross-eyed drunk. When Allen woke, he complained of mosquito
bites during the night.[8]

More recently, biographies of Ethan Allen published for young readers have repeated the tale of his purported desire for reincarnation as a
white stallion. Charles Stansfield, a Vermont collector of ghost stories,
reports sightings of the Great White Horse of the Winooski running
through the meadows of Allen's erstwhile farm in the river's intervale.
"Many are convinced that the phantom horse is the spirit of Ethan
Allen." A dead hero reincarnated as a white horse is a folk motif as
ancient as Alexander the Great's wish at death to be resurrected as a
white horse and as recent as the final scene of *Viva Zapata!*, Elia Ka-
zan's 1952 film scripted by John Steinbeck. The film concludes after
government troops of Mexico's corrupt President Porfirio Diaz kill
Emiliano Zapata, the leader of an early twentieth-century agrarian insurgency over land ownership. In the final scene, *campesinos* claim the
white horse they see running on the hills above their village is the fierce
spirit of Zapata. Verification of Allen wishing to return from death as a
white horse usually appears at the opening of this anecdote in the formula, "he told his friends many times."[9]

LOST CHILDREN, A HERO WITH FEELINGS,
SUSPICIONS OF TREASON, AND AN ALIBI

In 1824 and 1842 Zadock Thompson reported an incident from the life
of Ethan Allen that developed into the tale that Daniel P. Thompson
retold as a short story, "Ethan Allen and the Lost Children" (1848).[10]
The story develops the traditional folk theme of searching for lost children. Thompson focuses on the searchers' point of view to introduce
readers to the virtuous depths of Ethan Allen's feelings in a display of
his strong but gentle emotions. The story echoes ancient folk tales of a
stalwart woodsman rescuing babes in the woods. Allen's biographers
and Vermont's historians have recounted how in late May 1780 Ethan
Allen compelled a group of searchers to rescue a neighbor's two children lost in the woods near their home in Sunderland.[11] A variant of
once-upon-a-time tales, the incident's date is usually given in the first

sentence and the story told nearly verbatim in subsequent biographies
of Ethan Allen. Some cite Zadock Thompson's 1842 claim that he heard
the tale from one of the surviving children, then an elderly woman still
living in Williston. In all versions of the tale, Allen incites the searchers to a greater effort but does not himself rescue the children. They
are found only after he rallies the exhausted searchers with a "do-or-
die" stump speech in the manner of his earlier speech that quelled the
angry crowd at David Redding's trial in 1778. In this instance, however, Allen aims to save lives, not cause a death. As a man of deep feelings, he sheds tears that motivate the searchers to continue and even
increase their efforts to find the children. The Robin Hood of the Green
Mountains, conceived and reborn in the 1830s as a rugged Jacksonian
hero, nonetheless responds to the emotional requirements of the moment as a man of feeling. For Thompson's readers, Allen's eyes well up
in sympathy. He energizes the exhausted searchers to greater effort by
a heartfelt call for them to imagine how they would feel in the parents'
situation. With Allen's teary eyes the story celebrates a heroic leader of
men with the power of sympathy to induce change. A recent biographer repeats Zadock Thompson's estimate of seven hundred searchers
from Vermont, New York, and Massachusetts on the scene, while another says "dozens" came from neighboring towns.[12]

Henry Mackenzie's hugely popular novel *The Man of Feeling* (1771),
a widely influential product of the sentimental movement, allied sentiment and sensibility with true virtue and sensitivity, the marks of the
man of feeling. In America by the 1850s, sentiments and feelings had
become the prime matter of novels and short fiction generally written
by women. After performing good deeds, however, the genre permitted strong men to cry when "least able to fully verbalize" overwhelming emotions. Never short on words in a public moment, Ethan Allen in
this tale becomes a superhero of deep emotions taking to another convenient stump to compel his audience by sentiment to take the moral
high ground of action. Michael Riffaterre argues that a text's verisi-
militude depends on "the myths, traditions, ideological and esthetic
stereotypes, commonplaces, and themes" harbored by its audience.
Thus, nineteenth-century writers' portrayals of people and situations
that contemporary readers could relate to, in a language and within a
frame of reference familiar to all readers, reached a wider audience and

could be more persuasive than an abstract treatise. Generally, anecdotes framed as tall tales or legends reveal no authors. The original author(s) of "traditions" disappear in time's erosion of memory. The question — is it fiction or supported fact? — seldom uncovers an original author.[13]

With a modest hint of uncertainty in 1929, John Pell pronounced the lost children tale "a well authenticated tradition," meaning earlier unnamed authors knew of it, but he could uncover no known original source. Notwithstanding the doubt lurking in a "tradition," other writers have repeated the story without Pell's modest doubt, depending solely on his imprimatur of "well authenticated." Charles Jellison in 1969 shut off further discussion by asserting the tale was "too well documented to be doubted."[14] Zadock Thompson's reputed witness to Allen's role in the search, the younger sister Betsy Taylor, by then in her fifties, left no account to support Thompson's claim of Allen's tearful call to resume the search, nor does she appear in later claims for the tale's authenticity. He alludes to conversations with her and men of the Taylor family. Instead, after repeating Daniel P. Thompson's opening line, "In the last days of May," authors down the years have simply repeated condensed versions of his story, the moral of the tale usually explicated as a platitude suitable for an obituary or eulogy — "his friends could always depend on him" or "he was always ready to afford relief to the suffering."[15]

Zadock Thompson could have found the original source for his first account of the lost children story in *The Affecting History of the Children in the Woods* in its first Vermont edition (1809). A Hartford, Connecticut, edition had appeared in 1796.[16] Folklorists trace the lost children theme at least to the sixteenth century. Charles Perrault drew on it for his Thumbelina tale and the brothers Grimm retold it in the Hansel and Gretel story.

A background story to the tale of the lost children could begin with a spy's report to George Washington about Ethan Allen's activities in the early summer of 1780. The single surviving independent contemporary account of Ethan Allen's activities during the time when the children were lost spreads a shadow of doubt over all later claims to the story's historical authenticity. Rumors of Ethan Allen secretly negotiating with the British in Canada had reached George Washington by July 1780. Washington asked General Philip Schuyler in Albany to send a spy into Vermont to verify his suspicions about Allen. Schuyler sent John Lansing, his military secretary, and Peter Cuyler of Albany on that mission. They secretly engaged Isaac Tichenor, a political opponent of the Allen-Chittenden faction, the commissioner of the Continental Commissary depot in Bennington, and the future governor of Vermont, to make discreet inquiries about Allen's activities. Tichenor admitted to disliking Allen, but his sources' information came from Allen's close associates since the early 1770s — Deputy Commissary Joseph Farnsworth; militia Colonel Samuel Herrick, who had raided Skeensboro when Allen took Fort Ticonderoga; and Jonas Fay, the principal author of the Vermont Declaration of Independence, son of the landlord of the Catamount Tavern, and brother of Joseph who negotiated with Haldimand's agents. Tichenor passed on to Lansing and Cuyler their reports of Allen's travels and meetings in Vermont and Connecticut on government business from early May to July 11.

Allen went to Hartford to order gun powder for the militia on May 2, returned to Vermont on May 9, and seven days later disappeared, after "giving out he was going to expedite the conveyance of powder" from Hartford to Bennington, where he finally appeared on June 5, "after completing his journey."[17] One of the rumors that prompted Washington to engage a spy reported Allen in New York City consorting with the British on July 2. In a chapter titled "The Perfect Alibi," Pell conjectures that the calendar of Allen's movements "exonerates" him. Pell's sequence of events fails to explore the block of eleven days — his disappearance from May 16 to the second day of the search when he delivered the do-or-die stump speech, though Pell coyly concludes with the observation that the lost children story, "unlike most traditions, is dated, and just when a date comes in handy."[18] Questions remained unanswered: Did George Washington's original source of the rumor get the date wrong? If "regiments" of searchers witnessed the speech in Sunderland, why was the incident not reported before Zadock Thompson's newspaper report in the 1840s?[19] Where was Ethan Allen when the Taylor girls were lost and found? And who said so? Too dramatic to ignore and good fodder to describe a melodramatic hero, the irresistible tale of the lost children appears in nearly all of Allen's biographies.

THE "FLOWING BOWL" CALMS THE HERO,
A PRESIDENT TELLS AN ALLEN JOKE

Over the last 150 years, brief anecdotes about Ethan Allen in several biographies and novels have almost verbatim retold a tale attributed to James Rivington as a traditional account of Allen in New York probably during his captivity, "a tall figure" angrily marching through the city in "tarnished regimentals, a cocked hat and an enormous sword," to confront and avenge an insult to him by Rivington, the arch-Tory printer of the *Royalist Gazette*. The stories do not give an exact date of the event. Some versions say it occurred during Allen's parole in 1777, others state simply that it took place "on his sojourn there," and others give no date for the incident. The "enormous sword" appears in all versions, however, although as a British prisoner Allen could not have openly displayed or even possessed such a weapon. None of his fellow prisoners mention a sword in their recollections of Allen. He surrendered a sword at Montreal when taken prisoner in 1775. He hefted a "mucklehanger" (a naval broadsword) at Quebec a few weeks later when preparing to second a friendly British officer in an aborted duel of honor. Yet every version of Rivington's tale describes an "enormous sword" clanging on each stair step as Allen ascends to Rivington's second-story rooms. Engravings of Allen at Ticonderoga wearing the officer's uniform of a Continental regiment and flourishing a sword had circulated widely by the mid-nineteenth century, probably reinforcing if not serving as the source of his dress and weapon in the Rivington tale.

At first fearing Allen's violent inclination, the convivial Rivington immediately presses a "flowing bowl" of Madeira on Allen to distract him from his mission, and they soon consume three bottles of fine aged wine (some biographers say only two bottles) that seduces Allen into a friendly mood.[20] Benson Lossing's *Pictorial Field Book of the Revolution . . .* (1860) presented it as a traditional tale in a footnote without attribution.[21] The same tale appeared verbatim in *The Aethenaeum* (1874), London's leading literary magazine.[22]

Charles W. Brown's *Ethan Allen: of Green Mountain Fame, a Hero of the Revolution* (1902) retells a group of Allen anecdotes in a thinly connected narrative thread. After recounting Allen's intervention in the David Redding trial, Brown introduces Rivington's short tale of pacifying Ethan Allen with wine as "An anecdote of a different character told of Allen's sojourn in New York." Brown provides a nearly verbatim transcription of Lossing and DePuy. The latter introduces the tale: "Rivington, the king's printer, a forcible and venomous writer, had incurred Allen's enmity by his caustic allusions to him, and the hero of Ticonderoga swore he would whip Rivington the very first opportunity he had! How the printer escaped the threatened castigation," according to Brown, "was narrated in Rivington's own words."[23]

More recently, in 2005, Lucia St. Clair Robson's *Shadow Portraits: A Novel of the Revolution* retold a condensed version of the Rivington-Allen encounter in New York City. Once while free on parole in New York City, Ethan Allen "sought revenge for Rivington's libelous stories" about him. The clever Rivington deploys his Madeira, concluding triumphantly, "we ended good friends."[24] In these and several other retellings of Rivington and Allen reconciling over wine, the original insult to Allen remains a vague allusion by Rivington to "libelous statements" about the Green Mountain hero.

An anecdote attributed to President Abraham Lincoln, another brief tale, pairs the Yankee rebel with Britain's conqueror, George Washington. It may be the only scatological anecdote of Ethan Allen the quick-witted trickster. As Lincoln is supposed to have told it, Allen went to visit England after the war, but found his hosts there too fond of ridiculing Americans, especially George Washington, going so far as to hang a picture of Washington in the "backhouse," or toilet, to annoy the Hero of Ticonderoga. When quizzed about his reaction, Allen claimed to have found the picture's placement appropriate, however, because "there is nothing that will make an Englishman shit so quickly as the sight of Genl Washington."[25]

THE HERO'S WIVES' TALES, MISOGYNY

By the mid-nineteenth century anecdotal tales of real or imagined events in the life of Ethan Allen indebted to ancient folk tales for dramatic structure had become fully embedded in the literature and the lore of the Hero of Ticonderoga. Tales of shrewish and alluring wives provide fodder for two significant strains in the Ethan Allen story. In 1761 Ethan Allen married Mary Brownson, a woman he had known for several years from carrying grain to her father's gristmill. She bore him five children and died in 1783. Remarking snidely that Mary was five (sometimes six) years older than her husband, Allen's partisan biographers baldly and repeatedly contrasted Mary with their freethinker hero, invariably to her disadvantage. They portrayed her as illiterate and, worse, as a hectoring, whining Puritan shrew. While he wrote pamphlets and books, displaying his intellectual prowess, she prayed or scolded. Charles Jellison visits the shrewish wife theme several times, most egregiously when, without qualification, he reports that Allen's rented house in Bennington in 1780 "safely removed [him] from the strident whines of his wife for two years."[26] Other than describing Mary chasing her brothers from her home during their dispute with her husband over the dissolution of their lead mining venture in 1765, her spouse's biographers have rendered Mary speechless over two centuries.

Another anonymous tale of married life with Mary Brownson begins with Allen as the target of a practical joke. Some of Ethan's friends, the story runs, confronted him in the dark, wrapped in sheets. "Well," the undaunted, Ethan said, reining in his horse, "if you're angels of light, I'm glad to see you, and if you're devils, come on home with me—my wife is the Devil's sister." Displaying his reputed wit, he shifts the pranksters' target from himself and delivers the punch line at the expense of his wife instead. Like other tales about Ethan Allen, the story of this prank has roots in folklore. The Devil, in several folk tales, marries three sisters, eternal nags who impose burdensome tasks on him, watching his every move and caustically correcting his behavior. In the 1760s and 1770s, few households on the New Hampshire Grants or Vermont had a closet full of sheets to muck up in a midnight prank no doubt conjured up long after Ethan had died.

Propriety in defense of the Allen family's famous ancestor might have prompted composition of the frequently repeated religiose anecdote of Ethan and Mary's daughter Lorraine's deathbed question to Ethan. "Whose faith shall I embrace, yours or that of my mother's?" Lorraine reportedly asked her trembling father as he walked the room in great agitation. He replied, "That of your mother." The Sunderland historian said the Allen family denied the story, but "some of the Brownson family affirm that it is substantially true." Then he hedged: "There is nothing at all improbable in the story, and yet perhaps more has been made

of the anecdote than the facts would warrant," and concludes as a grudg-
ing afterthought that Mary Allen "was an excellent and pious woman"[27]
The Allen Memorial called her a "pious and most excellent woman."[28]

NO "TIME FOR THE WAITING GAME," SEPTEMBER WEDS MAY, WHO WAS SHE?

Accounts of Allen's second wife painted another portrait. Frances Allen's origins remained only vaguely known or perhaps intentionally
disguised until the late twentieth century. Her 1840s tombstone in
Burlington preposterously calls her Frances Montezuma. Benjamin H.
Hall's *History of Eastern Vermont . . .* (1858) calls her Frances Mon-
tuzan.[29] Her father, John Montresor, a captain in the 48th Foot Regiment during the French and Indian Wars and later commissioned in
the Corps of Engineers, was a cousin of Anthony Haswell, Ethan Allen's friend and the publisher of Bennington's *Vermont Gazette*, and a
cousin of Boston's Susannah Haswell Rowson, the author of *Charlotte
Temple: A Tale of Truth* (London, 1790).[30] Nearly two hundred editions of the romance place it among the most popular sentimental novels in American literary history. Rowson based her novel on her cousin
John Montresor's seduction and desertion of Anna Schoolcraft of Scho-
harie, New York, with their infant daughter Frances, for the rich and
beautiful Frances Tucker.

In a cautionary Richardsonian novel written "For the perusal of the
young and thoughtless of the fair sex," Charlotte dies after the birth of
the child. Rowson's cousin Montresor and his cruel treatment of Anna
Schoolcraft served as the novel's model for the corrupt rake Montra-
ville, seducer of Charlotte Temple. In the 1850s the novel was sold in
New York City representing Charlotte as a noted courtesan. About 1870
an advertising poster for a serialized version of Rowson's novel featured
a large portrait of the fictional Charlotte with the caption, "The Fastest
Girl in New York."[31] Rowson's sequel to *Charlotte Temple*, first published as *Charlotte's Daughter; or, the Three Orphans* (1828), later became known as *Lucy Temple*. Desirée Henderson, who has thoroughly
studied Rowson's novels, argues that the sequel novel "subverts the
didactic message of *Charlotte Temple* regarding a daughter's allegiance
to her parents and instead valorizes independence and even isolation as

FRANCES TUCKER MONTRESOR.
Frances Tucker, daughter of a West
Indies trader and former British army
officer, married John Montresor in
New York in 1764. They lived on
an island in Manhattan's East River
known then as Montresor's Island
(today's Randall's Island). Montresor
resigned from the army in 1778, and
they moved to England, where John
Singleton Copley painted Frances's
portrait. A riding oufit, a jaunty
black tricorn, and a red military
style jacket recall Montresor's military
dress in Copley's portrait of him.
*Source: The Art Collections of the United
States Department of State.*

the ideal state for young women." Henderson also demonstrates how
Lucy Temple, as a sequel, does not merely extend the story of its precur-
sor, but "enact[s] the breakdown of lineage dramatized in the novel."[32]

Frances Montresor's variously misspelled name suggests an intentional breakdown of lineage. The first report of General Allen's re-
marriage provided a first instance of lineage breakdown, with an error
similar to those found later in the accounts of his death and burial in
1789. The *Vermont Gazette* of February 21, 1784, announced: "Married at Westminster, on the 9th of Feb., the Honorable General Ethan
Allen, to the amiable Mrs. Lydia [*sic*] Buchanan, a lady possessing,
in an eminent degree, every graceful qualification requisite to render
the hymenial bonds felicitous." The error in her Christian name as it
appeared in her wedding announcement seems odd, especially as Anthony Haswell, the *Vermont Gazette*'s publisher, was Frances's cousin.
But her Allen descendants also later repeatedly misconstrued Frances
Montresor's family name as Montague and in the 1840s on the memorial stone marking her grave as Montezuma. Her misnaming suggests
Ethan Allen's surviving children and grandchildren knew little about
their mother and stepmother. As Henderson suggests, for Frances Allen
family lineage dissolved. Some of Ethan Allen's descendants also seem

to have harbored resentment or other adverse feelings about their stepmother. In 1791, working the southern Vermont court circuit in Bennington, the lawyer Samuel Hitchcock, the husband of Ethan Allen's
daughter Lucy, wrote to his wife that he planned to travel next to "the
other side of the mountain" to attend the court in Westminster. Since
Allen's death, Lucy's stepmother Frances Allen had lived there with her
aunt Margaret and Patrick Wall. Hitchcock then complained, "I shall
be obliged to call & See our *chaste, discrete & virtuous mother* — shall I
express a great deal of love to her on your account? — . . . But I should
be happily disappointed should she be from home." Crude sarcasm and
an urge to avoid Frances suggests strained, if not alienated, relations
between her and her stepchildren.[33] Whether accidental or intentional,
posthumous name changes tended to suppress memories of Ethan Allen's second wife.

Frances Montresor Buchanan was a principal heir to the estate of
the "enimical loyalist" Crean Brush, a colonial Irish lawyer who had
migrated to America in 1762 and quickly forged close ties to the political leaders of colonial New York. He had acquired about 60,000 acres
in New York lands much within the New Hampshire Grants for his
service to the Crown. A member of the New York Provincial Assembly, Brush was the chief author of the Assembly's infamous Bloody Act
of 1774 that declared Ethan Allen and his associates guilty of a capital
crime without benefit of trial.[34] Brush and his wife Margaret Schoolcraft, Frances's aunt, had raised Frances Montresor in New York City.
The natural daughter of Margaret's sister Anna (d. 1762) and John
Montresor conceived while he was on duty in Albany and the Mohawk
Valley, Frances at age sixteen married John Buchanan, an officer in the
King's American Rangers, in early 1777. He succumbed to wounds in
September 1777 shortly after the Battle of Brandywine Creek, leaving
his wife pregnant in New York.[35]

Except for William Czar Bradley's dubious eyewitness account of
Frances Montresor Buchanan marrying Ethan Allen, her story received
little attention in light sketches by writers far more interested in his life
than hers. Jellison, in an academic pun, called Allen's few years with
Frances when he had fallen from power in Vermont "emeritus years."
He was forty-six with three unmarried daughters at home when he married the twenty-four-year-old Frances Montresor Buchanan. He died

CREAN BRUSH.
Traveling eight thousand miles in
the 1840s to gather information and
images for his *Pictorial Field Book of
the American Revolution* (1850–52),
Benson Lossing sketched this image
of Crean Brush from a now-lost portrait of him at his grandson Henry
Norman's home in Caldwell (now
Lake George), New York. Lossing
believed the portrait was painted in
Ireland, when the subject was Major
Brush of the Dublin militia. Henry
Norman's mother, Brush's daughter,
could have brought this painting
from Ireland. Lossing transposed
the sketch to a wood block drawing
for Harper & Bros. to engrave and
publish in his two-volume illustrated
history of the Revolution. *Source: B. H.
Hall,* History of Eastern Vermont, *p. 603.
Courtesy of Special Collections, Bailey
Howe Library, UVM.*

MARGARET
SCHOOLCRAFT BRUSH.
By an unknown artist, the portraits
of Margaret Brush and Frances Montresor were likely painted in 1771 to
hang in their Westminster home until
the Brushs and Frances fled to Boston in 1775. *Fort Ticonderoga Museum.*

shortly after his fifty-first birthday by a few weeks, leaving her with
three young children of their own and his two adult daughters still living at home. The economic recession that struck after the war had re-
strained Allen's land business. Frances's share of Brush's estate made
her, at least on paper, among the richest young women in Vermont.

Two modern scholars differ over Allen's motives in marrying her.

Jellison defines her as an attractive "tease," and calls her Fanny, as she was once addressed in some brief, affectionate verses tenuously attributed to Ethan. He claims Allen's newly found passion blinded him to her Loyalist affiliations. Bellesiles gives her full widow's name, but mistakes her father for a French officer.[36] Passing over matters of the heart to find Allen's happiness at age forty-six based in his respect "for his wife's learning and wit," Bellesiles points to the "Dear Fanny" verse Allen inscribed in a gift copy of his *Reason the Only Oracle of Man*, claiming Allen loved her for her mind. Thirty years later her cousin Henry Rowe Schoolcraft noted her "intellectual physiognomy." That is, without giving details, she looked like an intellectual to him. Aided by the popular nineteenth-century "pseudo science" of physiognomy, analyzing facial features and head shapes was thought to serve as a gauge of character. Whether or not she read *Reason* or the couple debated philosophical questions remains unknown. In Jellison's version, the passionate groom found her youth and coquettish good looks irresistible. Randall says she taught French to her husband, a claim otherwise unremarked by his biographers.[37]

One biographer asserted that Ethan had married Mary Brownson for her father's assets. An unlikely speculation, however, as Allen surely realized when he counted the ten competing siblings.[38] But Allen's biographers leave unmentioned how or why Margaret Brush as executrix of the Brush estate, with assistance from the attorney Stephen R. Bradley, conveyed a large portion of Frances Buchanan's share of the estate, 3,200 acres of land in Westminster valued at £3,000 New York currency, to Ethan Allen on April 6, 1784. This tract of land conveyed to him without consideration of money constituted the single most valuable tract Allen owned in his land business.[39] From selective anecdotal stories and anachronistic interpretations Jellison finds Fanny a girlish tease in the mode of the 1960s, while Bellesiles sees Frances as a brainy, liberated woman of the 1990s. Marrying for money was a favorite theme of English and American novels from Emily Bronte to Henry James, but by the late twentieth century the mercenary motives of an older, cash-poor gentleman and hero who marries a wealthy, beautiful, young woman have shed their taboo. Yet the groom's calculations have remained unexplored in the many retellings of the traditional story of the couple's whirlwind courtship and marriage.[40]

William Czar Bradley (1782–1867) is usually cited as the eyewitness source for all subsequent accounts of the wedding.[41] The son of Stephen R. Bradley, Allen's lawyer, in whose Westminster home Frances Buchanan resided when she married Allen, young Bradley had not yet celebrated his second birthday when the wedding took place on February 9, 1784, in his parents' parlor.[42] An adult drawing on memory from toddler years raises suspicions about the influences and alteration of his earliest memories in the ordinary course of growing up and listening to others. The historian-psychologist Lea Weinerman has observed that memory "earlier than about 3.5 years is, for most of us, a blank slate. We all have what Freud first called 'childhood amnesia'—an inability to remember our earliest childhood." The age of earliest memories, generally considered a matter of cultural determination, very rarely happens by age two.[43] William Czar Bradley's version of the high-speed courting and the wedding itself probably represents an accretion of anecdotes learned later from his father and others. Aligning that tale with anachronistic versions of how Frances attracted Allen discovers the shifting relations of interdependent recollections and history. Reconstructing a personal moment of a hero's life from the retrieved memory of a witness still a toddler, while ignoring the self-interest and political accommodation that resonate from the actual moment, sharply slants the account toward sentimental fiction, with a warm glow of romance and heavy-handed humor. Accounts of Allen's second marriage contain many of the elements of romance novels, with a rugged, worldly hero meeting and sweeping up in his arms a young, attractive, and well-endowed widow. The story both grew in magnitude with the telling and retelling and apparently distracted investigative researchers from the less romantic aspects of the union. The tales, myths, and legends may have blinded students of Ethan Allen to the financial aspects of marriage to a woman with a claim to thousands of acres of prime land in New York, Vermont, and New Hampshire.

Most of the anecdotal stories concerning Ethan Allen originated in the mid-nineteenth century. More recent biographers have shown little interest in Allen's marriages beyond portrayals of Mary Brownson Allen as a scolding, but otherwise speechless spouse, near kin to the shrewish wives of folk tales and Shakespeare. Every account contains uncritical repetitions of William Czar Bradley's dubious version of Allen's proposal and marriage to Frances Montresor Buchanan as the stuff of sentimental romance. Curiosity about Allen's choice of a rich Loyalist widow and heir to a land-rich estate seems suppressed by the controlling power of the mythology of Ethan Allen, the hero invented in the second quarter of the nineteenth century. The evolving story of Ethan Allen as shaped and told in both anecdotes and full biographies was intended to teach and amuse readers. Increasingly, however, teaching gave way to amusement, in the form of a reputedly spotless popular hero.

A TELEVISION HERO: NAMED FOR WARSHIPS, FORTS, SCHOOLS, FURNITURE, AND CONSUMER PRODUCTS

The introduction of television in the mid-twentieth century further resurrected and revised Ethan Allen in anecdotes or brief tales of his adventures. These came in brief dramatic stories presented in twenty-five minutes of a televised program's half-hour of air time. In 1957, when western and frontier themes provided the staples of nightly television entertainment, a Canadian television series introduced a less aggressive Ethan Allen than the historians' or novelists' versions of him. Called *Hawkeye and the Last of the Mohicans*, the series was based loosely on James Fennimore Cooper's Leatherstocking Tales. Three of its thirty-nine episodes presented "The Ethan Allen Story." Following the "hero and sidekick" format of *The Lone Ranger*, a popular western series that ran nearly forty years on radio and television, the handsome John Hart played Hawkeye and the rugged Lon Chaney Jr., a second-generation film actor of few words, played his Indian sidekick, Chingachgook, the last of the Mohicans. On their weekly missions, they fought the forces of crime and evil on the northern frontier. The thirty-nine television episodes took place during the French and Indian Wars in an area ranging from the Hudson River Valley to the Great Lakes. "The Ethan Allen Story" bends the chronology of the larger television series by depicting the 1770–75 exploits of Allen and the Green Mountain Boys during their active resistance to colonial New York's claim to jurisdiction on the New Hampshire Grants, a dispute thinly sketched by the television script. The plot follows the simple formula of television westerns and their near-cousins, police and private-eye detective stories. Hawkeye and Chingachgook are commissioned by a Crown officer to investigate a complaint that Ethan Allen (played by George Barnes) has committed crimes verging on treason against the British colonial government. Arriving on the New Hampshire Grants, they learn otherwise; the local sheriff and a tax collector have victimized the settlers. Without gunshots or spilled blood, "The Ethan Allen Story" concludes with Hawkeye and Chingachgook departing the New Hampshire Grants to travel west on another mission as friends of Allen and the Green Mountain Boys.[44] For Canadian television audiences, an amiable Ethan Allen made his mark without blustering threats of annihilating his Yorker opponents and the creative foul mouthing found in many accounts of his antics during the "time of the antient mobb."

Allen's fame and name also appeared outside the print and electronic media. During the Civil War, the practice of naming forts and naval craft for American heroes drew on the story of Ethan Allen. The remains of an earthen fort in Arlington County, Virginia, bear his name. In 1861 Vermont troops assigned there guarded the western approach to Washington. Two Union Navy coastal defense ships carried his name. Remnants of a military base in Vermont named for him in 1894 continue to serve as a firing range and winter training area. That practice carried into the twentieth century when in 1962 the U.S. Navy christened the USS *Ethan Allen*, a nuclear submarine, a "ring tailed peeler" indeed, when it fired the first Polaris missile launched by the U.S. Navy's submarine fleet.

In the meantime, places, organizations, and consumer goods and services began to carry Ethan Allen's name. By the mid-twentieth century, a state highway as well as public and private elementary schools in Vermont had taken on his name. A Vermont milk bottler sold the quintessential Vermont product in bottles embossed with Allen's image in the customary posture of the Hero of Ticonderoga. A furniture manufacturer with two factories in Vermont presently sells products made and marketed by a corporation named for him. In Vermont it is difficult to avoid encountering Ethan Allen's name or an image that purports to represent him. The name appears on apartment houses, including one for senior residents. A limousine service delivers diners to a Burlington lakeside dock, where a tour boat bearing his name carries them

USS *ETHAN ALLEN*.
Commissioned 1961 and powered by a nuclear reactor. Length: 410 feet; beam
34 feet. Decommissioned 1983; recycled 1999. In Tom Clancy's novel *The Hunt
for Red October* the decommissioned USS *Ethan Allen* was destroyed to cover
the escape of the defecting Soviet submarine *Red October*. The navy named the
submarine for Ethan Allen "because of his contributions to democracy." *Source:
U.S. Department of Defense.*

over Lake Champlain for dinner and dancing. A modest Ethan Allen
shopping mall in Burlington displaying his name is visible from a
mock-Norman castellated tower dedicated to him in a city park on part
of his original Burlington farm. A South Burlington motel named for
him stands beside an antique shop guarded by the silhouette of a figure
with a tricorn hat and musket. Other hotels and motels around New
England display his name. A now-defunct private club for men in Burlington once discreetly printed his name on its letterhead and menus.
An Amtrak train displays Allen's name as it travels between New York
City and Rutland. Outside Vermont, his name appears prominently attached to many public and private places and enterprises. Ethan Allen
Elementary School, otherwise known as P.S. 306, stands on Vermont
Street in Brooklyn, New York. A state correctional facility for children
in Delafield, Wisconsin, once a "reform school" called the Hill School
for Boys, adopted his name in 1959. They called the school newspaper *Green Mountain Views* and their sports teams the Green Mountain
Boys. The school closed in 2011. What can possibly be remembered
from fact or fiction about Allen that led the Wisconsin Department of

Corrections to rename a correctional facility for children after him, except perhaps in a great hermeneutic leap connecting an obscure Victorian tale by Daniel P. Thompson about Allen encouraging a crowd of settlers to continue searching for a pair of lost children? The Wisconsin Historical Society reported that only the date of the school's name change survives on record; the name-change's initiator remains undiscovered.[45]

Suggesting that the naming of a "children's correctional facility" found inspiration in a story based on an ancient folk motif adapted to reveal the hitherto unspoken emotional depth of Ethan Allen's heroism is, admittedly, a bit of an interpretive stretch. But then, so too is Daniel P. Thompson's version of Allen. Nonetheless, like most of the latter-day applications, an Ethan Allen reform school indicates his unlimited polyvalent capacity to signify almost anything or, perhaps, even nothing.[46]

Twentieth-century consumerism welcomed Ethan Allen, finding many useful places for him. In the twenty-first century, remembering the forceful anti-Yorker, Hero of Ticonderoga, scourge of the Loyalists, poetic lover of a beautiful young wife, the Green Mountains Robin Hood, tearful rescuer of lost children, all of the above and more, among the disparate welter of places, consumer products, and institutions displaying his name apparently remains useful. Time and overuse have seemingly not drained content from the name. But will the iconic hero persist? Will a time come when Ethan Allen will become an empty image in service to commercial impulses? Or will he persist as a paragon of values of the sort that Henry Stevens and his nineteenth-century associates believed would serve Vermont well in troublesome times?

REMEMBERING ETHAN ALLEN IN CONTEMPORARY POLITICAL DEBATE

Participants in modern Vermont's political debates sometimes invoke Ethan Allen's rugged individualism to bolster support or opposition to a current policy issue. The Ethan Allen Institute, "a free market public policy research and education organization"—a politically conservative advocacy group—actively participates in many of those debates. On the bicentennial of Allen's 1789 death, the Institute's founding president

A REVOLUTIONARY IDEA ...
GET OUT AND VOTE ON TUESDAY!

Ethan Allen

ETHAN ALLEN
POLITICAL CARTOON.
Appearing two days before the
midterm elections of 1998, this well-
intended cartoon, perhaps unwit-
tingly, avoided Ethan Allen's
personal rejection of electoral
politics. *Source:* Burlington Free
Press. *Cartoonist Ted Hudson.*

chided Vermont's legislature for failing to be guided by Allen's expo-
sition of the fundamental holy writ of seventeenth-century property
rights, the theories that Allen used to support the legitimacy of New
Hampshire land titles. More recently four members of the Vermont
House of Representatives introduced H. 491, a bill proposing "to create
a single-payer health care system in Vermont to promote health, to prevent chronic health conditions, and to contain costs," anachronistically
calling it Ethan Allen Health.[47] The lively critic from the Ethan Allen
Institute opposed the plan as unnecessary and too expensive. To support his opposition to the bill he invoked the authority of Ethan Allen
as the "brawling, boozing, blaspheming giant . . . the outspoken champion of liberty and property," the familiar, mythic, creation of Allen's
nineteenth- and twentieth-century biographers.[48]

The contrasting afterlives and legacies of Ethan Allen suggest how
no single narrative, especially a lively one like Allen's captivity narrative, tells the full story. The victor's version of history, with its forgotten
or undisclosed alternatives, invites scrutiny. Winners' tales are usually
selective and incomplete, sometimes with a narrative more powerful
than mere facts. Tales mutate through many versions over time. Once
again those stories and their revisions intone Ethan Allen's apt advice
to Canadian merchants seeking their support in 1775 soon after Ticonderoga fell into American hands: "One story is good until another story
is told."[49]

MY UNCLE JERRY

There's much, he says, about Vermont
For history and song,
Much to be written yet, and much
That has been written wrong.

{ CHARLES G. EASTMAN, 1848 }

CHAPTER VII
─────────

SILENCE AND EXCLUSION

Murder, Slaveholding, and Plagiarism

────────

The evidence documents some of Ethan Allen's activities beyond dispute. On May 10, 1775, he and Benedict Arnold captured Fort Ticonderoga with eighty-three of the "valiant Green Mountain Boys" who had gathered at Hand's Cove in Shoreham. Allen's and most accounts gloss over the fact that roughly 40 percent of the triumphant force that pushed into the crumbling fort came from Massachusetts, New Hampshire, Connecticut, and New York. Allen did capture Fort Ticonderoga. The record clearly established his capture at Montreal on September 25, 1775. But Ethan's version of the incident in his captivity narrative still lacks probing analyses of his decision to launch that rash attack, after promising to join Montgomery in the siege of St. John. Moreover, did the promises of John Brown and Seth Warner prompt him to hazard it, as in Ira's version, written after Brown, Warner, and Ethan were long dead? The convention of town Committees of Safety gathered at Cephas Kent's tavern in Dorset on July 26, 1775, rejected Allen, and elected Seth Warner to command the newly organized Green Mountain rangers as a New York militia unit. He also wrote and published tracts forcefully stating the case of the New Hampshire titleholders against New York authority and for Vermont's recognition by Congress. This much and more has a secure basis in accessible, verifiable fact.

Guy Carleton, Lord
Dorchester, Governor
General of Quebec,
1768–78, 1784–96.
Carleton commanded the defenders
of Montreal who captured Ethan Allen
there on September 25, 1775. The year
after Carleton lifted trade restrictions
on Vermont timber and livestock exports to Quebec in 1787, Ethan, Ira and
Levi Allen visited Carleton, then 1st
Baron Dorchester, on his second commission to govern Quebec, to petition
for tariff-free trade of Vermont products
from Lake Champlain to markets in
Quebec and England. *Courtesy of the
National Archives and Library of Canada.*

The documentary record of other aspects of Allen's active life makes
clear statements, but Allen himself and subsequent generations of historians and biographers have rendered often contradictory interpretations about their meaning. In 1788 he clearly stated to Guy Carleton,
governor general of Canada, "In the time of General Haldimand's command, could Great Britain have afforded Vermont protection, they
would have readily yielded up their independence, and have become a
province of Great Britain."[1]

Did the Arlington Junto treat with the British with the purpose of
joining the British Empire, or did they, beginning with Williams's and
Ira Allen's accounts, cleverly bluff the British to defend Vermont's vulnerable northern frontier? The long documentary trail of both stages
of the Haldimand Negotiations has produced a sharp contrast of interpretations that remains vigorous more than two centuries later. After
the success of the New York land speculators at the Ejectment Trials in
1770, did Allen briefly work on behalf of New York as James Duane, the
only principal to leave a record wrote, or did he immediately take command of the Green Mountain Boys? In other cases, like Allen's death,
the contemporary record contains contradictions that have engendered
conflicting interpretations and have allowed license in telling the story.

His brother Ira, historians, biographers, illustrators, and others have also repeated events not supported by any evidence other than "tradition has it," "history says," and similar disclaimers that precede the retelling in works of a serious nature. The more dubious tales include Allen leading the rescue of two lost girls, his taking sacks of salt between his teeth and slinging the heavy bags over his shoulder, his having a tooth pulled to provide an example to a frightened woman who needed an extraction, the dialogue about religious conviction with his daughter Loraine as her death approached, or one John Graham said he "often heard him affirm," that after death he expected to live again as a white stallion.[2] The retelling of these tales usually employs the same dialogue and much of the same language, as if presented by an unnamed eyewitness, often word for word. In his captivity narrative Allen started the story of his twisting "off a nail with my teeth, which I took to be a ten-penny nail" that went "through the mortise of the bar of my hand cuff."[3] These stories have become part of the legend of Ethan Allen.

But the same serious writers who accept and repeat these stories have not followed up on other hints in the documentary record that might lead to a less favorable view of the hero. The rhetorical tactics of silence and exclusion worked effectively in *A Narrative of the Colonel Ethan Allen's Captivity*, in Samuel Williams's and Ira Allen's histories of Vermont, and in many subsequent biographies of Allen and histories of Vermont to construct the story of Ethan Allen. Early in his captivity narrative Allen selectively reported several significant incidents soon after the capture of Ticonderoga. Without details, he blithely turned the following day's drunken chaos into a lovely May outing: "the sun rose with a superior luster" as the fort's conquerors "tossed about the flowing bowl . . . and wished success to Congress."[4] After his subsequent blundering attempt to seize the British sloop at St. John, Allen returned to headquarters at the old fort and reported to the Continental Congress: "Provided I had but five hundred men with me at Saint Johns when we took the Kings sloop I would have advanced to Montreal."[5] He silently passed over how his command failures left his men defenseless and easily routed, while subsuming Benedict Arnold's leading role in capturing the British sloop and troops into "we." Nor did he mention Arnold's warning to cancel his mad, undermanned and ill-provisioned scheme against superior advancing British reinforcements.

Writing his *History of the State of Vermont* years later in London, brother Ira sought to persuade a British Admiralty Court to release a shipload of guns he had acquired in France, introducing readers to Ethan as "a proprietor of the New Hampshire Grants," without further discussion of his activities against Britain's colonial government in the land title controversy with New York or his role in taking Ticonderoga. *The Green Mountain Boys* (1839), Daniel P. Thompson's immensely popular novel, silently omitted Allen's capture at Montreal, lengthy imprisonment, and absence from the Bennington battle, but elevated the Hubbardton battle to center stage. Thompson's fictional character based on Seth Warner assumed the novel's lead role at the Hubbardton battle, but Ethan Allen resumes that role shortly thereafter when the novel returns to its fictional present.

Myth, fact, and fiction supported and configured by silence and exclusion have had their various ways in making up the story of Ethan Allen. Exclusion's purging power carried on with the frequent reprinting of Ethan's captivity narrative through most of the nineteenth century, with the continued popularity of Thompson's novel into the twentieth century, and with twenty-first-century biographies. In the course of time, as the story of Ethan Allen succumbed to the demands of new generations of readers, significant moments in the life and the story were shaped or excluded to satisfy the exigencies of those later times.

DID ETHAN ALLEN KILL ANYONE?

Historians and others have not seriously pursued the question of whether Ethan Allen took a human life. Considering that most of Allen's biographers since the 1830s have repeated his fierce threats to kill recusant Yorker settlers, destroy their homes, and level every building in Yorker settlements, only John Pell opened the question of whether Ethan Allen took a human life. He bathetically concludes, however, that "on most occasions, he treated his victims with unexpected leniency. The only casualty in the war of the New Hampshire Grants was a pitiable dog named Tryon."[6] Allen relates in the narrative of his captivity that one of the "centries" at Fort Ticonderoga charged one of his men with a bayonet. Composing his narrative in 1779 he recalled, "My first thought was to kill him with my sword." But, he continued calmly, "in an instant, [I] altered the design and fury of the blow to a slight cut on the side of the head," and transformed himself in memory into an oxymoronic nonviolent warrior.[7] He did not take a life in the Great Cow War at the pesky Tory nest in Guilford or at "the siege of Vallumcock" where he and the Vermont militia faced off the Yorkers over the West Union. No record attests to his taking a life while scouting for General Montgomery and the Americans who invaded Canada in 1775 or his having killed anyone in the fight that ensued in his ill-conceived thrust against Montreal. Yorker depositions document his violent language and behavior as the Green Mountain Boys terrorized Yorker settlers on the Grants and his threats to take lives. A few clues suggest that he might have killed at least one of his Yorker opponents. The conjecture begins with his second marriage in 1784, itself a confection of the mid-nineteenth century firmly embedded in the story of Ethan Allen.

The unquestioning repeated reliance on William Czar Bradley's account of Ethan Allen's marriage to Frances Montresor Buchanan as a whirlwind, sentimental romance may have had the effect of blinding students to the financial aspects of Ethan Allen marrying a woman with a claim to thousands of acres of prime land. And it may have also excluded consideration and investigation into the longstanding antagonism between the groom and the man who had raised the bride and whose landed wealth had enriched her, the arch Tory Crean Brush, the chief author of the New York Provincial Assembly's Bloody Act of 1774 that declared Ethan and his lieutenants guilty of a capital crime without benefit of trial.[8]

According to Benjamin H. Hall writing in 1857, when Brush took his family two hundred miles north to settle on the west bank of the Connecticut River in Westminster, his city fashion in clothing "contrasted strongly with the simple garb of the villagers, and for some time pomp and parade availed to conceal the defects of character." The country mice soon saw the flashy city mouse was really a rat. Hall established the dramatic structure of the conflict between the morally deficient Brush versus the heroic Ethan Allen even though he did not very much like Allen for his treatment of East Siders. He also reported that Brush, in a state of dishonor and despair, took his own life by gunshot.[9]

The Whig *Boston Gazette* published a notice in 1778 that Brush killed himself in New York, but the news story did not specify the manner of his apparent suicide. Many years later in New York City former Loyalist Timothy Lovell, who had lost most of his Vermont land to the Confiscation Court and was probably the next-to-last person to see Brush alive, certified Brush's death for an 1800 lawsuit brought in New Hampshire by Elizabeth Norman, Brush's Irish-born daughter, who had come to America in the 1790s to claim her portion of her father's estate. Her court action sought to recover some of her father's loans from borrowers in Walpole, New Hampshire. Lovell stated that he had visited Brush at his rooms, not another lawyer's office as Benjamin Hall and others later claimed, and sold him a load of firewood on the day of his death. Leaving Brush for an hour to arrange delivery of the wood, Lovell returned to find him dead, with his throat slit.[10]

Lovell's affidavit emerged recently from the surviving papers of Stephen R. Bradley, the Allens' and the Walls' lawyer, who also represented Brush's daughter Elizabeth in Vermont in her efforts to recover her share of her father's estate.[11] Lovell's testimony suggests that Brush did not die by his own hand. It buttresses a theory that could implicate Ethan Allen in the death of Crean Brush. This theory begins with questions not otherwise raised by Brush's death: would Brush kill himself less than an hour after ordering firewood to warm his rooms? Would he choose to slit his own throat, an uncommon and difficult suicide? Did the authorities ever find the weapon? Moreover, did Ethan Allen, in New York City at the time, have a hand in his death? The two had a history, which included their long-running animosity and Allen's subsequent campaign of vengeance against Loyalists, beginning with the hanging of Queen's Loyal Ranger David Redding within days of his release and return to Vermont, and his official work confiscating Loyalist property until it became potentially rewarding to welcome them back into Vermont.

While a prisoner on parole in New York City in 1777, Allen initially moved freely about the city. The British soon confined him to Long Island still on parole, but in August the British took him back to the city for violating parole and lodged him in the Provost Jail. Allen languished in the "Congress Hall," a large cell in the Provost Jail Loyalists frequented to observe and antagonize prominent Patriot captives.

The British commander learned that Allen had broken his parole by returning to the city on the Brooklyn ferry. Brush's cousin Richard

BRITISH PROVOST MARSHAL JAIL, NEW YORK CITY. New York's New Gaol served as a debtors jail from 1760 to 1776. The British army filled it with American prisoners of war from 1776 to 1782. After the war, it returned to holding debtors until 1830. *Source: Wikimedia Commons.*

Hill, then working on the ferry as a guard, would have recognized Allen, as he had refused to accompany Allen on the American expedition against Canada in September 1775.[12] Brush also could have encountered Allen on his parole-breaking visit to the city or even after his confinement in the Provost Jail, a place notorious for both the cruelty of its guards and, like the prison ships, the ease of escaping. An American privateer captured Brush and the Hill brothers on the brigantine *Elizabeth* headed for Halifax after looting Boston merchants' stores. Held in a Boston jail for nineteen months like Brush, who escaped jail in his wife's clothing and fled to New York, the Hill brothers also escaped. Richard made his way to New York, where he joined the British army's quartermaster's department as an inspector on the Brooklyn ferry in late 1777, effectively police duty. John also went to New York and served first as surgeon's mate in the 27th Regiment of Foot (Inniskillings) in 1777–78 and then in Francis Rawdon's Irish Volunteers in 1779. On ferry duty, Richard probably identified Allen breaking his parole as he crossed the river. The Hill brothers eventually went to Nova Scotia with other Loyalists in 1783. In the 1790s John ran the military brig in Quebec, when Levi Allen was imprisoned there under suspicion of plotting with brother Ira to annex Canada to Vermont and form a new republic.[13] The Hill brothers finally settled in Malahide, Upper Canada, after 1812.[14]

Throughout the war, prisoners on both sides easily escaped or broke parole to walk away and never return to their captors. When Allen was exchanged in the spring of 1778, most of the men taken prisoner with

him at Montreal had escaped at various places along the way from Canada to England, back to America, and finally to jail in New York. After
Allen and other prisoners landed at New York in late November 1777,
the British placed the remaining thirteen prisoners taken with him in
1775, along with eight added to them in Halifax, in a church, a make-
shift jail filled with prisoners. On their second night there, twenty-nine
of the prisoners, including most of those still with Allen from the Montreal fiasco in 1775, escaped. Of the original thirty-four shipped to England on the *Adamant* and returned to Halifax and finally New York,
three were exchanged, two died in captivity, and "all the rest at different times, made their escape from the enemy." In March 1778, shortly
after Brush's death, Allen's cellmate Elias Cornelius (1758–1853), a surgeon's mate of the 2nd Rhode Island regiment, escaped from the prison's hospital ward, where most inmates lay on their death beds. His
and other escapes from the lethal prisons of New York City suggest the
lightly battened British prisons allowed the captors to depend on the
feeble conditions of the prisoners to restrain them.

On August 14, 1786, eight years after Crean Brush's death, a poem
on the *Vermont Gazette*'s front page suggested that some Vermonters,
maybe many of them, might know something about Ethan Allen escaping a British jail in New York. The poem's opening line recalls Allen's braggadocio stunt soon after his capture by the British: "Allen
escaped from British jails, / His tusks broke by biting nails," an incident he reported in his captivity narrative. But in retelling his experiences as a prisoner in Cornwall's Pendennis Castle, in the Halifax jail,
in New York's Provost Jail, and in the holds of British warships carrying him from Quebec to England and back to North America, Allen
does not mention his own escape from any British jails, though he recalls the escapes of nearly all of the men captured by the British in his
Montreal fiasco in 1775. When fellow prisoners plot to murder their
British captors as they sail from Halifax to New York, he condemns the
escape plot and refuses to violate an officer's code of honor. In Allen's
accounts of his captivity, nowhere does a record or a later anecdote survive that he escaped from a jail. Residence in jails was not unknown
to the Allen brothers. Jailed on charges of blasphemy in 1773, brother
Zimri Allen and cousin Remember Baker escaped from the Salisbury,
Connecticut, jail. Brother Levi was imprisoned for debt in Connecticut

and Vermont in the mid-1780s and in Quebec by the British on suspicion of plotting a rebellion. Ira was imprisoned in France in the 1790s on suspicion of spying for the British. Yet the *Vermont Gazette*'s poet says Ethan escaped from jails. The plural "escapes" undoubtedly exaggerates, but there could be a kernel of truth in it. He could have escaped from the Provost Jail, if only briefly during the time that Crean Brush died. The *Gazette*'s poet might have imagined such an escape to make a couplet with nails, but it is no less credible that he and maybe many other Vermonters knew Allen escaped from a British jail and remained complicitly silent in deference to their hero and his wife Frances, who was raised by Crean Brush and his wife. Allen feigned incapacity before and after his imprisonment. While on parole he had roamed the streets of New York behaving in a manner that led British authorities to believe he had gone mad, a ploy he later admitted he used to extend the limits of his liberty. "Extreme circumstances at certain times," he wrote, "rendered it political to act in some measure the madman." "The enemy gave out that I was crazy and wholly unmanned."[15]

Allen had the motive and he could have had the opportunity and the means to dispatch Brush. Were he known to be free in New York—the necessary opportunity—Allen's and Brush's mutual hostilities provided sufficient motive to make the rebel prisoner a prominent suspect in Brush's death. An hour's absence from the prison to kill Brush would have presented difficulties, but with ultimate vengeance in mind, doing so possibly justified the risk. Allen could have established no better alibi than presumed imprisonment at the time of Brush's death. He had reason to hate Brush, and in captivity he developed a fierce animosity toward Loyalists.

And he might have had a weapon—a pearl-handled belt dagger with a double-edged blade, long identified as Allen's in the collections of the Fort Ticonderoga Museum. His Irish benefactors could have easily hidden it among their gifts of clothes, food, and wine given to him and his fellow prisoners aboard the *Sole Bay* at Cobh in February 1776. In a time when surrendering officers were not usually subject to body searches, Allen could have easily concealed and carried the knife. His captors searched him several times for letters or other papers. In his captivity narrative, moreover, he speaks of using a knife to open a hole in the floor to communicate with a new fellow prisoner in the cell below

him. For a man who often carried a sidearm and a short sword or cutlass, an eight-inch dagger blade could be "a small knife" and still serve
nicely for that task. Although long held by Fort Ticonderoga, however,
the dagger had been misidentified as belonging to Ethan Allen. That
error demonstrates yet another attempt to link something to the "hero,"
and like so much else it was wrong and misattributed.[16] Allen called
his Irish gift a "pen knife," an instrument that by the late eighteenth
century came in various lengths from four- to twelve-inch blades. Some
were straight blades, like the Ticonderoga dagger; others had folding
blades, a design easier to carry in a pocket. Ethan Allen could have hidden an Irish penkife during his captivity and used it to kill Crean Brush.

Patrick Wall (d. ca. 1820), a Boston tailor and friend of Margaret
Brush who accompanied her from Boston to New York following her
husband's escape from the Boston jail, might also qualify as a suspect
in Brush's death. An Irish immigrant with an otherwise thin record
of his origins, Wall married Brush's widow Margaret in June 1780.
In 1784 the Walls, with Frances Montresor Buchanan (a widow since
1777), returned to Vermont seeking to recover their shares of Brush's
estate.[17] Brush and Wall could have had a deadly conflict over Margaret's affections. Wall, his wife's good friend and perhaps her lover,
could have provided another suspect in Crean Brush's death. While
no extant information exists on the sexual relations of these three people, historian Clare Lyons's examination of the sexual culture of late
eighteenth-century Philadelphia illuminates how quickly and commonplace serial and casual sexual relationships developed in the urban plea-
sure culture of American colonial and revolutionary societies.[18]

The question of who killed Crean Brush — a vengeful Ethan Allen,
feigning madness, with the knife he secretly possessed in the Provost
Jail, or an amorous Irishman, Patrick Wall, with his tailor's shears,
Brush himself, or someone else altogether — lacks a convincing answer
more than two centuries later. Yet when a plausible suspicion arises, the
unquestioned traditional version of Brush's death as a suicide seems another dubious anecdote. Meanwhile, as Randolph Roth has shown, the
replacement of civil government by a British military occupation dissolved customary legal and social restraints on homicide.[19]

Like most of those anecdotes, Benjamin H. Hall's tale of Ethan
Allen and Crean Brush's longstanding enmity has retained currency in

a version composed in the mid-nineteenth century. Who killed Crean Brush? Silence allows the verdict of suicide in the dubious certitude of a winner's tale.

DID ETHAN ALLEN OR ANY
OF HIS FAMILY OWN SLAVES?

Almost six years to the month after Crean Brush's death, Ethan Allen and his young bride left Stephen Bradley's home with her baggage and guitar in a sleigh "with a magnificent pair of black horses and a black driver." The first published version of that event given in Henry DePuy's 1853 biographical treatment of Allen relied on an anecdote of "Hon. William C. Bradley (son of Stephen R. Bradley)." The most recent retelling of Ethan Allen marrying Frances Montresor Buchanan after a century and a half adds to Bradley's account, perhaps in the manner that Bradley embellished his telling. It has "Ethan's hired man, the freed slave Newport," assisting the couple. As Ethan wrapped "his bride in a great bear rug, he [the driver] snapped his bull whip over the horses' heads, and to the jingling of sleigh bells, the newly-weds raced off across the Green Mountains" in this happy portrait of a nineteenth-century pastiche.[20]

Critical studies of Ethan Allen, his brothers, and his descendants have not probed their relationships with African Americans. Though the Allens had close connections to the New Hampshire Grants and Vermont from 1770 on, they were born, grew up, and spent much of their adult life and times in Connecticut, where in those years one in four residents was black, most of them slaves. Connecticut was the last New England state to abolish slavery. The possibility that Allen and others in his family owned slaves runs counter to the cherished view that Allen represented a paragon of the struggle for liberty, especially for the common man against aristocratic authority. Yet through several generations of the Allen family's history, Ethan Allen, his descendants, and his brother Levi employed black men and women as laborers, farmhands, and domestic workers and, for Levi, as a trusted assistant in his business affairs. Family records leave almost no evidence of their black employees' legal status as free or slave. Writers of popular and academic histories of Vermont and biographies of Ethan and Ira Allen have remained largely silent on the matter, probably and incorrectly assuming Vermont's well known clarion for liberty, Article Two of the state's first constitution in 1777, firmly established that Vermonters could not have held another adult as chattel property.

Vermont's 1777 constitutional prohibition of adult slavery has often been cited to proclaim the state's lack of slavery and advanced position on racism. Though often unspoken and unexamined, the law permitted males under the age of twenty-one and females under age eighteen to be bought and sold in and out of state and brought into the state. Noble acts against slavery are also often cited to bolster that claim — Ebenezer Allen personally manumitting Dinah Mattis, a slave woman, and her child left behind at Ticonderoga by retreating British soldiers in 1777, or much later a Vermont judge's finding against a plaintiff suing to regain a run-away slave because "God gives no bill of sale."[21] Yet illegal slave ownership and trading and transporting slaves persisted despite the constitution. The legislature in 1786 reaffirmed both the existence of slavery in Vermont and the equality of all men with a statute that prohibited holding and transporting slaves for sale outside the state. The "Act to Prevent the Sale and Transportation of Negroes and Mo-lattoes out of this State" assigned a penalty of $100 on a person so convicted. But the constitution and the 1786 statute together only enabled slaves to bring suit to enforce the prohibition and punish slaveholding violators, a financially insurmountable block to freedom for the poorest of Vermont's poor. In his 1794 history of Vermont, Samuel Williams's discussion of the constitution gave probably the best contemporary description of the purposes and workings of Vermont's first constitution, but failed to mention its ban on adult slavery, as did John Graham's extensive letter on the Vermont Constitution and government.[22] Vermont's population expanded swiftly in the post-revolutionary decades, nearly doubling between the first federal Census of 1791 and 1800. Black men and women, some freed by their service in the war and others slaves brought by their owners, made their way to Vermont, most often from Connecticut, the main source of new settlers seeking cheap land. The U.S. Census allowed white households to count black Vermonters, slave or free, as "other persons." A toothless prohibition and silence on black slavery allowed it to continue both openly and covertly in Vermont deep into the nineteenth century.[23]

Following the slaveholding custom of single-naming a slave, accounts of Ethan Allen's death on February 12, 1789, identified Newport as the black farmhand who had driven Allen on a hay sled over the frozen lake from South Hero the day he died. According to the *Burlington Free Press*'s unsupported claims in the 1850s and later, Allen's black farmhands were free, not slave.[24] African American slaves with a single name appear in surviving accounts by other members of the Allen family. Early nineteenth-century Vermont court records also reveal occasional commercial transactions between Allen family members and black Vermonters whose names suggest they might have been slaves. Various members of the Allen family over several generations employed black men and women from the 1760s in slaveholding Connecticut until at least the 1840s in Vermont and elsewhere.[25] While some could have been free blacks, others were certainly slaves, in several instances slaves brought to Vermont by an Allen. Even those Vermonters who might have had moral qualms about slavery mostly acquiesced in its presence by their silence. Historians and Ethan Allen's biographers into the twenty-first century have accepted that silence without question, despite a few scholars pointing to the facts of the Allen family's slaveholding and urging others to look closely at the persistence of slavery even after its prohibition by the first state constitution.[26]

In October 1765, after Ethan Allen abandoned the iron foundry business in Connecticut, he moved on to another extractive venture, joining the slave-holding lawyer and politician Benjamin Stiles Jr. and other investors, including his brothers-in-law Israel and Abraham Brownson and his cousin Charles Scott. They took possession and began to work a lead mine in Northampton, Massachusetts, with three slaves, Tom, Cato, and Cesar.[27] Ethan supervised the unpaid labor of the black slaves, whose probable owner Benjamin Stiles could have hired out to the partnership.[28] The partners found the mine unprofitable and the partnership came to an unhappy dissolution in a dispute over Allen's unpaid wages. Twenty years later, seeking funds to support publication of his book *Reason the Only Oracle of Man*, Allen wrote to Stiles in Connecticut inviting his investment to help pay off Anthony Haswell's printing bill. Stiles's friendly reply offered no assistance.[29]

In 1778, living in Amenia, New York, and soon to be married, Levi Allen placed a notice in the *Connecticut Courant* for a run-away slave.

He offered no reward for the slave's return, and nothing indicates Levi recovered the slave. About 1779 he went to British-occupied St. Augustine, East Florida, and spent nearly five years there and in other parts of the South behind the British lines as a Loyalist merchant trader, British military courier, and leader of a British coast guard unit near St. Augustine. Though he mentions no slaves in his surviving records of those years, he could have owned at least one in a region where slavery prominently supported a labor-intensive agricultural export economy. In 1784, returning to Vermont, Levi purchased from Albany's Jacob Lansingh a slave named Prince. Later Levi complained from Bennington that Prince had an injury to his right eye. In a letter to Ira, he referred to Prince as a "servant," at the time a common euphemism for "slave," a practice satirically noted in the New York stage production of Royall Tyler's play *The Contrast* (1787). The play's republican hero Colonel Manly, having recently suppressed Shays' Rebellion in Massachusetts, visits New York with his Yankee batman, Jonathan. When asked if he is Manly's servant, the offended Jonathan indignantly replies, "Servant! Sir, do you take me for a neger,—I am Colonel Manly's waiter." Country bumpkin Jonathan and most of New England knew quite well that "servant" meant a black slave and as a white man he socially outranked slaves.

Levi entrusted Prince with commercially significant tasks in Vermont and St. John, Quebec, where Levi opened a trading post.[30] During business trips to Montreal and Quebec from St. John in the 1780s, he often left Prince with his wife Nancy and Mime, a French female domestic servant. As the winter of 1787 approached, he wrote to Ira in Vermont, seeking sufficient woolen goods to dress Prince and Mime for winter weather. In February 1789, Levi departed Boston for England ignorant of Ethan's death nine days earlier. Before embarking, he directed Prince to sell a "sleigh load of deer skins" they had acquired on the journey to Boston. Levi's voluminous business records contain nothing further on Prince's fate.

In the absence of positive evidence, the question, "Did Ethan Allen ever own slaves?" never appears in his biographies. Around 1900, however, John Ellsworth Goodrich (1831–1916), a professor of English at the University of Vermont, composed a "Reminisence" given by his wife, Ellen Moody Goodrich, of her "grandmother, Mrs. Judge

Penniman, formerly the wife of Ethan Allen."[31] Ethan Allen's widow
Frances Allen married Jabez Penniman in 1793. At the eloquently sentimental center of Ellen Goodrich's recollection of the Penniman and
Moody families' dynamics, she recalled an unnamed black woman and
her daughter Eliza who worked for them. She provides no dates of
death for them; the mother seems to have died sometime around Frances's death in 1834. After the elder Pennimans' deaths, Eliza lived with
and worked for their daughter Adelia Penniman Moody, Ellen's mother,
until her own death in the Moody house later in the century.[32] Eliza
and her mother's constitutional status would suggest they were free,
but a hint of slavery in Ellen Goodrich's account invites conjecture.

Mrs. Goodrich fondly recalls details of family life with increasingly
emotional details: "The servants of that old household used to grow up
in the house with the family." She remembered her own mother's stories about the black mother: "The old darky cook that we loved to hear
about was the mother of [Eliza] our inherited 'queen of the food-land,'
as we named her."[33] The old woman "would keep the children chained
to her side whole evenings, telling all sorts of strange weird tales. Closing her eyes and swaying her head she would break forth into wild
strains of melody with unknown words; and the music, unearthly as it
was, impressed these little listeners, filling their hearts with a kind of
veneration akin to reverence. Yes, even our old black Eliza did all these
entertaining performances in a lesser fashion, to our great edification;
and there still hangs about that tall gaunt dark woman, a flavor of mystery. We all loved her in a way. She was part of our lives."[34] How Eliza
and her mother became part of the Allen and Penniman families ap-
proaches, but quickly retreats from, full disclosure in Ellen Goodrich's
phrase "our inherited 'queen of the food-land.'" The sentimental tone
induced by the Moody children's sobriquet for Eliza could block further questions and divert from discussion a probable inference that
Eliza and her mother were chattel property at some time in their lives
with the Allen, the Penniman, and the Moody families. Possibly once
held by Ethan Allen, on his death in 1789 both mother and daughter
could have been inherited by Frances Allen as slaves (the mother illegally, the daughter, if under age eighteen, legally) and when she married Jabez Penniman in 1793 conveyed under couveture to Penniman,
and after the Pennimans' passing inherited by Robert and Adelia Pen-

niman Moody, Ellen Goodrich's parents. It also suggests that Ethan and Frances's black farmhands could have been slaves, one of them perhaps Eliza's father, but dispersed by illegal sale or manumission when Frances left her intervale home and farm to live in Westminster with Margaret Brush Wall and her husband. Neither the 1791 nor the 1800 U.S. Censuses list any black residents of Colchester or Westminster, though they could appear unidentified by race in the "Other" census category of household inhabitants.

Closer to Ethan in the Allen family lineage than his widow's granddaughter, his oldest surviving daughter Lucy Allen Hitchcock (1767–1842) and her son Henry H. Hitchcock (1792–1839) in fact legally owned slaves in Alabama and in Vermont, where slaveholding was constitutionally prohibited for adults, but silently transacted and tolerated. Henry Hitchcock migrated as a young lawyer from Vermont to Alabama in 1819 when the territory became a state. There he enjoyed a prosperous career as a lawyer and land speculator. His legal career in Alabama included his election as first attorney general of Alabama, appointment as U.S. attorney, and later election as chief judge of the Alabama Supreme Court. His private business affairs in agriculture, land, and commercial developments in Mobile required many slaves.

Lucy Allen married the lawyer Samuel Hitchcock two months after her father's death in 1789. Her husband died in 1818 in Vermont. Eventually she migrated to Alabama to live with son Henry until 1835. That year he accompanied her back to Burlington, where she resettled with two slaves she had brought from Alabama, Lavinia, age thirty-five, and her son Francis, age twelve. Writing in 1833 to her son Ethan Allen Hitchcock, a West Point graduate and career army officer, Lucy told him that her personal slave Lavinia was "the best servant in Alabama."[35]

When Lucy Allen Hitchcock brought her two personal slaves to Vermont in 1835, many Vermonters had already joined the growing national movement to abolish slavery. In 1786 the legislature had enacted a law intended to strengthen the constitutional prohibition of slavery. The Vermont Anti-Slavery Society had been founded in 1833; many towns then formed their own chapters. A bill introduced in the Vermont Assembly in 1791 intending to support and expand slavery in the state failed to pass into law, though it got more than twenty votes and anti-abolition remained strong in larger towns, including Burlington.

Lucy Allen Hitchcock's two black slaves from Alabama worked for her in Burlington for six years, until Lavinia's husband paid a manumission fee to Lucy shortly before her death, an illegal and unnecessary transaction in Vermont. The historians Marshall True and Harvey A. Whitfield have observed how the town's residents unsurprisingly "accepted slavery in their midst or remained blissfully and willfully ignorant of it." In those same years Zadock Thompson, Daniel P. Thompson, and others vigorously promoted Ethan Allen as Vermont's heroic defender of liberty and property. While Ethan Allen's only surviving daughter Lucy Allen lived among them, many, maybe most, of Burlington's four thousand citizens ignored illegal slave-holding. The only child of the state's revered hero still living in Vermont, probably rendered Lucy untouchable, so silence assured no scandal to raise questions about how an apparent heir to Ethan Allen's concepts of liberty and property could tolerate chattel slavery in Burlington.

Ethan Allen's grandson, the Honorable Henry H. Hitchcock, chief judge of the Alabama Supreme Court in 1837, owned many slaves during his active years. A rich man, Hitchcock advertised in Mobile's *Commercial Register* (October 27, 1837) for a "Ranaway Slave" named Ellis, who had "lost one of his ears."[36] As with the results of great-uncle Levi Allen's 1778 advertisement for a "Ranaway Slave" in the *Connecticut Courant*, we know nothing of Ellis's fate. The Panic of 1837 ruined Judge Hitchcock's financial affairs, and he died in 1839, a victim of the worst yellow fever epidemic of Alabama's history, bankrupt like great-uncle Levi Allen, whose death in Burlington in 1801 Henry's father Samuel Hitchcock attended and reported.[37]

Court records reveal that other members of the Allen family had brief commercial contacts with black Vermonters. The first such record of a black Vermonter in a land transaction with an Allen appears in one of several suits by Ethan Allen's heirs against Ira for maladministration of Ethan's and Heman's estates. Needing money, the Pennimans requested assistance from Ira to pay for the education and clothing of Frances's two sons by Ethan, Hannibal and Ethan. In a series of successful suits against Ira in Rutland and Franklin County courts, the Pennimans attached land Ira sold to eight Swanton residents, including "Amos Negro-alias Billings."[38]

The second court record concerns a lawsuit for payment of a debt

owed to the Burlington merchants John Jasper and Moses Catlin, hus-
band of Lucinda Allen (1776–1852), the elder Heman Allen's daughter.
Jasper and Catlin in 1811 sued Justin Warner in Chittenden County
Court. Warner owed $2.50 for goods charged to him by Jasper and
Catlin. He had requested on October 14, 1808, that "you will pleas to let
Nimrod have and charge the same to Justus Warner." Nimrod's single
name's biblical origins suggest he was black and at some point a slave.
He remains otherwise unknown; he could have been a slave or a common laborer who worked for Warner in exchange for goods or other
compensation. The "Negro" Amos Billings and Warner's Nimrod remain as obscure as Ethan and Frances's post-nuptial sleigh driver, who
might have been Newport.[39]

If Ethan Allen illegally owned Newport and other black farm workers, as well as a black domestic servant and her child, he would have
been little different from the slave-holding members of his family. But
no legends, myths, anecdotes, or indicative documents have survived
to help settle the matter with clues that might lead to verifiable records or reliable eyewitness accounts. Nonetheless, as with the revelation of Timothy Lovell's affidavit about Crean Brush's death, seemingly
impenetrable silence, intentional or otherwise, could still respond to
persistent probative searches into unexamined episodes in the story of
Ethan Allen.

WHO WROTE *REASON THE ONLY ORACLE OF MAN*?

Allen's exclusion of Dr. Thomas Young from any role in the composition of *Reason the Only Oracle of Man* presents a bold application
of silence and exclusion by Allen in some accounts and an example of
scholarly jousting between those who thought Young played a role and
those who deem the book all Allen's. Ethan Allen's *Narrative* details
his capture at Montreal and treatment by the British as they took him
to England in irons aboard the *Gaspee*. In 1776, three years before the
publication of the *Narrative*, John Leacock, a prominent Philadelphia
patriot, wrote *The Fall of British Tyranny, or American Liberty Triumphant* under the pen name "Dick Rifle." The play, printed twice in
Philadelphia and reprinted in Boston and Providence, does not have a

clear record of performance, but it was "well suited for dramatic readings by patriots." The play told the story of Allen's capture and voyage to England. By the time Allen reached Long Island under parole, "*The Fall of Tyranny* was in circulation." Allen might also have encountered it in Valley Forge, where he went directly after his release in 1778. "The similarity between Allen's *Narrative* and *The Fall of Tyranny* is uncanny." Allen exhibited no compunction about using someone else's words and ideas without attribution. In the play, "Leacock imagined a few moments in Allen's life, and Allen saw no reason to contradict a playwright who had made him a hero, and so he incorporated Leacock's scenes into his own memoir. In fact, he improved upon the drama, for he was a better writer. Leacock's Allen is a wooden, conventional hero; Allen's Allen bites the heads off nails." Allen made no mention of Dick Rifle's play that told his story before he did.[40] The captivity narrative in 1779 achieved his redemption as a self-invented man of action, a warrior and it demonstrated he had no compunction about using someone else's material as his own.

Reason, accepted as irrefutably Allen's creation, fills out and completes the self-portrait of a philosopher-warrior. The title page of the July 1785 preface to *Reason*, which Allen dated July 2, 1782, and in subsequent letters that discussed the book, Ethan Allen took sole credit for the work. Too long dead to protest his exclusion from authorship of the book, Young finally acquired an advocate in 1842. Zadock Thompson doubted Allen's sole authorship and offered two witnesses to support his critique. The preface briefly presents the origins and creation of the book with a retrospective opening like the captivity narrative's—"in my youth I was much disposed to contemplation, and at the commencement of my manhood, I committed to manuscript such sentiments or arguments as appeared most consonant to reason, lest through the debility of my memory my improvement should have been less gradual." He admitted he "was deficient in education . . . particularly in matters of composition." But his program of "scribbling" notes from his readings of "certain [unnamed] authors . . . [produced] unwearied pains" from studious application to "grammar and language, as well as the art of reasoning." Only "the Bible and the Dictionary" helped him to prepare the "treatise," that he cobbled together from "my old manuscripts" with the "scribblings," and "sundry passages from certain [again unnamed] authors [copied] many years prior to the completion of the subsequent manuscript."[41] As murky as most creation myths, Allen's account of the book's origins asserts that he worked hard to improve his skills in writing, rhetoric, and argumentation, and to expand his knowledge of the book's still unidentified subject matter using material from unnamed authors, some of which he copied as a deficiently educated youth. The preface is the work of a very self-conscious autodidact seeking to engage his readers in a confessional account of the book's origins.

Shifting to a mildly admonishing tone, Allen reveals the purpose of *Reason the Only Oracle of Man*. The book offers Allen's reasoned thoughts as moral exempla to guide those who "dare to exercise their reason as freely on those divine topics, as they do on common concerns of life [such as land and cattle], they would, in a great measure, rid themselves of their blindness and superstition, gain more exalted ideas of God and their obligations to him and one another . . . make better members of society, and acquire many more powerful incentives to practice morality [than from Christian doctrine]."[42] *Reason* offers a "how to" guide for moral self-improvement. Allen would have his readers believe that an uneducated man through diligence and common sense could produce a ground-breaking philosophical tract that would undermine organized Christianity.

Ethan's dissembling assertions in the preface did not accurately characterize his education or his claims to years of philosophical reflection. In asserting sole authorship, he also boldly misled readers. He attempted to present himself to others as a self-taught philosopher. His self-confidence in the task spilled into his campaign to raise money to pay for the book's printing. Seeking a loan from the Albany merchant James Caldwell to pay Bennington's Anthony Haswell for the printing of *Reason*, he promised to pay off the debt with the near perfect self-possession of an experienced land salesman and the foolish confidence of a novice chicken farmer: "I presume the Books will turn to money."[43] Soon thereafter, he enthusiastically told Benjamin Stiles, a former partner and slave owner in the failed 1765 lead mining venture near Northampton, that "the curiosity of the public is much excited, and there is a great demand for the Books." Allen anticipated "the clergy, and their devotees, will proclaim war with me." He correctly predicted the clergy's reaction: they will "put on the armour of Faith, the Sword of the Spirit and the Artillery of Hell fire."[44] Prepared to take the blame, he also eagerly sought the glory. But the book failed to sell as Allen had predicted. It had little immediate demand and no more than 50 of the 200 bound copies of the first and only printing of 1,200 books may have been sold or given as promotions. Unbound and bound remainder copies sat in Anthony Haswell's printing house after Allen's death until a fire of unknown cause destroyed them.

Allen sent copies of *Reason* to people he believed worth ingratiating in favor of his book. On a trade mission to Canada with Ira and Levi in 1788, Ethan carried a copy of *Reason* to Quebec as a gift to Governor General Guy Carleton, now elevated to the peerage as Lord Dorchester, perhaps to signify his peaceful intentions at their first meeting since Carleton had sent him in irons to Pendennis Castle in 1775. He forwarded his "Theological Book" to Hector St. John de Crèvecoeur in France, seeking approbation from "the old World." He asked Crève-coeur to lay it "before the academy of Arts and Sciences in Paris." He hoped that France's "learned gentlemen" might "be Somewhat diverted, with the untutored logic, and Sallies of a mind nursed principally, in the Mountainous wilds of America." If the lions "of the Capital of science" did not like the book, Allen would at least "have the satisfaction of reflecting, that I have made a bold attempt in Philosophy." He thought that his "reputation" would "depend in great measure on the reception that work may meet with, in the learned Cities, of Paris, and London." He yearned for the title *philosophe*.[45] At home, however, anonymous, purportedly European, critics lampooned Ethan and *Reason*. Haswell's *Vermont Gazette* in March 1786 reported the worldwide impact of the book with news from Boston of the arrival of the Sultan of Turkey's ship "The Siraglio" to convey "St. Ethan Allen" to Constantinople, to replace "the Mufti in that Empire who are all converted by the four copies of ORACLE OF REASON. . . . In this ship came four of the Grand Signior's Concubines, a present to St. Allen from the Grand Turk; and also the suit that Mahomet wore, when he was conducted by Gabriel to the throne above. It is certain that the Turks have changed the Style of their religion from that of Mahometism to that of, ALLEN-ISM."[46] No record of Allen's response to this news survives.

Reason, as well as Allen's letters seeking its support and favorable reception, avoid any mention of Thomas Young (1731–77), his former mentor and inspiration, who probably wrote much of the lengthy tract. Ira Allen recalled that "Ethan Began Early in Life to Dispute & Argue on Religious matters after an Acquaintance with Doct^or. Thomas Young a Deist my brother embrased the same Centiments."[47] About the same time Ethan developed his friendship with Young in the spring of 1762, he and business partners built a blast furnace to produce iron in the northwest corner of Salisbury, Connecticut, abutting Amenia, New York, in the Oblong. In June he married Mary Brownson, and with her probably took up residence in his brother Heman's house, where he had lived as a bachelor, before purchasing his own house in Salisbury in 1763. Young and his family lived across the New York border in nearby Amenia where he practiced medicine, played the violin, read, and wrote.[48]

John Adams would remember Young after he had left Amenia to settle in Boston as a "Scourge, a Pestilence, a Judgment," and said as long as Young lived there, "Boston will never be at peace." This "eternal Fisher in Troubled Waters" had an effervescent brilliance and a subversive bent. He helped organize the Boston Tea Party and promulgate the Pennsylvania Constitution of 1776. Shortly before his death in 1777, he suggested the name "Vermont" to the group forming a new state in the Green Mountains, and he recommended that they consider the Pennsylvania Constitution as a model for the new government. He had intellectual thirst, a copperplate memory, a flair for languages, and a love of dispute. Other physicians, including Dr. Benjamin Rush, thought highly of his medical skills. He taught himself the rudiments of Latin, Greek, German, Dutch, and French. A strident Deist and "zealous freethinker," Young pled not guilty of declaring Jesus Christ a knave and a fool in 1757. Back in court a year later apparently for a similar blasphemous offense, he asked for pardon from celestial authorities and the court. Young read widely in both classical and contemporary literature.[49] He was also a land speculator, and when that went sour, he wrote a tract fulminating against the "landjobbers," with a disparaging intent similar to that of Allen's own later attacks on his competitors in the land business.

By 1764, when Young and his family moved to Albany, Allen was on "very intimate terms with Young, had spent much time at his house, and fully imbibed all of his infidel notions." Collaboratively they might have begun to write or compile what two decades later became *Reason the Only Oracle of Man*. Heman's widow recalled years later, "Ethan Allen spent one summer at her house employed nearly the whole time in writing." She specifically recalled one evening that his intense concentration distracted him from hearing her first call to supper.[50] After Young's death from fever in June 1777, his widow moved back to Dutchess County, where Allen eventually retrieved the manuscript and seems not to have worked on it until about 1782 at the beginning of his withdrawal from Vermont's political affairs.

Suspicions about the identity of the book's author gained traction in 1852 when the Vermont historian Zadock Thompson suggested that Allen "rewrote, altered, and arranged" parts of the manuscript he had retrieved "into the form of a book."[51] Later scholars have concluded it "probable . . . that he wrote relatively little of it. In putting himself forward as the sole author of the book, Allen laid himself open to the charge of intellectual dishonesty, if not downright plagiarism." Comparing *Reason* with Allen's "other writings" leads to the conclusion "that some other person beside himself was concerned in its composition."[52]

With only one school term at a Connecticut parson's school Ethan Allen lacked proficiency in Latin or Greek sufficient to read and understand *Reason*'s frequent references to sources in those languages. Medical terms and discussions of medical theory, especially a lengthy, accurate one on the circulation of blood, strongly point to Young's authorship. The book makes hundreds of references to "God," but not once does it use "Jehovah," under whose authority Allen purportedly captured Fort Ticonderoga. As a preemptive rebuttal against charges by the orthodox clergy that his book promoted the heresy of Deism, Allen disingenuously claims ignorance of the matter: "As to being a Deist I know not strictly speaking, whether I am one or not, for I have never read their writings," though as a young man he spent many discussions with Thomas Young, a noted Deist.[53] In a confusing contradiction to that earlier profession of ignorance, however, *Reason* launches a lengthy discussion of Deism, the theological core of Young's beliefs and clearly the work of an author other than Ethan Allen. The author's persona in the preface — a homegrown, untrained, professedly ignorant philosopher and "hardy Mountaineer" at war with orthodoxy — dissolves when the text reveals itself as the work of some other unattributed author. A modern student of *Reason*'s authorship, George Pomeroy Anderson, concluded his analysis of "Allen's Bible" with the harsh, but fair judgment that Allen's "consummate vanity made him nothing more than a presumptuous, stumbling stranger in the dim land of metaphysics."[54]

In Allen's own time, criticism and accusations circulated in Vermont.[55] In 1788, Haswell's *Vermont Gazette* carried a front-page letter attacking the book. The published sources of Allen's arguments for Deism were well known by the 1690s. Critiques of corruption in the political power of Christianity, a favorite topic of seventeenth-century Deists, could be found in Charles Blount's (1624–93) *The Oracles of Reason . . . In Several Letters to Mr. Hobbs and Other Persons of Eminent Quality and Learning* (1693), which an otherwise unidentified G. Woolston in London accused Allen of reprinting. For Blount and Allen, reason displaces revelation and miracles. In his discussion of natural law, Allen tortuously deploys Thomas Hobbes's Cosmological Argument for the existence of a creator-God.

Allen claimed *Reason the Only Oracle of Man* as solely and entirely his own book, though it was largely written by another, a friend no longer in position to dispute him. Allen did not acknowledge his relationship with Young. His only recorded reference to his former mentor appeared in several unsuccessful petitions that he presented to the Vermont General Assembly in 1786 for a grant of land to Young's family "who are left Low & [in] Indigent Circumstances." The petitions requested the state grant land to widow Young to express gratitude for "our former Worthy friend Doctr Thomas Young," who disinterestedly helped form "this Government into Existence" and "to whom we Stand indebted for the very name of [Vermont]." The petitions recommended the formation of a committee in which "the Circumstances may be more fully Represented." The committee did not form, the matter ended, and Allen did not publicly mention Young again.[56]

Modern historians' treatments of Allen's *Reason the Only Oracle of Man* and his claim to sole authorship are generally similar, differing only in their various degrees of admiration for Allen's accomplishment. Pell generalizes about *Reason* as the crowning statement of a lifelong "rebellion against Calvinistic determinism . . . [Allen] was the slave of Freedom."[57] Pell avoids the authorship debate by calling Allen "an editor or reviser" of Young's text, accepting the latter role as probably closer to accurate.[58] Jellison argues that, while it may not be Allen's original work, "it is pure Allen from beginning to end" because "few men understood [nature] better and enjoyed greater rapport with it than Ethan Allen. He was, after all, a child of the forest." Allen, a Connecticut-born farmer, turned iron worker and lead miner, occasional deerskin hunter and finally land speculator barely qualifies for "child of the forest."[59] In 1989, four years before the publication of his *Revolutionary Outlaws*, Michael Bellesiles published an article in *Vermont History* that called *Reason* "the most important work" of Allen's life, "an act of enormous political courage" that made him the only revolutionary hero to author a book of philosophy as well as the first Deist book published in America. Bellesiles claimed full authorship for Allen despite the historians who gave Thomas Young "credit for writing most of the book." "There is only one problem with this widely accepted historical fact: there is not a shred of evidence for it." He goes on to refute point by point the historians who saw Young's hand in the composition of *Reason*, especially the arguments of Anderson's article "Who Wrote 'Ethan Allen's Bible'?" Bellesiles asserts without support that Zadock Thompson's witnesses to Ethan's visits to Young in Amenia, Jehiel Johns, about eight years old and a resident of Amenia when Allen visited Young there to read and discuss questions of the day and times, and Abby Wadhams, Heman's widow, for Ethan's summer of writing on spiritual matters at her house, in their old age had faulty memories, which he can no more prove than others can provide airtight proof of Young's authorship. And if either or both were correct, "the shred of evidence" does exist, nullifying Bellesiles's premise and much of the argument that followed. Bellesiles thinks that the mid-nineteenth century writers, in this case Zadock Thompson, tried to rehabilitate Allen by separating him from the anti-establishment tract to emphasize his role in the founding of Vermont and in winning the Revolution. Their "too oft told tale" became accepted wisdom.[60] He is generally correct about the mid-nineteenth-century revival of Ethan Allen, of course, but he fails to show how Thompson's attributing a partial role to Allen in writing *Reason* would downplay his Deism and emphasize his role in the founding of Vermont. Later Bellesiles's monograph treated *Reason* as a religio-philosophical statement of historical importance that distinguishes Allen in New England's persistent debate between faith and reason. He devotes a full chapter in *Frontier Outlaws* to summarizing Allen's views and placing him in New England's history of religion, but does not mention Young as Allen's mentor or Allen plagiarizing Young's work.[61] Less enthusiastic for *Reason* than his full-length biographers, John L. Barr, the compiler of *The Genealogy of Ethan Allen and His Brothers and Sisters*, notes in a biographical sketch of Ethan Allen that the book "was something of a hodgepodge of English Deism." He accepts Jellison's characterization of Allen's role as an editor of Young's manuscript and notes, extending that estimate to absolve Allen of wrongdoing. According to Barr, plagiarizing "was not unusual in the eighteenth-century. . . . it was not always considered dishonest to borrow from another writer."[62] Actually, Britain has had an anti-plagiarism law since 1709. Though Britain's copyright law was not enforced in its North American colonies, ninety-one years later it served as the template for the U.S. Copyright Act of 1790.[63]

Willard Randall has Allen tracking down the widow Young from Philadelphia to Dutchess County to bring home "the opening chapters of the book." Avoiding the sole authorship matter, he regards the rest of the book as basically Allen's, treating *Reason* as a statement of Allen's belief system and a reflection of Vermont's democratic religious culture. He also "finds it unimaginable" that Allen did not share with Young's widow some of the money he made on the sale of fewer than one hundred copies of *Reason*. No accounting of the book's few sales survived the fire that destroyed most of *Reason*'s remainders. Of the modern biographers of Ethan Allen, Michael Bellesiles fully supports Allen's authorship of *Reason*. His argument in defense of Allen's exclusive authorship relied on discrediting Zadock Thompson's authenticating witnesses and "first and only" claims—the only revolutionary leader to write a book of philosophy and the first American book on Deism. Yet all the modern biographers have accepted without question Thompson's reliance on equally elderly witnesses in the Taylor family's lost children story. William Czar Bradley's account of Fanny and Ethan marrying in his father's house in 1784, also a tale Zadock Thompson relied on in the 1840s, has been retold by all of Allen's biographers without questioning a memory acquired at age two and still reliable in Bradley's sixties. The Vermont Historical Society website reports that William Czar Bradley had a talent for storytelling "from a young age."[64]

A question of some import never arises in these biographers' observations on Allen's *Reason*. How did a distribution of so few copies of the book manage to circulate sufficiently to achieve the influence in American cultural history they attribute to it? Allen told Benjamin Stiles that 1,500 books were printed and 40 bound copies were shipped to New York in November 1785.[65] A few others were given as gifts. Haswell and Russell's initial printing produced only two hundred bound copies before the fire that G. W. Matsell mentions in his 1836 reprint destroyed the remaining bound and unbound copies. That reprint and its subsequent iterations in 1854, and J. P. Mendum's also in 1854 and in 1940 and 1972, and an "Ethan Allen Modernization" in 2008–9 did not give the book wide circulation. Charles Clendenen performed the modernization because he thought "many readers never finish reading this work, because it is just too convoluted. Readers have always had to fight their way through a dense fog of words to get to Allen's meaning."[66]

Excluding the dead Thomas Young completely from *Reason* without acknowledging any role for him in its conception and composition completed Allen's self-invention project. His partially borrowed captivity narrative redeemed him as a warrior. With *Reason* he became a self-acclaimed philosopher. He sought approval from Crèvecoeur with a platitude. Even if Paris rejected *Reason*, "I shall have the satisfaction of reflecting, that I have made a bold attempt in Philosophy, though unsuccessful."[67] As he told his readers in 1779, he was fearless before his enemies and his critics, because "To be timorous of death . . . was inconsistent with the character of a philosopher or a soldier."[68]

Reason's modern readers do not find Allen's critique of orthodox religion an engaging exercise. Although, at some level, Allen's or Young's satirical humor deconstructing God's harsh treatment of Adam and Eve (over an "indiscretion with a snake and an apple") or Moses posthumously reporting his own death might still draw a chuckle. Reason prevailed to dominate Western culture with little or no help from Allen's very sparsely distributed book.

This examination of the powers of silence and exclusion in the history of the story of Ethan Allen has mixed results. It does not resolve the issue whether Ethan Allen ever killed anyone, though if he did, Crean Brush comes close to filling the victim's role.

Historians remain silent by not addressing such matters, though clues and evidence have long been accessible for examination. Conclusive arguments pro or con for Allen the slave owner and for some members of his family are variously persuasive. Given the silent presence of continued slavery in Vermont for many years after his death, a persuasive answer to the question of Ethan Allen as a slave owner awaits a diligent researcher discovering a bill of sale, an entry in an elusive record that Pell claimed without support as "$69,823.36," or a record of manumission with Ethan Allen's distinctive signature sealing the deal.[69]

Questions prior to the query "Who killed Crean Brush?" remain unasked. Could Ethan Allen have killed or murdered another person, especially a significant opponent? Consider his behavior leading the Green Mountain Boys' aggressively violent treatment of Yorker settlers and New York authorities between 1772 and 1775. Prominent examples include attacking a Yorker deputy sheriff from behind and beating him to the floor of a tavern accompanied by threats to attack and burn a New York sheriff's house. Allen also directed the flogging of Yorker settlers, threatened to demolish or burn down more houses, and made other death threats that he followed within a year by his advice to Richard Montgomery and Philip Schuyler in September 1775 to kill more Indians to discourage their alliance with Britain.[70] Shortly thereafter Allen and a feeble force of Canadians and Yankees engaged Montreal's defenders for an hour-long firefight in the only combat action of his life. All of this suggests a man capable of extremely violent speech and behavior who could beat or kill others in a terror attack, or in a war, or *mano a mano* against Crean Brush. Allen's motive? — revenge against the crown piece of Brush's legislative career, the Bloody Act of 1774 that declared Allen guilty of a capital crime without a trial. Silence on that matter has been penetrated. The question of who killed Crean Brush remains tentatively, though not convincingly, answered.

Another prior question invites consideration in the matter of "Who wrote *Reason the Only Oracle of Man*?" Competent scholars have not accepted or have failed to identify a meaningful role for Thomas Young in composing *Reason*. Michael Bellesiles denies an author's role for Young, and Charles Jellison proposes something less than full disclosure. Neither Bellesiles and Jellison nor other biographers suggest a prior or alternative question: Did Ethan Allen use material in the twenty-year-old

Young-Allen manuscripts he retrieved from Young's wife without recognizing it as Young's work? He did "borrow" from other writers some of the scenes in *A Narrative of Colonel Ethan Allen's Captivity*. Future biographers of Ethan Allen who preserve the historian's necessarily skeptical distance between themselves and their subject will, as have all others before them, feel the attraction to the existing story of Ethan Allen, sometimes drawing them into the story so closely as to forget to ask some prior questions that may penetrate silent exclusions that call out for further investigation. Moreover, they will have to deal with and resolve the question of whether Ethan Allen really engaged in negotiations with the British authorities in Quebec for the purpose of allying independent Vermont with the British Crown.

THE HERO KEEPS HIS REPUTATION

When it came to the Haldimand Negotiations, the real Ethan Allen did not wish to stand up. In the late spring of 1781 the British pressed the Vermonters who had conducted negotiations with them for more than a year to take concrete steps necessary to bring Vermont into the empire. The preceding fall the Vermont legislature had heard rumors of the negotiations and accusations of treasonous behavior. Ira Allen, at the center of the Haldimand Negotiations, took actions to extricate himself and his co-conspirators from the jaws of the vise closing from Vermont on one side and the British on the other. His destruction of evidence, alteration of documents, and dissembling statements contributed an effective combination of deceit and pettifoggery. Governor General of the Province of Quebec Frederick Haldimand, impatient with the pace of the negotiations, sent agents to the June 1781 session of the Vermont Assembly in Bennington to assess the Vermonters' seriousness. They observed the scene from the gallery of the "Meeting House." Agitated by the possibility of treason by the state's leaders, the Assembly loudly demanded a meeting "on the subject of Colonel [Ira] Allen's mission to the British in Canada." A committee of the Assembly did not find Ira's oral representations at the meeting adequate and requested that he provide "the writings" for the inspection of the committee. Ira produced the doctored and selective papers and accompanied them with an oral explanation of "sundry" matters. He revealed to the Assembly that he had "discovered among British officers a fervent wish for peace." In this context, his explanation of negotiations for a prisoner exchange satisfied the Vermonters for a time. When that evening Ira met with the "Canadian spectators," they also accepted his explanations, "perfectly satisfied." "Is it not curious," Ira asked rhetorically, "to see opposite parties perfectly satisfied with one statement, and each believing what they wished to believe, and thereby deceiving themselves!"[1] Ira

SIR FREDERICK HALDIMAND,
GOVERNOR GENERAL OF QUEBEC,
1778–86.
General Haldimand was a Swiss native
who served in several European armies.
A distinguished veteran commander of
the Germans and Swiss troops of the Royal
Americans during the French and Indian
War, in 1780 Haldimand opened negotiations with leaders of the Vermont government, including Ethan and Ira Allen, to
bring the independent state of Vermont
into alliance with the British Empire.
The negotiations entered into a second
phase that continued until 1783.
Portrait painted by Sir Joshua Reynolds.
© *National Portrait Gallery, London.*

had certainly deceived the Assembly, and telling the story for exoneration and posterity in his *History*, he deceived his readers by claiming to
have also hoodwinked the British agents.[2]

Sooner or later every student of early Vermont history and Ethan
Allen must confront those notorious negotiations, for in the meaning
ascribed to them lies the key to the interpretation of many events before
and after.[3] The story that his brother Ira told about their activities on
behalf of Vermont, subsequently embellished by historians and biographers, helped make Ethan the mythical embodiment of Vermont. Revisionists later found much of Ethan's character doubtful, self-serving,
and probably disloyal. These opposing conclusions about Allen turn
more on the interpretation of the Haldimand Negotiations than on any
other factor. Both groups of historians read the same documents, especially after the Canadians published a calendar of the Haldimand papers, many created by the Allens. Ultimately, each beginning with a
different premise, both groups believed, as Ira would have it, what they
wished to believe.

Biographers and historians in the mid-nineteenth century who made
Allen an icon and centerpiece of Vermont's early history established
their premises and wrote in an environment of perplexing change they
regarded largely as troubling evidence of economic, social, and moral

decay. All of them, except Benjamin H. Hall, who lived in Troy, New York, and confined his study to eastern Vermont, found reason to extol Ethan Allen, build Vermont's self-esteem, and promote the values they attributed to him that they hoped to see in themselves and that would help shape the state's future. Those from out of state like Henry DePuy, who readily acknowledged his debt to Zadock Thompson, Hiland Hall, Henry Stevens, and other Vermont historical authorities, contributed to the movement. The Harvard historian Jared Sparks, who had published the first of the "heroic" Ethan Allen books in 1834, engaged in a lengthy correspondence with Henry Stevens, a founder of the Vermont Antiquarian and Historical Society, who collected material to support Sparks's writing and expounded to him ideas about the nobility of Vermont's founders.

HISTORY TO THE RESCUE: VERMONT'S HISTORIANS REMAIN INTERESTED

The books that turned Ethan Allen into an icon appeared at a time when the nation relished heroic biography and the "Life and Times" genre. The nation welcomed the filiopietistic biographies of the founding fathers with adoring books on Washington, Adams, Jefferson, Franklin, Patrick Henry, and others. States also celebrated their founders. Virginia had its own pantheon of revolutionary leaders, Massachusetts had both of the Adamses, Rhode Island had Nathanael Greene, New Hampshire had John Stark, Kentucky had Daniel Boone, Tennessee had Davy Crockett, and Vermont had Ethan Allen, all larger in reflection than in life and all symbols for their states.

In Vermont, though the experiences of the nineteenth century and especially the Civil War increasingly drew the attention of historians, the treatment of Ethan Allen did not subside or change. Nor did the impulse to address contemporary issues through the past. While many of the matters that had plagued the state between Jefferson's Embargo in 1807 and the middle of the century had receded by the end of the Civil War, Vermonters still thought that they had serious problems. In 1884 Governor John L. Barstow painfully told the legislature that "our beloved State is not keeping pace with others in material prosperity and development." In his farewell speech he lamented, "The census of 1880 again shows that our rural population and wealth are decreasing, while our villages and cities gain only a little more than enough to compensate." Barstow pointed to the reduction of Vermont's congressional seats from three to two as a stark reminder of Vermont's falling behind.[4] The revolution in transportation created by the railroads that provided welcome ease of movement and product also opened the state to competition and regulatory problems. The railroads also moved some towns downhill to the river valleys their tracks followed. Textile mills and other factories crowded along the same waterways. Marble and granite quarries and sheds produced some new landscapes. Growing grain and the sheep craze had largely passed, leaving much farmland abandoned and transforming Vermont agriculture into many small dairy farms often deemed marginal and unprofitable. The population remained stagnant, having barely increased from 326,073 in 1860 to 343,641 in 1900, a meager growth of 0.5 percent in four full decades. This invited troubling comparisons to the national rate of more than 140 percent.[5] Without an influx of immigrants—French Canadians working in the fields, woods, and mills; Italians in the stone industry; the Irish who had provided unskilled labor and had begun to experience upward mobility; and smaller numbers of other ethnic groups—the Vermont population would have declined. Old-line Anglo-Saxon Vermonters often found the different cultures of these new residents disquieting and further evidence of decay.

Before 1850 the sense of decline stemmed from people's perceptions more than the reality that "long mystified and concerned Vermont historians" and masked "important changes . . . in the composition and distribution of Vermont's population and consequently the reconfiguration of economic, political, social, and cultural life in the late nineteenth century."[6] Relying on contemporary records and perceptions, Harold Fisher Wilson labeled the period the "winter" season in Vermont agriculture.[7] The traditional description of "rural New England in the Gilded Age depicted the era as a bleak time of stagnation and retrenchment."[8] Paul M. Searls's more recent study *Two Vermonts* between 1865 and 1910 redefined the dichotomy as one of growth and stability dividing post–Civil War Vermont into "uphill" and "downhill" communities.[9] While other scholars have challenged the accuracy of the notion of decline, Vermonters saw themselves divided along basic values.[10] Those "with 'uphill' values were characterized by their affinity for the localized, informal, cooperative communities of pre-capitalist America. To be 'downhill' was to have opposite inclinations toward competitiveness, formality, contractual relationships, and comfort with concentration of power in increasingly larger institutions." Searls entitles his final chapter "The Failure of the 'New Vermont,'" or the "downhill" ethic. This environment mystified and troubled historians living through it.[11]

Ethan Allen's biographers and those writing in the late nineteenth century about Vermont in its formative years clung to the positive, heroic elements of the Vermont story, which helped provide confidence in times perceived as difficult. They saw no reason to question the past as seen by respected historians like Zadock Thompson and Hiland Hall who created the template from which their successors wrote. Some of these later writers had grown up reading Thompson and other Allen disciples.

Their histories of early Vermont demonstrated little familiarity with the trends in the historiography of the American Revolution. In the late nineteenth century, punctuated by the formation of the American Historical Society in 1884, as the United States began to explore its own imperial destiny, a new cadre of professionally trained historians largely working in the academy began to look for the meaning of the Revolution in British colonial and imperial policy and the question of home rule. "No taxation without representation," the slogan learned by every school child, symbolized this approach. The slogan, however, failed to note that between 1760 and 1775 Americans moved from being loyal subjects to denying the British Crown any rights over them. As Vermonters continued to lionize Ethan Allen, the nation and historical scholarship moved into the Progressive era. In his very influential *History of Political Parties in the Province of New York, 1760–1776* (1909), Carl Becker deflected the question from imperial relations to a focus more on a sociopolitical perspective, less about home rule and more about who should rule at home. This led to an examination of the conflicts among the colonists and less emphasis on the struggle with England. While Allen's defiance of New York's colonial authorities and later hostility toward New York's revolutionary government or the attack on Fort Ticonderoga and the Canadian expedition of 1775 clearly appear in these themes, the literature that addressed him did not fit in that contemporary Vermont historiography.

The academic studies of the American Revolution had no obvious impact on turn-of-the century Vermont chroniclers, possibly because none of those writing about Allen and Vermont held faculty positions or had trained in the developing programs in graduate studies to become professional historians. Vermont history remained comfortably entrenched in its filiopietistical shell. Professor Samuel Franklin Emerson taught history at the University of Vermont (UVM) from 1881 until he retired in 1923. UVM did not have an historian with an earned Ph.D. until 1910. Professor Henry Wells Lawrence, who taught a course in U.S. history, left after 1911, and the next doctoral-trained historian, Clarence Russell Williams, joined the faculty in 1923, replacing Emerson as an associate professor "pro tempore." Williams taught basically the same curriculum adopted in 1906 that focused on classical times and Europe with the exception of one course in U.S. history. In 1892 Norwich University hired Edwin L. Whitney, who held a Harvard Ph.D. in history. He quickly moved to the position of university librarian. Middlebury College's history faculty offered American history courses in the early twentieth century. From 1908 to 1916, Assistant Professor of History Archibald Darius Wetherell (d. 1916), Middlebury class of 1905, taught "American History from 1783." Allen Marshall Cline, who earned his Ph.D. from the University of Michigan (1907), taught "American History" as professor of history, 1920–26, and as professor of American history, 1926–52. These trained historians did not exhibit an interest in Vermont's past nor did the catalogue descriptions of their courses.[12]

Rowland E. Robinson, perhaps the best of Vermont's nineteenth-century writers, built a solid readership as a nature writer publishing in *Scribner's Magazine, Forest and Stream, Hearth and Home, The American Agriculturist*, and other mass-circulation magazines. His skillful and popular Danvis tales, local-color fiction written in the dialects of Vermonters and French Canadians living in Vermont, earned him the reputation of "a masterful regional observer and writer."[13] Writing with the assistance of his wife because of his blindness, Robinson accepted the assignment to write a history of Vermont in Houghton Mifflin and Company's American Commonwealth series.[14] His uncritical, though skillfully written, history of the state appeared in 1892 and followed the script written by his predecessors that he probably had read to him as part of his preparation. Robinson depicts the Green Mountain Boys as "honest backwoods yeomen," who embodied "the same spirit . . . as the men who fought at Lexington and Bunker Hill." In the same vein, he portrays the capture of Ticonderoga as a "means to unite with their countrymen."[15]

Robinson's characterization of Allen repeats the familiar refrain of his predecessors. Ethan exhibited "hearty good-natured fellowship and rough manners," though Robinson unlike some other writers detected that he could also "assume the deportment of a fine gentleman," an observation Allen would have approved. Robinson paid homage to Allen's "undoubted bravery [and] his hearty good-natured and rough manner." His "rude eloquence was the sort to fire uncultivated backwoodsmen, whether he harangued them from the stump . . . [or] in the gray pages of his ill-printed pamphlets." The same Ethan Allen appeared in Robinson's 1898 novella *A Hero of Ticonderoga*, a fictional local-color narrative told in dialect by Nathan Beaman, a young boy from Shoreham, Vermont, who accompanies Allen on his adventures. Beaman joins Allen in thwarting Yorkers, capturing Fort Ticonderoga, and heading down Lake Champlain in bateaux to capture the king's sloop at St. John. This account has Allen safely returning to Ticonderoga and omits the rash endangerment of his men in Canada and their disorganized, headlong retreat. The tradition of Nathan Beaman guiding Allen is pure fiction, which historians had debunked many years earlier.[16] By now Allen's promises to adhere to military discipline in return for General Schuyler allowing him to join the American invasion of Quebec had become an "invitation" by "the generals [Schuyler and Montgomery]," as Allen had claimed in his *Narrative*. In Robinson's version, John Brown "proposed to Allen that they should attempt to capture Montreal," and he repeats Ethan's dramatic account of shielding himself from an Indian by thrusting Loyalist Peter Johnson in front of the native attacker. Though the "attempt upon Montreal has generally been characterized as rash, if Brown had not, for some unexplained reason, failed to perform his part," Robinson concluded, "it is more than probable that the undertaking would have succeeded." He saw it as "one of those daring enterprises which if successful receives the highest praise," but when unsuccessful becomes "foolhardy."[17]

Robinson quotes Allen's June 16, 1782, letter to Haldimand with its claim that a "majority in the Congress and a Number of the principal officers of the Continental Army" continually plotted against him and its unambiguous statement that "I shall do everything in my Power to render this State a British province." Robinson emphatically declares, "There was no treason." In the effort to avoid an invasion of their state, the Vermont negotiators may not have exhibited "the most exalted devotion to the faithless Congress," but "they never sought to work injury to the Confederation from which they were excluded." Ignoring the evidence that the vast majority of Vermonters did not wish to rejoin the British, Robinson deals only with the concept of treason against the United States and not Vermont. With a legalistic but unconvincing twist of logic, he asserts "the Vermonters could not plot . . . treason against a government in which they had no part."[18] Citing Allen's "bold, daring, and resolute" nature, Robinson accurately declares that "Vermont has given him the first place among her heroes."[19] A well-known Vermont writer had skillfully laid another stone on the popular monument to Ethan Allen's glory.

In 1892, the same year that Robinson's history of Vermont appeared, Henry Hall's posthumous *Ethan Allen: The Robin Hood of Vermont*, written "to make plain the vivid personality of a Vermont hero to the younger generations," added more print and no new information to the cult. The book fit into the contemporary juvenile fiction genre of historical heroes who overcame hardship and achieved success. His widow's brief preface, light on analysis and heavy on eulogistic praise, claimed that "Mr. Hall's well-known habit of accuracy and painstaking investigation must be the guaranty that this 'Life' is worthy of a place among the volumes of the history of our nation." The book prints many documents and offers a measured account that follows the pattern first established in the 1830s. Despite the Haldimand Negotiations, Hall believed "Ethan Allen [was] always a patriot." He cites six reasons, mostly shallow evaluations of character rather than policy. With Hall's juvenile-targeted biography, the cult of Ethan Allen reached another segment of a broad national audience, linking his defiance of New York and capture of Fort Ticonderoga with Robin Hood, the audacious merry champion of the poor and scourge of aristocracy and hierarchical government.[20]

Between 1899 and 1903 Lafayette Wilbur published his *Early History of Vermont* in four volumes. He did not deviate from the pattern established by those he followed and to a large extent relied on. An amateur from Jericho, Vermont, privately publishing through a local printer, Wilbur demonstrated the power of Allen's hold on a growing public. By then Allen the Vermont hero had been fully transformed into a hero of the American Revolution. Wilbur ties the "sleepless and untiring" Allen to the ideals of the Revolution—"the systematical and bloody attempt by the British at Lexington" had inspired the capture of Ticonderoga. He appropriates much of his description of Allen from the florid, overblown address of Lucius Chittenden at the dedication of the Allen monument, itself an expansive element in the Allen myth. Allen's "ever active and dauntless spirit, by pen and voice, as well as the sword, warred against the most desperate and powerful enemies . . . and largely contributed to the establishment of a State and Independence of a Nation."[21]

On the Haldimand Negotiations, Wilbur concludes that "the armistice entered into by General Allen and others was not only approved by the Vermont authorities but was for the benefit of both Vermont and the Confederacy. Ethan betrayed nobody, but served his State." Wilbur neglects to mention that the only "approval" by "Vermont authorities" came from the coterie of conspirators themselves. When in 1780 the General Assembly "arraigned" Allen over suspicions about the negotiations, "he was acquitted of all disloyalty and public confidence was restored to him." The "aspersion against him did not serve to dampen his patriotism," even though Ira Allen had doctored the documents presented to the General Assembly and Ethan noisily resigned his commission as general of the Vermont militia. Wilbur does observe that Allen's services became "less prominent than before his capture," but he labels it "a mistake" that "he had lost his energy and zeal both for the nation and the State." Allen's diminished public presence occurred not because of "a decay of his powers," or a "change in his views towards the State and Country," but simply because occasions for "striking service did not occur again."[22] A zealous but not skilled amateur, Wilbur borrowed heavily from his predecessors and in the process his four-volume history added to the monument to the hero.

The last and by a wide margin the best and most useful of the histories of Vermont issued before challenges to the Ethan Allen story appeared in Walter Hill Crockett's five-volume *Vermont: The Green Mountain State*. Crockett, the director of publications at the University of Vermont, usefully carried his well-researched story of Vermont through World War I, but he devoted almost two of his five narrative volumes to the period before 1791 and statehood. He devoted an entire chapter to the Haldimand Negotiations. Though he did not document his sources, or publish a bibliography, clearly he had seen the calendar of the Haldimand correspondence printed by the Public Archives of Canada. Crockett's predecessors had relied on Allen papers, Vermont documents, and others on the fringes of the negotiations, but he became deeply suspicious that the discussions had gone well beyond the cover story of a prisoner exchange. Crockett frequently quotes from Haldimand's reports to George Germain, Britain's secretary of state for colonial affairs, from reports of Justus Sherwood, the former Green Mountain Boy turned Loyalist and leading negotiator for the British, and other documents and correspondence that make clear that he mined the Haldimand material for evidence to make his seemingly predetermined case and ignored less favorable evidence.[23]

In the first Vermont account to make use of the calendar of the Haldimand papers available in the 1885–89 *Report of the Public Archives of Canada*, Crockett noted that with the "Haldimand correspondence, printed by Canadian authorities, it is interesting to note the fluctuation of opinion concerning the sincerity of the Vermont leaders, confidence alternating with suspicion and distrust."[24] Crockett began his defense of Ethan and his associates by isolating evidence that Haldimand and his representatives doubted the Vermonter's sincerity. He quoted Haldimand's assessment that by "the uniformity of Ira Allen's conduct, that he must be the most accomplished villain living if he means to deceive us." On Jonas Fay, Crockett quotes Haldimand's suspicion, that "He professes so much honesty, accompanied by so many gestures of sincerity, that he seems to overact his part. He is certainly perfectly honest, or a perfect Jesuit: we have too much reason to fear the latter." Crockett concludes that Vermont had cleverly managed to forestall British military action on the lightly guarded northern frontier while at the same time putting pressure on Congress for recognition. The Vermonters "accomplished abundantly and exactly" their objectives through the extended negotiations. "Many persons in and out of Vermont viewed the Haldimand negotiations with severe disapproval and were inclined to look upon the action of Vermont leaders . . . as little short of treason-

able. The charges made are so serious that they deserve the fullest and
fairest consideration."[25]

Crockett's consideration began with a ringing and unsupported statement: "No men in America were more radical in their devotion to liberty, or more resolute in its defense, than the Green Mountain Boys."
Even those who disliked Allen and his associates, Crockett asserted,
"would not deny their shrewdness and sagacity." As nothing had hap-
pened "to change the attitude of the people of Vermont toward Great
Britain," Crockett colorfully concluded, "Ethan and Ira Allen and
Thomas Chittenden might have agreed to deliver Mount Mansfield,
with the same probability of keeping their agreement that would have
been in promising to transform Vermont into a royal province of Great
Britain." He underscored the point because he asserted that Allen and
Chittenden personally hated the British, the former for his captivity
and the latter for having to abandon his farm in Williston because of
the British military threat.[26] Crockett's stout exoneration cited a self-
serving "Certificate for the Protection of Ira Allen," in actuality a round-
robin letter, written and signed by the participants asserting that Ira
went to Canada for the sole purpose of a prisoner cartel. Crockett does
not mention a second round-robin letter Ira prepared for British eyes
that did not exonerate the conspirators. He quotes others with no inside
knowledge of the motives of the participants, including a recollection in
the 1840s by Daniel Chipman that his brother Nathaniel, "a principal
actor in all public transactions of the day and often an opponent of the
Allens," had found nothing but "merriment and exultation" in duping
the British. Nathaniel Chipman, a young lawyer, likely convinced of the
participants' innocence by their assertions and the round-robin letter,
forged the documents for Ira that achieved a stay from the Assembly.
He also penned the letter from Thomas Chittenden to George Washington proclaiming Vermont's attachment to the United States, explaining
why circumstances dictated their seeking a truce with the enemy. Writing during the time the iconic Ethan Allen was emerging in the story of
early Vermont, Daniel Chipman did not mention his brother's personal
and political enmity for the Allens and their associates. In March 1780,
for example, Nathaniel Chipman and Matthew Lyon, a close associate
of the Allens, secretary of the Governor's Council, and future son-in-law
of Thomas Chittenden, engaged in a fist fight.[27]

Crockett would not write anything that could besmirch the honor of the Green Mountain State or its heroes. Allen's "career is so closely interwoven with the early annals of Vermont that one inevitably suggests the other." Allen had rendered "splendid service" and embodied the qualities, "which in earlier days, have made chieftains and kings, namely a commanding presence, a strong right arm, great personal valor and a natural capacity for leadership."[28] The research and detail in *Vermont: The Green Mountain State* lent substantial weight and gravitas to the story of Ethan Allen.

REVISIONISTS EMERGE;
TRADITIONALISTS RESIST

As Crockett wrote, a doctoral student at Yale examined the Haldimand Negotiations for his dissertation "Vermont and Great Britain: A Study in Diplomacy, 1779–1783." Clarence W. Rife, after a thorough review of the archival material, initiated the revisionist position when he reached a very different conclusion from Crockett and all of the previous Allen biographers and historians. Rife, the first professionally trained historian to concentrate on an early Vermont subject, recognized that "the task of arriving at the truth is a manifestly difficult one," as the explanation of saving the frontier from invasion "has become settled tradition with almost every writer who has approached the subject."[29] Looking at the same archival material in the Haldimand papers from which Crockett found exoneration, Rife declared that Chittenden, the Allens, and their inner circle had negotiated "to offer or accept, terms of cessation of hostilities with Great Britain without the approbation of any other body of men." Without the news of the American victory at Yorktown, "undoubtedly" Chittenden would have introduced to the Vermont legislature "Haldimand's proclamation," with its "proposal of a change of government." "Heated controversy, perhaps even bloodshed, would have followed. Whether the Vermont conspirators could have brought the legislature to favor a policy of neutrality followed shortly by a reunion with Great Britain must be left to conjecture." With the promise of the war "to terminate in favor of the United States, the wise policy for these Vermont opportunists was to cover up the past and to maintain that the negotiations with the British [billed as a cartel for prisoner exchange] were merely a ruse to safeguard them against invasion."[30]

After the Continental Congress "rebuffed" Vermont overtures to join the Union in 1782, "Vermont leaders then turned more readily to Great Britain and in July tried to renegotiate a reunion," an initiative ultimately thwarted by instructions to Haldimand from London. Rife asks, with the military threats against the frontier gone, why negotiate? Along with the archival record, Rife points to the return of prisoners, the generous treatment of Loyalists, the British agreement to recognize Vermont expansion in the East and West Unions, and the Allens' efforts to populate northern border towns with Loyalists as further evidence of the seriousness of the negotiations.[31] This second phase of the Haldimand Negotiations with no British threat to the frontier proved Rife's analysis that the Vermonters had negotiated in earnest.

Aware of Rife's challenge to the standard story of Vermont, in 1927 Henry Steele Wardner published the first serious hint of an attack on innate love of liberty and instinctive dislike of hereditary station and tyranny as the driving forces behind Ethan Allen's written and reported statements and actions. Toward the end of *The Birthplace of Vermont: A History of Windsor to 1781*, a book devoted to the Town of Windsor and not to Vermont's larger political history, Wardner questioned the activities of the Vermont leaders. With Benedict Arnold's defection and John Andre's execution as a British spy in the immediate background, Wardner found that "The daring of Justus Sherwood [Haldimand's principal negotiator] and Ethan Allen in actually discussing in secret conversation a plan for bringing Vermont over to the British side is one of the high and glaring spots in Vermont's hectic history."[32] Wardner does not track the Haldimand Negotiations, but he thought it more than suspicious that "whatever portions of the charges and testimony" when the General Assembly in November 1780 confronted Allen "that had been reduced to writing were conveniently destroyed," making it difficult to pursue a "bona fide trial." Wardner questions the sincerity of Allen's rage at the insinuations of treason that provoked his resignation as brigadier general. His resignation "left him even more free than before to guide Vermont's political affairs and safer from court martial." But "in some quarters his reputation for integrity had been permanently impaired."[33]

Wardner's opening salvo, which in four years he would turn into a full broadside, had no apparent influence on the important, well-documented biography of Ira Allen that immediately followed the publication of *Birthplace of Vermont*. In 1928 James B. Wilbur brought out a two-volume biography of Ira Allen, useful for the evidence he uncovered and a year-by-year account of events and activities in early Vermont.[34] Wilbur may have completed his research in the early 1920s in advance of Rife's and Wardner's work, though his bias may have led him to dismiss them in any case. Wilbur "zealously defended Ira Allen's version of the state," which Wardner had referred to as Ira's efforts "to make his own exploits as a rescuer bulk as large as possible" and "to extenuate his own questionable methods." Wilbur sought to rescue Ira Allen from "national obscurity and occasional slanders and place him firmly on the pedestal reserved for Vermont's noblest son." He employed "tortuous arguments and convoluted reasoning" to refute "every possible accusation against Ira Allen," producing " a total whitewashing of the character, actions, and writings of Wilbur's hero to such an extent that it weakened his case."[35]

A year after Wilbur published his life of Ira Allen, John Pell, scion of the family that owned and restored Fort Ticonderoga where Ethan Allen vaulted onto the national stage, published the first modern biography of Allen. Pell diligently pursued primary evidence and located some documents not previously seen. But he constantly asserted knowledge of his hero's state of mind, took the congenial narrative beyond documentary support, and rarely failed to recite popular stories and anecdotes of Allen's outsized feats and monumental utterances, often ascribing them to "tradition" (meaning unverified).

In his acknowledgments, Pell expressed his gratitude to Wardner and thanked Clarence Rife for sharing his "unequaled knowledge of the Haldimand intrigue." Though he cites neither the Haldimand papers nor Rife, Pell weaves a narrative that argues with Rife in concluding that after 1782, when "it became clear that Congress intended to repudiate Washington's promise [to secure Vermont's entry into the Confederation], Ethan, as well as Ira, Chittenden, Jonas [Fay], Joseph [Fay] and the rest of the real leaders of Vermont, turned away in disgust. And from that time on they did everything in their power to render Vermont a British Province." Rumors circulated that because Ethan had accepted the pay of a lieutenant colonel, his conduct "was treasonable business." Pell asserts that "as a citizen of the independent Republic of Vermont, he was pursuing the course which he believed was most likely to benefit his State," and "Great Britain offered recognition as an individual Province, free trade with Canada, and no war debt."[36] Pell lays out the elements of the trade craft of Allen's dangerous "intrigue" and "apostasy," but he does not draw a conclusion as to the political morality of the intrigue, and he ignores that a vast majority of those living in Vermont would have thought the negotiations inappropriate if not treasonous against the state and nation. Instead, Pell moves facilely and without a seam from the elements of the Haldimand Negotiations to Allen's sudden romance and marriage to Frances Montresor Buchanan in 1784, ending with romantic speculation into their life together before Allen's death in 1789. Pell understood that the Allens treated with the British in earnest, but he did not draw the obvious conclusion. He also had an appreciation for the importance of land and open commerce with Canada in Allen's calculations, though he did not probe the dowry in land that came with Allen's bride.

Within two years of the appearance of Pell's biography, the Vermont Historical Society invited Wardner to address its Annual Meeting at the House of Representatives chamber in the Vermont State House. With a certain irony the Society, a major element in the nineteenth-century development of Ethan Allen's iconic status, invited the public reinterpretation of the Haldimand Negotiations and, to a lesser degree, the nobility of Allen's motivations.[37] Wardner's performance ushered in nearly a half-century of revisionism punctured by a few well-crafted and popular exceptions. The editor's introduction to the published version of Wardner's text broke with tradition, claiming that Wardner had examined the "historical dogma" and "cut through the prejudices," demonstrating that "the conduct of Vermont's first citizens was nothing short of treason to the Colonies."[38]

Wardner told the audience that the idea of serious negotiations with Haldimand would cause "our Vermont historians to hold up their hands in horror at the thought of Ethan Allen, Thomas Chittenden and their intimates contemplating the conversion of Vermont into a British province." "Vermont historians, with one marked exception [Rife], from Samuel Williams, who brought out his first edition in 1794, down to

Mr. Crockett in 1921, would have us understanding that Vermont for the purpose of averting an invasion from Canada, was deceiving the British into the mistaken belief that the people of this State were really preparing their State to become a British province." He included Ira Allen, "who always had a narrator's ambition to tell a story for all it was worth," among the influences on the historians who ardently espoused that "for three years Vermont met British overtures with such perfect acting" that they fooled the British into believing Vermont would turn to them.[39]

Wardner traced the history of the Haldimand Negotiations, developing the military situation on the Vermont frontier, the strained and threatening relations with Congress and with New York and New Hampshire, and the internal conflicts in Vermont. He posited that Colonel Seth Warner, Colonel Samuel Herrick, Colonel Thomas Johnson, and General Jacob Bayley exemplified those "who thought that the winning of American Independence was the chief work of the day." He found it "equally as a fact that Ethan Allen, Thomas Chittenden and Dr. Jonas Fay were leaders of that element which thought that the first duty was to safeguard the political integrity of Vermont." Their behavior in the Haldimand Negotiations would pivot on that aim, and with that supposition Wardner would find ample reason to excuse what some would label treason.[40] With his conclusion that the Vermont leaders held Vermont independence foremost, Wardner recognized that though the Allens had treated in earnest with the British and not tried to dupe them, their behavior had the understandable, even noble, motivation of preserving Vermont. Subsequent students who could not plausibly deny the reality of the negotiations would employ this argument to defend their heroes. Wardner had certainly punched a major hole in the century-long effort to make Ethan Allen a hero of the American Revolution, but he had not besmirched Allen's reputation as a principal defender of Vermont.

This motivation explained why Ethan Allen did not report the secret visit of Justus Sherwood as a spy, a Loyalist banished by the Vermont legislature with the penalty of flogging or death if he returned, especially with the recent hanging of Major John André as a spy in mind. It also explained the sudden favorable treatment of Tories. Wardner detailed the fake reports to the legislature, the destruction and forgery of documents, and the double sets like the round-robin letters prepared for different eyes, Ira Allen's "amazing misstatements," "the half or quarter truths," hiring the lawyer Nathaniel Chipman to draft letters and reports, and the constant effort of Ethan Allen, the leader of the movement, "to run with the hare and follow the hounds." Wardner deemed the duplicity appropriate to the protection of an independent Vermont. He explained that the complexities of the rapidly changing political and military events, rather than a change of purpose by Allen and his associates, created twists and turns in the negotiations.

Wardner broke ranks with "the opinion of Jared Sparks and our Vermont historians." He thought "as the Revolutionary War progressed, several Vermont leaders, when prospects of recognition of Vermont's statehood by Congress were discouraging, had serious intention of the State becoming a British province." He thought "they generally kept faith with the British" in the negotiations. He labeled the "cartel" for an exchange of prisoners a "stage-play." He endorsed James Truslow Adams's view in his 1926 *New England in the Republic* of the "complacent conclusion" of Vermont historians about the motives of the Vermont leaders. In his denials of a serious intent to join the British, they "may or may not have been telling the truth. Neither of the brothers paid much attention to that when it served their purpose to ignore it. When Allen said bluntly that what he was after at all costs was to save his property, he was probably nearer to the truth than at any other time in the negotiations."[41]

Wardner strongly espoused the view of Allen's seriousness in making Vermont a British province, but he did not develop the self-interested motivation Adams had suggested. That change would come in the 1930s as American historiography, in part stimulated by questions raised by the Great Depression, turned more to economic analysis. Though Matt Bushnell Jones in his 1939 *Vermont in the Making, 1750-1777* did not directly address the Haldimand Negotiations, he did lay out the motivation for Vermont independence and for its leaders seeking to preserve their prerogatives. In a detailed, carefully documented legalistic study, Jones, an attorney, saw the dispute with New York as less "a struggle between freedom and oppression than a contest between two competing groups of entrepreneurs determined to safeguard their own investments in disputed land titles."[42] "Much has been written," Jones noted, "depicting the grantees of the New Hampshire Grants as actual or prospective settlers on the land, innocent and confiding beyond most human kind, while claimants under New York grants are seen as rich, crafty, scheming men of affairs bent on wrestling their small farms from these settlers. The fact is that, except for the occasional but not numerous settlers under soldiers' grants, most of the original grant-ees, whether under New Hampshire or Vermont, were keen speculators who had no intent whatever to settle on their grants and, in fact, never did so." Allen might articulate the case for the common settlers against the Yorker aristocrats, but Jones found neither the Vermonters nor the Yorkers acted "like archangels."[43] Wardner had decided that the "Al-lens—Ethan and Ira—had no enthusiasm for the republican form of government"; they would accept life in a British province if it meant they could protect and populate their enormous tracts in northwestern Vermont and market their produce down Lake Champlain and down river to the port of Quebec.[44] Jones's firm and detailed analysis strongly buttressed Wardner's position.

Following the scent laid down by Rife, Wardner, and an import-ant article on the importance to Vermont of commerce with Canada, a Columbia University graduate student, Chilton Williamson, began researching a dissertation that would evolve into the first professional monograph reinterpreting Vermont's early history.[45] As Williamson worked, two formidable books aimed at popular audiences appeared within months of each other, taking opposite views of the Allens and the Haldimand Negotiations.

A staunch, unwavering support of the standard version of Vermont's past and Allen's iconic role, the last one for half a century, came off the typewriter of Frederic F. Van de Water. A successful popular writer, Van de Water bought a farm in West Dummerston in 1932 and moved there two years later. Aroused by "a fresh environment," he turned his writing interest to Vermont, and began to publish a series of books about life in the country and novels set around Ethan Allen and the exploits of the Green Mountain Boys.[46] His 1941 *The Reluctant Re-public: Vermont, 1724–1791*, a fast-paced and congenially written his-tory of early Vermont, concentrated on Ethan Allen's most active years between the late 1760s and the early 1780s. Van de Water's effective storytelling burnished the heroic story of Ethan Allen that the revision-ists had only slightly tarnished. Allen and his followers slew the aristocratic British and Yorker dragons on behalf of the Revolution and noble yeomen settling small farms with an innate sense of equality and democracy. Van de Water's lively representation of his principal players energizes his narrative. He found "among the lank and shabby states-men who talked through their noses and, ill-advisedly, were derided by their more worldly [Yorker] adversaries, the Allen brothers stand first — Ethan the whirlwind, the earthquake and the fire; Ira the small voice; Ethan who stamped an impression of himself deep upon the state he served; Ira who is very substance of the state itself."[47] Van de Water himself proudly wore the stamp of Ethan's impression.

In *The Reluctant Republic* Van de Water made one of the last and most eloquent statements extolling clever Vermonters defending their naked frontier and pressuring Congress for recognition through the Haldimand Negotiations. "The simplest and most plausible explana-tion of the whole thing," he wrote, "is that Vermont was in desperate straits; that she needed most sorely at the moment a lever and a shield — the first to move Congress into admitting her into the Union, the second to protect her temporarily from Canadian invasion." The Vermont lead-ers "knew that any attempt to reinstate the Crown was unpopular as to be chimerical"; thus they never seriously tried to consummate it.[48] Van de Water's emphasis on creating archetypal characters, however well portrayed, did not form an adequate basis for analysis. He neglected the geographical imperative of the Champlain Valley's connection to Can-ada and the raw contest for the validation of land titles that might have tempered his view of the negotiations.

The Reluctant Republic "boiled down to a modern restatement of [Rowland] Robinson, [Zadock] Thompson, Samuel Williams and oth-ers, made all the more appealing and delightful by Van de Water's skillful pen."[49] The book had sufficient impact in the popular history market to merit a reprint in 1974, and without other monographs on these early years in print, it became a textbook in a university course on Vermont history and was selectively excerpted for an anthology of ar-ticles on Vermont also used as a college text.[50] Van de Water pumped new oxygen into the traditional story of Vermont with a larger-than-life Ethan Allen at its center.

Within months of the appearance of *The Reluctant Republic*, Charles Miner Thompson, grandson of Daniel P. Thompson whose popular fiction had played a large role in constructing the heroic view of Ethan Allen, published *Independent Vermont*, a study focused on the years from 1777 to 1791. Thompson "flatly rejected" his grandfather's tale, declaring that the stories about Ethan Allen's physical prowess "sound more like the exaggerations of the tellers of tall stories in taverns, like folklore rather than fact." Allen "was a braggart who heightened the color and overstated the importance of everything he did."[51] Thompson thought after the Ejectment Trials in 1770 that "as long as he lived, he [really] did nothing except buy and sell land, for his activities as a politician, pamphleteer, and soldier, however they may have flattered his vanity and ministered to his love of power, were all shrewdly calculated to help his speculation." This lodestone guided Ethan's approach to treating with the British, and "the Allens and their followers were seriously thinking about uniting with Canada."[52]

Thompson provided no documentation (nor a bibliography) except when identifying a document in the course of his narrative. He quotes from "Telemachus" as proof of the seriousness of the "Vermont plotters," but the teasing document has disappeared or remains hidden in a box in some archive or private collection.[53] Thompson, who does quote from Justus Sherwood's journal, discusses the "half-truths," document forgeries of the "conspirators," and the sham of the prisoner cartel ("The business of the cartel was really no business at all"). He laments the "absence of any confidential letters . . . except by inference," but "there is little mystery about the affair other than the mystery." He concludes, "The conjecture need not be accepted, but surely the presumption in favor of their willingness to join Canada is strong." He notes that after Yorktown and the apparent American victory "the negotiations with Haldimand did not cease."[54] Thompson's not especially good or original history made the new interpretations of the state's past available for the first time on the popular level. How much readership that wartime publication received remains a question, and certainly it did not attain the reach of Van de Water's *Reluctant Republic*.[55] The story of Ethan Allen concocted over nearly a century retained a firm grip even after two decades of revision. That grip would begin to weaken as a cadre of professional historians began to revise it, but it would not entirely lose its hold, especially in the popular imagination and memory. In fact, it would eventually re-establish its position.

THE REVISIONISTS PERSIST

Several decades dominated by revisionism began in earnest in 1949 when the Vermont Historical Society published Chilton Williamson's doctoral dissertation *Vermont in Quandary: 1763–1825*. Williamson's geopolitical study examines the natural connection of the Champlain Valley with Canada and the St. Lawrence River in the years between the British conquest and the completion of the Champlain and Erie Canals in the 1820s that "opened" the valley to the south and west. He begins with a self-evident fact: "The physical geography of Vermont," he posits, "has had a profound influence on its history," and men adapt themselves to it.[56] Basing his account of the Haldimand Negotiations heavily on the Haldimand, Clinton, and Germain papers, those of Loyalists Justus Sherwood and William Smith, owner of New York patents in Vermont, and the Allens' and other materials generated in Vermont, Williams dedicated two full chapters to them. One detailed the first phase aborted by the American victory at Yorktown, and the other discussed the more damning second phase of the negotiations on their resumption in 1782 with the war all but over.

Williamson expressed no doubt that the Allens, Chittenden, and their associates negotiated with the British in good faith. The Vermonters hoped that the British would recognize the New Hampshire titles, permit the election of civil officials, open commerce through Canada, and defend the state against incursions from New York or the United States. For their own protection, the conspirators attempted to conceal the real nature of the negotiations. And well after the fact, for posterity, Ira Allen began the historical cover-up by influencing Samuel Williams's treatment of the affair.[57] Williamson quotes Sherwood, who "described Ethan and others as impelled by self-interest rather than loyalty to Great Britain." Sherwood told Haldimand, "It appears that they have two Strings in their Bow that they may choose the strongest, which they are not able to determine till it is better known how Mr. Washington succeeds in the present campaign against Cornwallis at Yorktown." Williamson agrees that the Vermonters did have two strings, looking for recognition of the New Hampshire titles from Congress and, failing that, from the British.[58] Williamson portrays Allen and his associates as driven by land titles and commercial objectives that continued even after the Haldimand Negotiations collapsed, and he discusses those in the chapter on "Quebec's Commercial Dependency." He makes no judgment about what others chose to label as treason or to defend as clever Yankees duping the British for the protection of Vermont's northern frontier, describing the behavior and its motivation, but assessing them only in commercial terms.[59]

In 1968, H. Nicholas Muller III wrote his doctoral dissertation on the "Commercial History of the Lake Champlain-Richelieu River Route: 1760–1815." It detailed and often quantified the commercial relations and strengthened Williamson's hypothesis. While Williamson concentrated on politics, Muller's dissertation documented trade and the impact of politics on it, arguing that the Canadian market played a dominant role in the commercial life of the Champlain Valley. Muller also published an essay that examined the oligarchic character of early Vermont government; another two articles discussed the Haldimand Negotiations, both arguing that Allen and the conspirators, motivated largely by economic factors, determined to make Vermont a British province.[60] In a 1974 critical appraisal of Frederic Van de Water's *The Reluctant Republic* he sided with the revisionists about the seriousness of the negotiations and "the sizeable financial stake the leaders had in protecting their vast land holdings," concluding that "even if [Ethan] Allen's actions are interpreted as looking out for Vermont first, it was a mean and rather private vision of the state he had helped to create."[61] In discussing the attempted cover-up in Ira Allen's *History*, Muller wrote, "One version best fits the facts: the Allens seriously attempted a reconciliation. Applying A. L. Burt's apt metaphor, 'the master key of his guilt' opened the door. Then instead of having to pick lock after lock, we pass right through."[62] Only by the assumption that Allen pursued the Haldimand Negotiations with sincerity does the evidence add up.

After Muller's dissertation and two decades after *Vermont in Quandary*, Charles Jellison's *Ethan Allen: Frontier Rebel* dismissed Allen's previous biographers with the exception of John Pell, who through sound research rescued "Ethan Allen from the limbo of folklore to which he had been assigned by generations of partisans and popularizers." In a breezy style with thin documentation sometimes supported by the myths and legends of folklore that encrusted the Green Mountain hero, Jellison's treatment of the Haldimand Negotiations demonstrated

the growing influence of the revisionists. "Reality in this case was obviously treason," he wrote, "or at least intended treason. The evidence
surely supports this conclusion." Recent discoveries in British archives
"leave absolutely no room for doubt. Ethan and his Arlington friends
were bent on delivering Vermont to the enemy." And "it is clear beyond
any question that as the negotiations progressed and the pieces of the
dangerous transaction began to fall into place, Ethan and his accom-
plices became firmly committed to the idea of taking Vermont back to
the British Empire."[63]

Jellison refutes Rowland Robinson's facile conclusion that the conspirators could not have committed treason against a United States
that did not recognize Vermont, citing the Vermont General Assembly's 1779 legislation that declared anyone giving assistance to enemies
of "this state, or the United States of America guilty of high treason."
He rejects "the contention that his property in the north was the principal, or even major, determinant in deciding Ethan to throw his lot with
the British," concluding that "it seems much more likely that Ethan
was moved to act as he did mainly by a genuine concern for the future
of Vermont." Jellison rejects Williamson's hypothesis of Allen's self-
interest and harkens back to Wardner's declaration of guilt tempered by
the nobility of concern for the beset, fledgling state. This schemer, prevaricator, self-promoter, land speculator, aspiring traitor, and impulsive
military leader still managed to inspire the admiration and affection of
a biographer who had read much of the evidence.

ETHAN ALLEN TRIUMPHANT:
THE TRADITIONALIST ASCENDANTS
REGAIN THE STORY

With Williamson, Jellison, and Muller, the revisionist pendulum had
swung its full arc, and would begin to swing back. The next accounts
would provide the Allens, Chittenden, and their associates a gentle landing that would become increasingly softer. J. Kevin Graffagnino's narrative in his doctoral dissertation "Revolution and Empire on the Northern
Frontier: Ira Allen of Vermont, 1751–1814" ably followed the "serpen-
tine path" of the negotiations. He quotes Justus Sherwood's acknowledgment of the Allens' self-interest. Ira "and his family," Haldimand's

negotiator wrote, "have a large fortune, which they do not intend to lose, if there is a possibility of saving it; at any hazard, he is determined that Congress shall not have the parceling of his lands to their avaricious Minions."[64] Graffagnino points out that the Allens "looked north" to counter New York and Congress, but his account of the negotiations other than recounting Ira's role does not judge the motivations and seriousness of the Vermont participants. A short synthesis in the excellent one-volume history of Vermont published in 2004 by the Vermont Historical Society takes a similar pass on judgment. It asks, "Were the Allens serious?" It responds to the question by indicating the division among the historians and concluding "whatever the case," Cornwallis's loss ended the first phase and British diplomatic concerns ended the second phase.[65] The softening of the revisionists had begun.

In 1993 Michael Bellesiles published his revised dissertation as *Revolutionary Outlaws: Ethan Allen and the Struggle for Independence on the Early American Frontier*, Bellesiles sees Allen as the primary force behind events on the Grants from 1770 to his captivity in 1775 and in Vermont from his return in 1778 to 1784. The publisher touted the book as demonstrating that "more than a legendary Revolutionary War hero," Allen led a "group of frontier subsistence farmers united in their opposition to New York elites and land speculators."[66] Bellesiles clung to this view in assessing the Haldimand Negotiations, portraying Allen as successfully guiding the Vermont ship of state between the Scylla and Charybdis of the British and of New York and Congress. In this account "Allen's top priority remained Vermont's independence and security. . . . Nothing short of a series of unmitigated disasters culminating in an invasion by the Continental army would make union with England attractive, and even then the whole affair would have to be conducted slyly." In Bellesiles's view "the core" to protecting Vermont lay in "persuading Congress to let Vermont into the Union."[67] Clearly influenced by the trend in the late 1960s into the early 1980s to interpret the American Revolution from "the bottom up," viewing it from the experiences and everyday life of the common men and women rather than the educated and wealthy white founding fathers, Bellesiles interpreted Ethan Allen as creating a democratic polity, and accordingly, he tended to downplay economic motives.

For the first three years of the negotiations Bellesiles's Allen skillfully practiced the art of disinformation with the British, Congress, American military leaders including Washington, Stark, Schuyler, and Warner, and Vermonters as "a study in contradictions and evasively noncommittal." Allen "mastered the art of mixed messages to keep Vermont afloat." In the second phase of the negotiations after Congress's refusal to recognize Vermont, Allen filled his letters to Canada "with encouragement, but when Haldimand pressed for a meeting, Allen managed superficially to agree, while in fact refusing. Stating his desire for such a personal encounter with the British commander, Allen thought the time not yet propitious. Just a few more months, he assured Haldimand time and again." Bellesiles turns to Ira Allen's conclusion in his *History* that the negotiations "were from necessity," and they addressed the "'mutual interests' of security and trade."[68] The Haldimand Negotiations had only a small role in Bellesiles's larger and more valuable work in which he sees Ethan Allen as the representative of "the resistance of independent agricultural communities against the machinations of dishonest governments under the control of wealthy speculators intent on stealing the land of the poor."[69] This view of Allen, though better researched and presented, echoes the views of Allen's commitment to egalitarian polity developed in the nineteenth-century celebration of the Revolution and largely overlooks the Allen brothers' commitment to securing land for themselves.

Robert Shalhope's *Bennington and the Green Mountain Boys: The Emergence of Liberal Democracy in Vermont, 1760–1850* probed the "democratic individualism of the Green Mountain Boys" and the contest among competing groups to shape Vermont polity that became liberal democracy.[70] The Haldimand Negotiations have a small role in Shalhope's work, which sees them mostly as weakening the Allen-Chittenden faction's control over the Vermont government. He does point to the importance of land in their venal calculations. "Through their control of the sequestration and confiscation of Tory land and personal property these officials had not only created a powerful faction that enabled them to dominate the political life of the state but had personally benefited by buying up choice plots of land as consequence of the sequestration program." The group achieved the same end through awarding themselves "land grants within the state, becoming proprietors of hundreds of new townships created under their own administration." They also took advantage of their offices, in Ira Allen's receiving his surveyor general's pay in land and taking a "handsome Reward" to improve the opportunity for others to obtain "a choice grant of land."

Shalhope calls the Haldimand Negotiations "a complex and tangled affair." He recognizes the conflicting position taken by historians, but downplays the revisionists and concludes that "Bellesiles presents the most balanced and reasonable account of these negotiations."[71] But with his concentration on the political factions in the 1780s, Shalhope sees "the Haldimand negotiations, with their distinct hint of treason," lending an advantage to Isaac Tichenor and his ally Nathaniel Chipman in their effort to weaken the Arlington Junto and move the state toward the "hierarchical elitism of federalist gentlemen." This approach ignores Nathaniel Chipman's role as an attorney working for Chittenden and the Council to author documents to satisfy the Assembly and Congress about the benign nature of the negotiations.

With Shalhope's endorsement of Bellesiles the pendulum swung even farther away from the revisionists, and in 2011 it completed the swing with Willard Sterne Randall's *Ethan Allen: His Life and Times*. Randall returned the story to the work begun by Jared Sparks, Zadock Thompson, Daniel P. Thompson, Henry DePuy, and Hiland Hall. With a polished style, a keen eye for the interesting and dramatic, and the skills of a practiced storyteller, Randall has greatly refurbished the iconic Ethan Allen, at least in the popular mind. Rolled out with much fanfare, including a review in the *Wall Street Journal*, author lectures and appearances on radio, and a full two-page review in *The New York Review of Books*, Randall's biography garnered attention in Vermont and beyond.[72] A national book catalogue offered it with the enticement, "While Ethan Allen's legend has endured through four centuries of American history, he remains perhaps the least understood of America's founding fathers. Randall finally gives a three-dimensional portrait of this venerated leader of the Green Mountain Boys, a man who was a mythical figure even in his own time."[73]

Randall does not succeed in elevating Allen to the status of founding father. In re-creating his three-dimensional hero, Randall recounts and sometimes embellishes most of the larger-than-life anecdotes of Ethan's prodigious strength, crude oratorical power, and reputed sensitivity for the unfortunate, many generated in the nineteenth century long after Allen's death in 1789. Randall overstates Allen's military leadership and accomplishments. He develops one or two of the three dimensions with plausible but undocumented activities and knowledge of Allen's thinking. And, like Bellesiles and to a lesser extent Crockett, Pell, and Jellison, he regularly has Ethan occupy center stage. He ignores the revisionists and entirely exonerates Allen and his associates from any consideration in the Haldimand Negotiations of seriously casting their lot with the British. In placing Ethan Allen as the prime mover in charge of the negotiations, as he did in the development of Vermont, Randall also joins others who have not asked whether Ira and politically sensitive Thomas Chittenden, the subject of an earlier biography co-written by Randall and his wife, Nancy Nahra, would have risked their lives putting a boastful, often bibulous man who had committed serious blunders as a leader in the past. With some chronological challenges, Randall quotes from Allen's June 1782 letter to Haldimand in which he indicates that "the last refusal of Congress to admit this State Into the Union has done more to awaken the common people to a Sense of their Interest and resentment of their Conduct than all which they had done before." Allen closed the letter with the ringing declaration, "I shall do Every thing in my Power to render this State a British province." Randall asks, "Did Allen mean it, or was he only wedging the door open for future ties between Vermont and Canada?"

Randall answers successively "no" and "yes," though the question presented a false dichotomy with its either-or choice.[74] Certainly Ethan and Ira Allen's subsequent activities to the time of Ethan's death and beyond demonstrate their view of the imperative of trade with Canada and through it to Britain. The revisionists also answered the first question in the affirmative. For his part Randall embraces the traditional view that the Yankees had exchanged prisoners, protected the northern frontier, and put pressure on Congress for recognition.

With Randall's *Ethan Allen* the story of Vermont with Ethan at its epicenter has come full circle, returning to where it had begun with Samuel Williams and Ira Allen in the 1790s and subsequently in the middle two quarters of the nineteenth century greatly expanded with legends, myths, and fiction. The heroic Ethan Allen developed from perceived needs to address problems encountered by Vermont, and the reaffirmation of that view in the sixty years after the Civil War had also addressed perceived Vermont issues. The late twentieth- and early twenty-first-century rejection of revisionism seemed more attuned to telling a good story that would sell to an audience hungry for heroes.

The physically imposing, bold, brawling Vermont yeoman and stout defender of the rights of Americans, the military hero resplendent in his garb, rudely eloquent and forceful in his oratory, and articulate in his writing, master of many guises from the rough frontiersman to a gentleman philosopher had firmly secured his place in the popular mind and imagination. His persona left little room for the self-interested land speculator, unprofessional militia officer and mob leader, schemer looking for the main chance, and truth-challenged man who would lead Vermont into the British Empire.

Ethan Allen had good reason not to stand up, to keep his activities secret. And that clandestine stance served all of the interpretations that followed. He could not avow he would lead Vermont into the British Empire, nor could he tell the British that he simply led them on.

When it's not about the money,
it's about the money.

{ ANONYMOUS }

EPILOGUE

THE HERO LIVES

Who was Ethan Allen? The pattern of his life and the limited reliable details of his deeds and character reveal several configurations of the man. Broad, bland strokes in earthen tones lay out the first thirty-two years of Allen's life. From his birth in 1738 on a Connecticut subsistence farm until 1770 and his involvement with the New York Ejectment Trials, Ethan Allen led an unremarkable life. Few surviving records only partially document his youth and early adult life. No mileposts suggest his future prominence in public affairs. His father's early death in 1755 left him responsible for the family farm and his mother and siblings' welfare. He strayed from that obligation only once, following a recruiter's drum in 1757 to a battle on Lake George that ended before he arrived. By 1760 the Allens had sold the family farm. With their shares, brother Heman opened a general store in Salisbury and Ethan bought into an iron foundry partnership in 1761, the same year he married Mary Brownson of Roxbury, Connecticut. They lived near the iron forge and had two children by 1765.

The iron forge partnership fell short of profit expectations and dissolved in a violent financial dispute and litigation. In subsequent extractive ventures, Ethan unsuccessfully sought silver from an old mine near Roxbury. In 1765 he joined six partners, including Mary's brothers Abraham and Israel Bronson, his cousin Charles Scott, and Benjamin Stiles Jr., a Roxbury lawyer, in an attempt to revive an abandoned lead and silver mine near Northampton, Massachusetts. Like the foundry, the lead mine failed, this time with animosity between the Allens and Mary's brothers. To avoid creditors the Brownsons migrated north into the lawless Green Mountains, advising the Allens to do the same.

Ethan, Mary, their two children, and Ethan's brother Zimri moved only as far north as Sheffield, Massachusetts. For at least the three following winters Ethan traveled north into the Green Mountains to hunt deer for their skins. That business decision kept him on the downward course of his earlier commercial ventures. Insatiable demands for buckskin clothing in Britain and its American colonies for more than a century had significantly depleted New England's wild deer population. Normal winter kill and increasing human predation had reduced deer numbers even in the lightly settled Green Mountains.[1] Hunters and skinners occupied a very low-level niche in the New England economy. After the French and Indian War, the fur trade had moved west from Albany and Montreal to exploit the still abundant populations of fur bearers around the Great Lakes and in the Ohio River Valley. Ethan repeated his winter hunts in the Green Mountains, while brother Levi hauled pots, pans, and textiles to the Great Lakes to trade with the native people for furs, bringing home hard cash money and gifts to share with his mother and siblings.

Ethan spent his winters scouring the uninhabited vastness of the Green Mountains in a business that brought slim profits. Perhaps prompted by Heman and Levi trading in Susquehanna Land Company shares, Ethan, while hunting on the cheap land of the New Hampshire Grants, might have recalled his father's speculation in Susquehanna shares in the Wyoming Valley of Pennsylvania.[2] After buying and selling a few parcels of undeveloped land in Connecticut, Ethan tried speculating in New Hampshire Grants titles in 1769–70. As a boy, he had displayed persuasive skills that might support his aspirations to an economic and social status above the rank of farmer, iron monger, lead miner, or deer skinner. A less physically demanding enterprise than his previous ventures, land speculation offered opportunities for a sharp salesman to earn good money buying and selling distressed New Hampshire grant titles. Like many young colonials with limited working capital on Britain's American and Australian frontiers in the eighteenth and nineteenth centuries, Allen shifted from hunting for skins to hunting for land.

More substantial profits from selling New Hampshire grant titles came easier than tracking deer at night over snow-covered mountains, and Ethan Allen had fully committed to land speculation by 1770.[3] In that year, however, a New York court invalidated a group of New Hampshire titles that overlapped New York titles and ordered the defendant settlers ejected from their farms. Ethan Allen's assistance to investors in the grants during the trial and after earned him a new, prominent, but precarious position on what came to be known as the New Hampshire Grants. The New York ruling threatened the validity of his own investment in New Hampshire titles and hope of expanding his business.

After the Ejectment Trials, however, Ethan Allen would in less than three years emerge from an unremarkable life of limited expectations as a small-scale land speculator to become a widely known author of newspaper articles that crudely borrowed from English philosopher John Locke's theory of property to defend the Grants settlers right to own land they had improved. Additionally, he would also violently resist New York's efforts to assert authority over the New Hampshire Grants and simultaneously with members of his family acquire large tracts of wild land, much of it in the Champlain Valley.

West of the Green Mountains, invalidating New Hampshire titles had triggered violent resistance to New York asserting jurisdiction on the Grants. Backed by his cousins Remember Baker and Seth Warner, Ethan Allen became the leader of a forceful agrarian insurgency against New York claims to rule over the Grants. Mobs of settlers with New Hampshire titles attacked New York surveyors on the Grants, burned houses of New York titleholders, humiliated and physically attacked New York officeholders on the Grants, and threatened to kill Scots tenants living on a New York settlement at Panton if they returned and to annihilate Durham-Socialborough (today's Clarendon), a town of overlapped New York and New Hampshire titles. Disguised as Indians, they destroyed crops and maimed cattle of other settlers who held land by New York titles. Known widely as the Green Mountain Boys, the insurgents led by Ethan Allen and his kin wreaked havoc across the region from 1772 to 1775.

In January 1773, apparently unmoved by New York's feeble attempts to suppress the Green Mountain insurgents' campaign to purge the Grants of New York titleholders and sympathizers, the brothers

Ethan, Ira, Heman, and Zimri Allen, with cousin Remember Baker, formed the Onion River Land Company and quickly bought a bundle of New Hampshire titles from brother Levi. In May, Ethan and Ira boldly went unnoticed into the Province of New York and bought titles to large tracts of land in the Champlain Valley from Benjamin Ferris of Quaker Hill, Duchess County, and Edward Burling of White Plains, wild lands originally acquired from New Hampshire's Governor Benning Wentworth in 1763.[4] A year later after the terror attack at Panton, New York's Provincial Assembly passed and the governor proclaimed a Riot Act, quickly renamed the Bloody Act of 1774 on the Grants. The law declared Allen and his chief associates felons guilty of capital offenses and offered substantial dead or alive rewards on them. In 1774 Allen published a lengthy attack on New York's treatment of the Grants settlers, *A Brief Narrative of the Proceedings of the Government of New-York*. By April 1775, on the brink of war between Britain and its American colonies, the Onion River Land Company owned titles to more than 65,000 acres of the New Hampshire Grants concentrated on Burlington Bay and the Onion (Winooski) River Valley, most of it purchased from original investors for a penny an acre and generous credit terms.[5] By early 1775 Ethan Allen's energetic defense of New Hampshire titles in newspapers and political tracts, teamed with the terror tactics of the Green Mountain Boys, paralleled the increase of Onion River Land Company holdings. The populist rhetoric of his *Brief Narrative* defended individual farmers with small, improved plots. He left unsaid the Allens' growing personal interest and the wealth they sought in acquiring large tracts of New Hampshire Grants titles. Meanwhile, Ira and Remember Baker surveyed townships and clashed with New York survey teams north and east of Burlington during 1774 and early 1775.

War with Britain came to the New Hampshire Grants on May 10, 1775. Ethan Allen led a group of the Grants' insurgent settlers and other revolutionaries from Massachusetts, Connecticut, and New York to capture the old British fort at Ticonderoga. News of the first successful attack on a British stronghold encouraged the colonial Patriots and diverted combative energies on the Grants by an unspoken truce from the land title dispute with New York to mounting an invasion of Canada. Most of the Onion River Land Company's assets became a war zone; and most of its principals — Ethan only briefly — would be involved in the Northern Army's invasion and retreat from Canada in 1775–76 and repelling Burgoyne's advance south in 1777. Ethan Allen's foolish misconduct in attacking Montreal in the early days of the invasion kept him a British captive until 1778.

In May 1775, as Ethan Allen's captivity narrative and his post-victory correspondence with revolutionary Congresses in New York, Connecticut, and Massachusetts make clear, he saw taking Ticonderoga as a grand opportunity to "signalise" himself—to capitalize on the fame and glory he would earn by a great victory over the British in Quebec. After the success at Ticonderoga, however, the war, like Ethan Allen's earlier ventures, proved an inglorious flop, earning him thirty-one months as a British prisoner. Many settlers in Dorset, Bennington, and other westside towns with New Hampshire titles had condemned Ethan Allen and the Green Mountain Boys' terror tactics during the insurgency against New York before the war. Memories of Allen's role with the insurgency, together with recent reports of his leadership failures after taking Ticonderoga, as well as a bungled sortie against St. John, doubtless cost him an expected colonelcy of the new Green Mountain regiment in July 1775. Late that month at a convention of ten Committees of Safety in Dorset a large majority gave command of the regiment to Seth Warner. Allen eventually wrangled a place as observer on the general staff of the American expedition against Canada in the days before the September invasion. With only 130 men in a poorly conceived, undermanned, and outgunned scheme, as a civilian without authority, he failed to take Montreal and was captured on September 25. Throughout his captivity, he demanded, sometimes successfully, that his captors treat him as an officer, though he had no commission. His insistence on the title "Colonel Allen" nearly cost the lives of fellow American prisoners when, claiming his obligations as an officer and gentleman, he threatened to reveal their planned mutiny to the British ship's captain, who had treated Allen and several other American officers as gentlemen, and to fight them in his defense. The near-mutineers, perhaps astounded by Allen invoking a privileged officer's code of conduct against them, cancelled their plan. Nor did he mention his good fortune when they held back from killing him after his threat to expose them.[6]

Exchanged for a British officer and in Vermont by June 1778, Allen needed money to support his family and his own pretensions.

Without an active land business, his sole source of income, a temporary thirty-one-month commission in the Continental Army paying $75
per month, would have left him deep in debt and possibly bankrupt,
the frequent fate of low-paid Continental officers. Volunteering for active duty without enthusiasm later in July, he reported to Continental
General Horatio Gates that he had "plenty of Business," and probably
the army already had "plenty of officers."[7] Ethan Allen badly needed
money in 1778; discounted for inflation, his monthly pay of seventy-five
Continental Congress dollars was worth four silver dollars.

Allen was in prison during the founding of Vermont and the glorious victories over the British at the Walloomsac and Saratoga; his return was initially acknowledged by a modest cannon salute. He had
persuasive skills to rescue himself from the ranks of the dishonored and
discarded and resume the hunt for fame and glory. Soon after his arrival in Vermont in early June, Allen seized on the opportunity to mol-
lify an angry crowd about to lynch an "enemical" Tory. In the course
of a day he convicted Private David Redding of the Queen's Loyal
Rangers of unspecified charges and pleased the crowd with a hanging as Governor Chittenden had ordered. The military code for treating officers he had insisted his own captors afford him forgotten or
ignored in the case of Private Redding, Allen's conduct in that affair
confirmed he was still an aggressive and volatile figure. Back in the
hunt and a hero again, at least in Bennington, he then wrote *A Narrative of Colonel Ethan Allen's Captivity Containing His Voyages & Travels etc. . . .* (1779) and, like the born-again author-heroes of popular
Indian captivity narratives, redeemed himself as a warrior before the
world at large.

Ethan Allen had found the way to money that would support him
and his family. Redding's hanging in 1778 and the publication of his
captivity narrative in 1779 firmly secured his prominence and political
influence in Vermont without submitting himself to a popular election
and the mercy of the voters, whom he probably did not trust after the
"old farmers" had kept him from leading the Green Mountain regiment. Equally important, a long relationship with Governor Thomas
Chittenden, an old friend from Connecticut and a pre-war customer of
the Onion River Land Company for a large parcel of land in Williston,
as well as other friendly members of the Governor's Council, including

his brother Ira and Timothy Brownson, another relative of his wife, earned him a seat on the Vermont Confiscation Court. Ethan Allen avoided electoral politics in the independent state of Vermont, even refusing to take a seat when the town of Sunderland elected him to the Vermont General Assembly. He sat with the Governor's Council and the General Assembly, freely participated in their deliberations, and represented those bodies as an envoy to Congress. His friends in power first found him a seat on the Confiscation Court. Low-hanging fruit, Loyalist lands seized by the state invited sharp dealing by the Court, including Allen's crass attempt to seize brother Levi's Vermont land. Levi fought him in the pages of the *Connecticut Courant*, concluding the family feud by reminding his brother that he had aided him during his captivity in the Halifax jail and on parole on Long Island. Then he challenged Ethan to a duel in Bennington. Levi appeared on the field of honor, but Ethan went elsewhere without comment on the incident.[8] Ira certified paying £150 on Ethan's behalf to purchase three hundred acres of choice intervale farmland in Burlington confiscated from Loyalist William Marsh. Lacking an official receipt of payment and signed only by Ira, this certificate of the transaction strays suspiciously wide of the Confiscation Court's official records. The records are ambiguous on other land transactions involving the Allen brothers, but Ethan seems to have recused himself from the Court before enlisting a group of associates to petition for a grant of two large islands in Lake Champlain north of Burlington, subsequently known as the Two Heroes. The Governor's Council appointed two receivers to collect the fees for the Two Heroes grant from the associated grantees, Thomas Chittenden and Ira Allen, but Ira Allen's treasurer's records contain no reports of payments received in this matter.[9] Records of the General Assembly for his diplomatic missions to Congress indicate that as an unelected, paid advisor to the governor and Council Ethan Allen had secured great political influence and reliable compensation for his services.

The legislature sent Allen as envoy to Congress in late 1778 ostensibly to petition for Vermont's admission to the United States and to dampen concerns over the secession of sixteen New Hampshire towns on the Connecticut River and their union with Vermont. But Allen and Governor Chittenden personally opposed both measures as potential threats to the Arlington Junto, a power bloc led by Chittenden and his closest advisors, prominently including Ira and Ethan Allen. Ethan failed to secure the state's admission to the United States, when New York, New Hampshire, and Massachusetts objected. On Allen's return home he misrepresented Congress as willing to accept Vermont if the union were dissolved. His reward for defending the junto's power may be reflected in his appointment to lead the Vermont militia. Though other Vermonters had more military and battle experience than Ethan Allen, and in several cases the wounds to show for it, none enjoyed the same level of influence in the Governor's Council and the General Assembly or struck as much fear in the government's opponents. The Council appointed him commander of the state's militia in 1779 and the Assembly concurred. The following year, Governor Chittenden sent Allen to Guilford in southeast Vermont with one hundred men to quell settlers still loyal to New York who had refused Vermont militia service. He threatened to devastate the village and annihilate its residents. Guilford capitulated and Governor Chittenden pardoned the ringleaders.

With Chittenden's approval in 1781, ten New York towns on the west border of Vermont complained that their state government had abandoned them and, like the East Unionists, petitioned to join Vermont. Deliberations between Vermont and residents of the proposed West Union prompted New York Governor Clinton to send a small force of militia to suppress the secessionists. Vermont in turn called out five hundred militia and stymied New York's eighty at the Walloomsac River. General Ethan Allen appeared on the scene in a pseudo-military outfit and calmly observed the peaceful withdrawal of the militias without further disturbances. From the point of view of Governor Chittenden, Ira and Ethan Allen, the Fays, and a few other immediate associates, there had been far more interesting business afoot between the Arlington Junto and General Frederick Haldimand, Britain's governor of the Province of Quebec.

Despite Allen's disclaimers and oaths he would never become a Benedict Arnold, generous proffers of land and military leadership came several times from his British captors during his imprisonment in England and New York and, when free in Vermont, directly from the British in Quebec in 1780–82. They certainly came often enough and with promises of sufficient rewards to set a man thinking seriously about his future. The terms Britain offered to Allen included an independent Vermont politically allied with the British Crown as a colonial province. Ethan Allen could imagine himself a colonel of a British-paid provincial regiment and receiving extensive additional land. Commensurate with the regimental colonelcy, in the civil sphere he would advance to the head of an elite landed gentry of Loyalists and increase the Onion River Land Company's vast landholdings. Once settled and cultivated, their land in the Champlain Valley could freely send produce to the nearby markets in Montreal and Quebec and beyond to England. Beginning in 1780, under the pretense of conducting a prisoner exchange, Ira with other participating conspirators went to Canada to negotiate the exchange and subsequently to clarify and negotiate the matter of Vermont's leaders turning away from the United States to ally with Great Britain. From the beginning Ira Allen led Vermont's negotiators, representing his group's positions face to face with Haldimand's agents. The British initially contacted Ethan, and he received their messengers at his home in Sunderland and at the blockhouse in Castleton, but he excused himself from meeting their agents on their Lake Champlain gunboats, claiming caution against assassination by agents of New York or George Washington. Washington did suspect Ethan Allen of meeting and conspiring with the British, and he sent spies to flush him out in the summer of 1780. Their reports cleared Allen, but Washington's suspicions continued, and he refused to exchange a British officer for battle-hardened Gideon Brownson, Mary Allen's brother, an original Green Mountain Boy, then a prisoner in Montreal. Washington said he still suspected Ethan Allen of treason. The Brownson family and members of the General Assembly openly accused Ethan and Ira of treason. Ira presented an account of the prisoner exchange to the General Assembly, but Ethan's accusers again charged him with treasonously conferring with the enemy. Ethan angrily resigned command of the militia. Articles of impeachment accused Ethan of treason, but the document disappeared overnight before a hearing could be held. A battered British army under Charles Cornwallis surrendered to a Franco-American coalition army at Yorktown, Virginia, in October 1781, bringing an end to both active war and the first phase of the Allens negotiating with the British. Ethan Allen's biographers have consistently said he led and directed the Vermont side of the Haldimand Negotiations. Yet Ira, Chittenden, and the Fays had far too much experience in dealing with Ethan

than his biographers allow. They were also too smart to risk their lives following a boastful bumbler fond of the "flowing bowl" in a scheme requiring secrecy, tact, and self-control, trademark skills of successful politicians seldom displayed by Ethan Allen. The negotiations reopened for a second round in 1782, further suggesting Allen's seriousness.

Accessible records of Ethan Allen's life from the end of the war in 1781 to his death in 1789 are limited. Usually cited events include brief reports of Mary Brownson Allen's and their daughter Loraine's deaths in 1783. Biographers' stories of his 1784 marriage to Frances Montresor Buchanan have been taken nearly verbatim from William Czar Bradley's report of the event composed as an adult, purportedly witnessed by him at age two. Some correspondence survives about Allen's failed promise to resurrect the Green Mountain Boys—the "antient mobb"—to intervene in a title dispute in Pennsylvania's Wyoming Valley and other letters reveal his initial sympathy, but later disdain for Shays' Rebellion when the Massachusetts rebels sought refuge in Vermont. The rebellion's spillover to Vermont triggered a venomous tirade from him against an uncontrolled populace that also suggests "sour grapes" over his loss of political influence as Vermont's population grew and changed.[10]

Allen's influence on public affairs had waned, but not his need for money. He published *Reason the Only Oracle of Man* (1785) as solely his own work, though he had plagiarized roughly 75 percent from manuscripts of his dead mentor Thomas Young. Allen never mentioned Young's name in the book and it sold fewer than five hundred copies. In 1784, after the peace with Britain was settled, the Allens opened discussions with Guy Carleton, Quebec's new governor general, on developing free trade relations with Canada. British spies reported that the Allen brothers were recruiting Loyalist settlers from Vermont and New York to their borderland townships. By late 1788 they had twice gone to Quebec to sell timber rafts laden with forest products and conferred once with Governor General Carleton to discuss Vermont's commercial relations with Quebec and Britain. Writing to John Wheelock at Dartmouth College after dining with Carleton and his staff, Ethan dismissed Carleton's staff for their conversational shortcomings.[11] No record survives of a conversation on military tactics between Allen and Carleton, whose regulars, militia, and Mohawks handily routed Allen and a motley mob of Canadian farmers and raw American militia men attempting to capture Montreal in September 1775. Allen would probably have directed the conversation from events at Montreal over ten years past to repeat a refrain from a letter he wrote seeking an audience with Carleton when the brothers arrived in Quebec that brought in reply an invitation to dine with Carleton and his staff. He liked the "policies of General Haldimand" toward Vermont, Allen wrote several times, and probably said as much to Carleton.[12]

Ethan and Ira dissolved the Onion River Land Company in 1784, and distributed its inventory between them. Levi had set up as a trader in Quebec on the Richelieu River at St. John, and the Allens developed a grand plan to carry on individually in the land business from bases on the Onion River in Vermont and the Richelieu River in Canada. Having succeeded in winning an extraordinary trade agreement with Carleton allowing enumerated items into Canada contrary to their proscription under British mercantile laws, they extended their plan to establish a direct market connection with England. One significant geophysical obstacle stood in their way. The Richelieu River's shoals and rapids between St. John and Chambly required a canal to allow seagoing ships to sail from Burlington to England with Champlain Valley produce. Such a project would require a Crown license and a great deal of money, so Levi Allen set out for London in February 1789 on the day before Ethan died in Burlington. Beginning with Samuel Williams's and Ira Allen's histories of Vermont in the 1790s, Ethan Allen's biographers in later generations reshaped his story. Recollections of him included frequently repeated legends and myths, often modern reworkings of ancient folk tales meant to represent the reality of his life. Remembering Ethan Allen lived on synonymously with "the story of Vermont" and its creation as an independent state.

By the mid-nineteenth century, in uncertain and confusing times, some Vermonters sought a hero, a symbol of values they had seemed to have lost. They found it in Ethan Allen, who had become an icon in the histories of early Vermont and to a lesser extent in the creation of the early American republic. For the remainder of the century and throughout the twentieth and into the twenty-first century, the frequent publication of books about him, especially those aimed at popular audiences and young readers, sustained his iconic status. Icons are very efficient tools, and engravings and statues of Ethan Allen also told viewers about him without so much as a word. Iconic images presented a generic if bland visage, but in a popular nineteenth-century engraving his full figure poses aggressively in a crudely conceived uniform with a threatening sword in hand that succinctly says it all. It's Ethan Allen, the Hero of Ticonderoga.

Beginning in the mid-nineteenth century, Vermonters assigned to Allen their own cherished and idealized values. A century later, Dorothy Canfield Fisher, a well-received novelist and commentator on matters of concern to Vermont and the nation from the 1930s to the 1950s, appraised Ethan Allen for his role in her version of the Vermont story. In *The Vermont Tradition* (1953) Fisher considered Allen a passionate man, "as few men are, wildly passionate. Not passionate about women, not about power over others, not about getting money. He was passionate about an idea—the ancient idea that men and women live best and most fruitfully in as much freedom and equality as is possible. He was the voice of Vermont. He still is." Fisher was wrong about Allen's lack of passion for "money." She was also wrong that the idea that thriving in freedom helps folks "live the best and most fruitfully" was an "ancient tradition." The ancients for whom that ideology actually worked best lived comfortably, even extravagantly, from the labor of slaves or the rents of their tenants. And she was wrong also that Allen is the voice of Vermont. But she did express and even buttressed a prevailing view.

Despite his central role in a clandestine scheme to ally Vermont with the eighteenth-century British Empire, Ethan Allen became a hero of the American Revolution. With evangelical enthusiasm, an elite group of Victorian Vermonters promoted a story of Ethan Allen that would compel social and moral reform in a community they believed had fallen from the high standards of its revolutionary origins. Their efforts led generations of Vermonters to conceive, erect, and maintain a cult of personality that celebrated and honored him, a man they had never seen and mostly knew from his captivity narrative and Daniel P. Thompson's *Green Mountain Boys*, canonical texts for learning the story of Ethan Allen.

The story of Ethan Allen has been transformed since the 1830s to present a hero configured by comedic or tearful treatments in a consistently sentimental avoidance of events and actions that could otherwise have diminished his popular appeal. In the mid-twentieth century, the U.S. Navy named a nuclear submarine for him in honor of his "contributions to democracy." During the first war fought by the United States more than two hundred years earlier, Ethan Allen had plotted a British alliance for Vermont and a favored place for himself within the empire. Congress and the Navy Department during the Cold War were not above making it up in Vermont. More recently and equally myopic, a Vermont newspaper's political cartoon presented a sketch of Allen, musket at the ready, commanding citizens to vote in a coming election. Later, the anachronistic admonition "What would Ethan Allen say?" in a debate over state-run health care in Vermont elicited not so much as a nod of the head in agreement or dissent from the Vermont legislature. After nearly two and a quarter centuries since his death, Ethan Allen's grip on collective memory even in Vermont may have weakened as a moral force for reform, if in fact he ever really fulfilled that role in the magical thinking of Henry Stevens and the founders of the Vermont Historical Society. Modern consumerism, however, certainly continues to find him useful and congenial.

What do we conclude from this study of the story of Ethan Allen? We know that Ethan's brother, who needed validation as he faced financial ruin in Vermont and the British Admiralty Court, wrote about Ethan and the history of Vermont. Wiley Ira, who had scrubbed a critical section of Samuel Williams's first history of the state, launched the posthumous veneration of Ethan. We know that a disinterested Connecticut farmer and a failed entrepreneur eager for the main chance eventually embarked on the nearest accessible path to wealth through land speculation by amassing depressed and questionable New Hampshire titles. Ethan Allen endeavored assiduously by any means at hand for the last half of his fifty years to secure legal recognition for those titles, including contemplation of allying Vermont with the British Empire. We know how a seriously flawed and compromised military leader became depicted in print, in statuary, in engravings, and in paintings as a military hero decked out in a faux uniform brandishing a sword. We know how a frontier ruffian who aspired to genteel distinction learned how to present and promote himself through his publication of Lockean political tracts, the popular best-selling narrative of his captivity that turned failure into fame, and the opaque homespun philosophy in the largely plagiarized *Reason the Only Oracle of Man*. We also know how later generations of Vermonters answered their own needs and secured Allen's memory in scholarly and popular minds that persists despite attempts at revision. The real Ethan Allen does stand up, but few have seen him.

APPENDIXES

Vermont Historiography, 1807–50:
Change and Response

The emergence of Ethan Allen as an iconic Vermont figure and the founding father of Vermont occurred in the decade of the 1830s. By 1850 it had become fully accepted. Henry Stevens, a founder of the Vermont Historical and Antiquarian Society (hereafter the Vermont Historical Society) in 1838, and his contemporaries deliberately "invented" the new Ethan Allen in response to social, economic, and political developments they found perplexing and disturbing. Stevens, who achieved varying levels of success as an innkeeper, farmer, turnpike investor, and merchant, participated in local politics and twice represented Barnet in the legislature. He kept his ties in Montpelier active. Members of the upper middle class to which Stevens aspired and Vermont's intellectual elite feared society had become soft, that "the old hearts of oak are gone."[1] They would look to the past for regeneration. In March 1843 Stevens wrote to David Baldwin, treasurer of the Vermont Historical Society, that Vermont must return to Allen and other heroes who had secured Vermont's independence and statehood. Stevens wanted to "address the current social problems with the same spirit that had once inspired the Green Mountain Boys." This analysis of the manufacture of Ethan Allen as a hero in part rests on the Vermont response to significant change and the historiography that delineates it.[2]

Historians see the years between Jefferson's Embargo in late 1807 and the middle of the nineteenth century as a distinct period of transformations in Vermont. Contemporaries noted the changes, though they did not have the context and perspective of hindsight to delineate their experience as an "era." The historical and other literature details the economic dislocations, changes in agriculture, uncertain and hesitant development of manufacturing, revolution in transportation, the beginnings of urbanization, migration from the state, and drastic slowdown in population growth. It studies the perceived consequences and reactions to these perplexing changes, and the volume and quality of the historical literature on the 1807–50 period rivals the concentration on the years from exploration to statehood in 1791. Many of these studies explicitly select 1807 and 1850 as the inflection points when, according to the consensus of historians, Vermont entered into a new era and four decades later turned a corner. This body of literature informed the thinking of John J. Duffy and H. Nicholas

Muller III, which they first articulated in *An Anxious Democracy: Aspects of the 1830s* (1982), and then in several journal articles they published in England and the United States. Publications by other scholars have added to, refined, reinforced, and reiterated the hypothesis, often in detailed analyses of particular aspects of it.[3]

The one-volume treatment of Vermont history by Michael Sherman, Gene Sessions, and P. Jeffrey Potash, *Freedom and Unity: A History of Vermont* (2004), presents an excellent overview based on current scholarship. It discusses the period under the chapter title, "Years of Optimism and Anxiety, 1807–1850," dates that deliberately bracket the years from the Embargo to mid-century. It points to the Panic of 1837 as the "fundamental divide between optimism" and the "more anxious outlook of the following decades." This useful book provides a comprehensive overview and an excellent bibliography of both monographic and journal literature.

Scholars continue to consult, refine, and expand three major mid-twentieth-century studies of Vermont history. Lewis D. Stilwell, *Migration from Vermont, 1776–1860* (1948), has remained an influential work. It first appeared in published form in 1937 as a very lengthy article in *Vermont History*. In "a composite biography of about eight thousand Vermonters who left Vermont," Stilwell detailed the pace and reasons for the migration.[4] David M. Ludlum's doctoral dissertation at Columbia University came out in book form in 1939 as *Social Ferment in Vermont, 1791–1850*, and then in 1948 as part of the Vermont Historical Society's planned, but never completed, ten-volume Growth of Vermont series, which also reprinted Stilwell. Ludlum wrote about "the period of unrest preceding the Civil War," a time he argued, "the Green Mountain State was noted for its radicalism," as Vermonters "lent their support to many movements to change social and political institutions."[5] The third basic work on the period, also begun as a doctoral dissertation, Harold Fisher Wilson's *The Hill Country of Northern New England: Its Social and Economic History, 1790–1930* (1936), defined "northern New England" largely as Vermont and to a much lesser extent New Hampshire and Maine. Later advertised though never published as volume 10 in the Growth of Vermont series, this study took a rather negative view of Vermont agriculture, largely because of adverse economic, geographic, and demographic forces. Taken together, these three volumes form part of the core of Vermont historiography for the first half of the nineteenth century.

More in-depth monographic studies still rely to some extent on Stilwell, Ludlum, and Wilson, employing them for context, building on them, adding to their narrative, and sometimes using them as a foil for revision. As a body of scholarship, they provide a rich description of the general change, anxiety, and responses to it. P. Jeffrey Potash in the published form of his Ph.D. dissertation, *Vermont's Burned-Over District: Patterns of Community Development and Religious Activity, 1761–1850* (1991), probes deeply into "The Dynamics of Change in Addison County" and its links to "The Second Great Awakening in Addison County." His detailed research in Addison County lends itself to extrapolation to the entire State of Vermont.[6] Randolph Roth in *The Democratic Dilemma: Religion, Reform, and Social Order in the Connecticut River Valley of Vermont, 1791–1850* (1987), also based on a doctoral dissertation, discusses the troublesome, almost bewildering changes in Vermont. In a chapter titled "From an Era of Promise to Pressing Times, 1815–1843," Roth argues that the difficult to comprehend changes created an environment in which Vermonters through avenues of revivalism, moral reform, perfectionism, and political reform sought to establish a social order that reconciled their ideals with their perceptions of the harsh reality of living in a flawed society.[7]

The Vermont Historical Society's published an abridgment of T. D. Seymour Bassett's *The Growing Edge: Vermont Villages, 1840–1880* (1992), a monumental though not widely available 723-page Harvard dissertation, "The Urban Penetration of Rural Vermont, 1840–1880" (1952).[8] As he discovered new evidence and had new insights, Bassett year by year annotated his work in lengthy marginal notes and new pages that he inserted in the bound copy of his dissertation. In *The Growing Edge* and his larger dissertation, Bassett does not explicitly address "anxiety," but his chapters with detailed and heavily documented discussions on country towns, French Canadian and Irish immigration, urbanization, transportation, industry, a variety of social movements, and other topics provide the material to develop that theme. In another work, *The Gods of the Hills: Piety and Society in Nineteenth Century Vermont* published by the Vermont Historical Society in 2000, Bassett drew from his dissertation, articles he published, and four decades of investigation. *Gods of the Hills* contains the well-researched work of a mature scholar that places the revivalist impulse and other reform movements with a religious tincture in their denominational contexts.

Wilson in *Hill Country*, among the first scholarly studies of agriculture in the northeastern United States, focused heavily on Vermont. Wilson regarded 1830 as the beginning of agricultural "autumn" in Vermont that morphed into "winter" in 1880. In his analysis, by 1830 Vermont agriculture, the major economic activity in the state, had already experienced its best days, and would thereafter have to adjust to changing market conditions, the competition from the West, and the limitations of the soil and growing season. His discussion of the early "autumn" years concentrated on the sheep boom and the dislocation it created for the rest of agriculture and "External Causes of Distress." Wilson and others tend to downplay the impact of the 1823 Champlain Canal, which with the opening of the Erie Canal in 1825 made Vermont vulnerable to competition from the burgeoning agriculture of the West and abetted out-migration.[9] Howard S. Russell's *Long Deep Furrow: Three Centuries of Farming in New England* (1976) provided an account of farming changes and practices with little attempt to explore the consequences for the broader society in which they operated. But Russell does help set the context and offer details of the farming experience that created anxiety.

Christopher Harris in his provocative, relatively unknown and revisionist dissertation at Northeastern University, "The Road Less Traveled By: Rural Northern New England in Global Perspective, 1815–1960" (2007), convincingly refutes the standard understanding of Vermont agriculture despite how those farming perceived it. Harris's global context, command of the modern theory and literature, and statistical analyses lead him to very different conclusions about the health of agriculture in Vermont in the first half of the nineteenth century. Harris rejects the seasonal analogies of decline: "Indian Summer," "sunset," "autumn," and "winter," though he recognizes that the contemporary literature on which Wilson and others based their accounts supports the negative seasonal imagery. He cites Wilson, Stilwell, and Percy W. Bidwell and John I. Falconer, *History of American Agriculture in the Northern United States, 1620-1860* (1925), and quotes Michael Bell's assertion that the "decline of New England agriculture remains one of the best-known, generally accepted themes in American historical geography."[10]

Harris does not accept that theme and argues that the "new agriculture and the industrialization of the first half of the 19th century came out of a society of highly skilled men" who participated fully in the "new modern industrial society." The sheep craze and "the changes in the Yankee farming mix meant the northern countryside began to look different: first, stripped woodlots, then fields abandoned to forest and farms consolidated. Many of these changes signaled decay to outsiders with notions of how things should look." This, "especially in Vermont, gave rise to a mythology of decline and loss, some of it real, most of it apparent." All of this spawned "an incessant literature of decline."[11] Harris asserts that the "population decline occurred as rural industry dried up, not as agriculture declined. The transient population that fed on rural industry moved on, and birth rates plummeted. National industrialization meant market consolidation with little use for small quantities of produce from diversified farms." Vermont farmers pulled back from the market and diversified, became more self-sufficient, and often turned to barter. They exhibited "a rediversification of income sources." Harris convincingly argues that the Vermont farmer thrived, but he concedes that contemporary and historical observers alike saw it much differently. The perceived decline in Vermont agriculture sparked and fed the various responses.[12]

Harris cites the work of Hal S. Barron, *Those Who Stayed Behind: Rural Society in Nineteenth-Century New England* (1984), who almost entirely limits his primary research to Chelsea, Vermont. Barron anticipates Harris's refutation of the nature of the depopulation "for which northern New England is so famous." He thinks the "historians of the region have long spoken . . . in terms of extraordinary decline and decay," a "portrayal . . . so bleak that one gets the strong impression that rural New England was particularly cursed," an impression that helped fuel revivalism. Barron questions this traditional picture, "often derived from the writings of biased contemporary observers who did not live in the older communities and tend to take their editorializing and anxious portrayals of 'deteriorating' conditions at face value as evidence of social realities."[13] The same intellectual elites who worked to establish Ethan Allen as a hero saw decline rather than "normal" transformational "characteristics of older agrarian communities." In 1848 George Perkins Marsh, Vermont's leading intellectual, spoke to the Agricultural Society of Rutland County. He snobbishly labeled the Vermonters who had left the state "deserters." They had "abandoned the blessings of a well-ordered home in New England amidst rural beauty . . . to live among the miry sloughs, the puny groves, the slimy streams which alone diversify the dead uniformity of Wisconsin or Illinois."[14] Like Stevens before him, Marsh thought that Vermonters had gone soft and needed the moral backbone of an Ethan Allen. Marsh made much of his own illustrious career living abroad, which might have qualified him as a "deserter."[15]

The shrinkage of the local market, as Harris later argues, with "the dwindling number of local customers effected more subtle changes in the business of local craftsmen and merchants." Barron's detailed analysis of persistence in Chelsea demonstrates that out-migration occurred more in the nonagricultural sectors. He also notes the migration to cities and factories, a theme developed by Thomas Dublin in *Farm to Factory: Women's Letters, 1830–1860* (1981), which includes young women's migration from Vermont farms to mills in the state and beyond in New England. The long and useful introductory essay, which cites Wilson and Stilwell, discusses the young women's migration from the farm, the changes they experienced working and living in an urban manufacturing society, and some of the impacts on those who stayed behind. The book contains the letters of four young women, including the "Mary Paul Letters" at the Vermont Historical Society. Before leaving Vermont, Mary Paul grew up in Barnard and Woodstock. Dublin quotes Zadock Thompson's judgmental and snide appraisal in his 1842 widely hailed and read *History of Vermont, Natural, Civil and Statistical*. Thompson believed it all "too common" that "farmers' daughters" returning from the mills to the farms had grown up as "young ladies, [who] play the piano . . . [and] spend their father's surplus funds on fine clothes."[16]

The "social ferment" created by these attitudes naturally spilled over into political life as causes moved "away from moral suasion to controversial strategies of legislative coercion." Scholars have investigated and written about the shifts in the Whig Party, Jacksonian politics, the Liberty Party, anti-slavery politics, and the Anti-Mason movement. Vermont became entangled in the Anti-Mason enthusiasm, an essentially anti-establishment movement, more than any other state. It provided the only Electoral College votes for an Anti-Mason presidential candidate, elected an Anti-Mason congressman, and sent Anti-Mason William Palmer of Danville to Montpelier for four consecutive one-year terms as governor. Silas Jenison, the first Vermont-born governor, filled out Palmer's last term and won election on a combined Whig Anti-Mason ticket.

Robert Shalhope in *Bennington and the Green Mountain Boys: The Emergence of Liberal Democracy in Vermont, 1760–1850* (1996) develops a convincing argument about the way in which "individuals busy creating a nineteenth century liberal elite" turned to their version of Vermont's founders and "innocently viewed themselves as the same sort of resolute democrats as those who fended off New York aristocrats, defeated the British, and forged an independent republic." Whigs, Jacksonian Democrats, and Anti-Masons all saw themselves as "the true heirs of Ethan Allen and the Green Mountain Boys," claims that Shalhope sees as "political manifestations that swept the state," creating cultural icons to "ease or even obscure the anxieties and contradictions" they felt so keenly. They easily ignored much of the historical record and placed Ethan Allen and the Green Mountain Boys on an exalted pedestal.[17]

These works and other, often more specialized, monographs on topics as diverse as human geography, women, railroads, ethnic groups, literacy, perfectionism, education, and political movements, often cause-oriented, delineate conditions in the first half of the nineteenth century in Vermont. They all discuss change, and many deal with the perceived anxiety created by the change. The better local histories, Zadock Thompson's 1842 three-part *History* and Abby Maria Hemenway's comprehensive five-volume *Vermont Historical Gazetteer*, discuss these topics. Stilwell, Wilson, Ludlum, and other historians have mined these local treatments for much of their evidence. The extensive literature in scholarly journals, particularly in *Vermont History*, published without a break since 1930, elucidates particular parts of life in Vermont between the Embargo and mid-century and contributes immensely to the understanding of a society in transformation.

The literature of the years from 1807 through 1850 only superficially deals with the Panic of 1837, "which did not generally abate until 1843." The synthesis in *Freedom and Unity* asserts that six years of bank panic and deep recession "marked a fundamental divide in Vermont between the optimism of the post revolutionary era—undergirded by economic growth and revival and reform idealism—and the more anxious outlook of the following decades."[18] Though Vermont legislative reports stated that "her citizens had suffered perhaps less than those of other states" they acknowledged that in "1837 the business and credit systems received a serious shock," and that the Panic "continued to make conditions extremely hard in Vermont throughout 1840."[19] The changes in the presentation of Ethan Allen coincide almost exactly with the Panic of 1837, perhaps by an unrelated chronological accident and perhaps not. The history of Vermont, while not ignoring it, has not sufficiently drilled into the Panic of 1837.

Historians and others since Stilwell, Wilson, and Ludlum have laid out the fundamental story of Vermont between 1807 and 1850 and have provided different interpretations, often more nuanced than straight-on revisions. They all agree that those who lived in those years and recorded their thoughts or took actions generally found themselves living in perplexing, disquieting, confusing times marked by major upheavals in which they perceived elements of economic and social decay. In this environment the figure of Ethan Allen emerged as a durable hero for the times.

The Vermont Historical and Antiquarian
Society: Documenting and Promoting a Hero

Created by an act of the Vermont legislature in 1838, the Vermont Historical and Antiquarian Society (VHS) for more than two decades remained a small, elite organization dominated by an inner circle led by Henry Stevens. Beginning with Massachusetts in 1791, by 1825 the five other New England states had established historical societies. State historical organizations had also formed in New York, Pennsylvania, Virginia, Kentucky, and Louisiana before the creation of the VHS. The Society was born in an era when Vermonters organized around causes like the Anti-Mason Party, anti-slavery, the Vermont Bible Society, temperance, school and prison reform, and others. It sought to preserve the historical record, especially during "that transition state," as former Congressman William Czar Bradley observed, "when the men who can furnish the facts connected with the establishment of the State have nearly all passed away and those who by intimacy with the founders have received their information from the first sources are passing likewise."[1] Stevens, a compulsive and indefatigable collector who had worked for decades to assemble the records of Vermont's founding generation and to promote their veneration, lobbied for the legislation. He sought an institutional framework and support to house his collection and to forward his agenda of celebrating Vermont's founders in general and Ethan Allen in particular.

The act of incorporation charged Stevens of Barnet and Oramel H. Smith, Daniel P. Thompson, and George B. Mansur, all from Montpelier, with "collecting and preserving materials for the civil and natural history of the State of Vermont." The act vested the incorporators with the responsibility of electing a president and "other officers as they shall judge necessary," and it authorized Stevens to call the first meeting of the organization. Section 3 prescribed that "the library and cabinet of the said corporation shall be kept in the town of Barnet," Stevens's home.[2] The initial library and cabinet consisted of Stevens's collection.

The incorporators waited until October 1840, when the legislature and other state officers gathered in Montpelier, to hold the first meeting. With nine other well-respected "Associate Members," including former two-term Governor Silas Jension, they named Stevens president and librarian, a position that later became keeper of the cabinet, and Thompson and Mansur secretaries, one "Recording," the other "Corresponding." They adopted a constitution and by-laws that provided for a committee of three to consider proposed members "for their approbation"; if approved by the committee, "the names of the candidates, with the names of the members who proposed said candidates, shall be entered into the book of nominations," to "be balloted for at the next meeting of the Society." The officers with the associate members probably constituted themselves as the nominating committee and elected twenty-three members whose names appeared on the rolls in 1841, "very probably without their knowledge or consent."[3] The following year another twenty-two entered the membership rolls. By the end of the 1840s VHS membership had grown only slowly and numbered fewer than seventy.

Stevens and his colleagues loaded the membership list with the state's political and intellectual elite.[4] The roster did not include many Democrats or those who had espoused Jacksonian positions. Forty-eight of the members held or had held political office, with most holding more than one office during their careers. The membership included seven governors, five of whom held office consecutively from 1835 through 1844, and one lieutenant governor. Nineteen served in the Vermont Assembly, three as members of the Council abolished in 1836 when Vermont established the state Senate to which nine VHS members won election. Two worked as the secretary to the Vermont Senate, including the influential DeWitt Clinton Clarke who would own the *Burlington Free Press* which supported the Whigs. Three of the VHS members served in Washington as U.S. senators and another eleven as congressmen. At least 25 percent of the members had legal training, and nine served as state's attorney for their county. Eighteen sat on various benches, including five on the Vermont Supreme Court where two became chief justice. Because Vermont statutes did not establish qualifications, including legal training or membership in the bar to serve as a judge, and the assistant (side) judges won office in partisan elections, the number of VHS members with legal training remains uncertain.[5] Other politically active members of the Society included three U.S. collectors of customs, a county sheriff, several clerks of large towns, the quartermaster-general of Vermont, two who held the office of Vermont secretary of state, a state auditor of accounts, a U.S. marshal, the U.S. comptroller of the currency, and the minister to Chile. Several also sat on the Council of Censors that met every seven years and served on the constitutional conventions that regularly followed to consider the recommendations of the censors.

If the VHS could muster political influence, its members also included, in addition to DeWitt Clinton Clarke, many of the best-known historians and publishers. Six owned and published newspapers located in Burlington, Montpelier, and Middlebury. E. P. Walton, who owned *The Vermont Watchman* and the *Green Mountain Patriot*, compiled and edited the eight-volume *Records of the Governor and Council* and began the annual publication of *Walton's Vermont Register*. William Slade, who served as governor, edited the *Columbia Patriot* (Middlebury) and assembled and published the *Vermont State Papers*. Zadock Thompson, whose histories of Vermont had a wide following in the state, and Governor Hiland Hall, who followed his distinguished legal and political career with the publication of the authoritative *Early History of Vermont*, leant historical gravitas to the Society.

The rolls also carried Charles W. Eastman who, while he served a single term in the Vermont Senate, had made an impact with his newspaper and his published compilation of poems written by Vermonters. University of Vermont Professor George Wyllys Benedict, who like Eastman, served a single term in the state Senate and for a time owned and edited the *Burlington Free Press*, had more influence as a distinguished academic. The members also elected Samuel Read Hall, the author of curricula for teachers and the founder of the normal school movement. Daniel P. Thompson, VHS recording secretary, politically active and the publisher of anti-slavery *The Green Mountain Freeman*, had made a major contribution to burnishing Ethan Allen's story with his extremely popular novel, *The Green Mountain Boys*.

Most of VHS membership had associated with each other regularly in Montpelier when the legislature gathered in October. Chittenden and Washington Counties had the largest number of members, smaller groups came from Addison, Orleans, and Bennington Counties. Even Essex County had at least one member. Most secured room and board in the capital and remained in town during much of the legislative session and certainly during the week. The membership included very few identified with farming, by far the largest occupation in Vermont, or industry, and those who did often had a strong Montpelier connection. Araunah Waterman, a farmer who owned a "woolen factory" in Montpelier, managed to serve as a town representative, a state senator, and a judge in the Washington County Court. After leaving the governorship following two terms in 1842, Charles Paine concentrated on his railroad and related activities with the Vermont Central Railroad, which bypassed Montpelier.

Most of the exalted group of men remained passive members, not taking an active role or attending the Annual Meetings. Stevens organized the first full-scale Annual Meeting for October 1841 that he hoped would prove "useful in waking up the people of the State in connection [with] the subject" of Vermont's past.[6] Stevens spent several months promoting attendance and seeking a speaker.[7] George B. Mansur, the Society's recording secretary, who lived in Montpelier, simply could not attend.[8] Nathaniel Chipman, a state leader and staunch political enemy of the Allens, Chittenden, and their coterie in the 1780s and 1790s, could not attend because of the ravages of age, "infirmness," and "failure of sight."[9] His brother Daniel thought that the Society had "the promise of high importance," but he did not have it "in my power" to deliver an address because of "a nervous disorder — neuralgia."[10] Zadock Thompson, whose ideas had helped motivate Stevens's promoting of Ethan Allen, begged off because of poor health. He had also approached Professor George Wyllys Benedict, who also declined. Benedict, who would live for another thirty years, was "sick with consumption," Thompson reported.[11] There was "no service I would rather do" than speak at the meeting, declared William Czar Bradley, the son of Stephen Rowe Bradley a founding father and Ethan Allen's attorney and in whose home Allen had met Frances Montresor. But he claimed he could "not make it compatible with my situation." He admonished Stevens that the time had come "for the Society to exert itself," even if he would not.[12]

Eventually Stevens succeeded in enlisting speakers to provide a program at the annual October meetings in Montpelier. Hiland Hall spoke at the 1842 meeting, Stevens addressed the members in 1843, and George Perkins Marsh provided the program in 1844. The 1846 presentation at the Annual Meeting on the "Deficiencies in Our History," by John Davie Butler from Norwich University defined the purposes of the Society that Stevens and his associates had envisioned. For his well-received efforts they elected him as an associate member.

After beginning with a brief recitation of the dreadful condition and the loss of many of the treasures of Vermont's early history, asserting that Governor Thomas Chittenden's papers "were sold to a pedlar with paper *rags*." and "The *maps* captured at the Battle of Bennington were used as *curtains* until all, save one, perished," Davis admonished the Society members to rectify the situation both in preserving documents and objects and in writing the early history of Vermont more forcefully.[13] Butler called on the historians to recognize and stress that Ethan Allen and the Green Mountain Boys had determined to capture Fort Ticonderoga two weeks before "the men from Connecticut arrived in Bennington." He demanded that historians uncover why John Brown had failed to assist Allen at Montreal. "The answer to it might show that the blame of Allen's finding captivity for himself, when he sought to capture Montreal, is not to be charged solely to his own fool-hardiness."[14] He called for a stronger defense of the Allen-Chittenden faction in defending both Vermont and the United States in conducting the negotiations with Haldimand.[15]

Butler asked that the members "rejoice that we have a State [Historical] Society," recognizing its "low estate," but "knowing that all beginnings are small." He demanded support for the Society from "Statesmen," "Politicians," "Scholars," and "Rich men." "Is there no hope," he asked, "of any further aid from the State? Shall not this State, like so many others, perfect its archives, or shall the only State that redeemed its revolutionary paper money at par neglect to finish securing even its own laws and journals, and the records of its courts?" He noted that other states, led by Massachusetts, had begun to publish their records, pointing out that "even Georgia has procured the copying of twenty folios regarding her history in British public offices." If we leave the history of Vermont "to be written by foreigners . . . it will be the play of Hamlet with the part of Hamlet omitted."[16]

Well aware of his audience, Butler praised the work of "our President"; he has "gathered fragments from lake to river, from Massachusetts to Canada, he has spent three months together in the collections of sister states, or the general government; he has secured correspondents in Canada, and in the person of his son [Henry Stevens Jr.] broken through the Chinese wall of English exclusiveness, he has found the laws and journals of the legislature given up for lost," and "he has saved letters by the thousands that were ready to perish." Stevens, Butler asserted, had concentrated on the Revolutionary era, and "we ought to be grateful that he has exhausted none of the mines of investigation," but more remains. "We must seek for sermons, histories, and biographies, hoards of newspapers, or those thrown away like autumnal leaves, journals in manuscript, letters sent out of the State to those from whom the settlers came forth."[17]

Butler's address formed the centerpiece of the Society's first publication. It also printed the VHS charter, constitution, and by-laws; the Vermont declaration of independence; and the proceedings of the Vermont convention of June 4, 1777, at which it agreed to the first constitution. The pamphlet closed with the faux "Song of the Vermonters" hailed by Stevens as a 1779 product "substantiated" by a long note linking the heroic poem to Vermont's defiant declaration and maintenance of its independence. A quotation from Ethan Allen's March 9, 1784, letter to Congress that "Rather than fail, I will retire with my hardy Green Mountain Boys to the desolate caverns of the mountains, *and wage war with human nature at large*," followed the "Song" and ended the booklet. Butler had forcefully articulated Stevens's and his colleagues' agenda in forming the VHS that had included venerating the founders.

By 1860 the Society had forced Stevens to give up the presidency, secured legislation to drop "Antiquarian" from its name, and adopted the practice of making out of state luminaries "Honorary Members." After some decades of relative somnolence it went on to develop a broader vision than that of its founders. But by 1860 it had largely succeeded in its initial purpose of working to preserve, interpret, and transmit Vermont's heritage to help shape society through the use of the past. The Society and its leaders stood at the center of the creation of Ethan Allen as the embodiment of the robust democratic values they attributed to Vermont. They conveniently ignored that Ethan Allen would have fit in more comfortably with their hated Jacksonian political enemies, many of whom participated in slaveholding and robust drinking. The Society provided an institution to sustain the creation of a hero fit for Vermonters.

The Vermont Historical and Antiquarian Society: Early Membership Roll

Member	Election Date	Category/ office	Residence	Positions Held
Allen, Heman "Chili"[1]	1842	Associate	Colchester	Judge, Vt. rep., Congress
Allen, Heman "Milton"	1842	Associate	Milton	Vt. rep., Congre
Benedict, George W.[2]	1841	Councilor	Burlington	Vt. senator
Bradley, William Czar	1842	Associate	Westminster	Vt. rep., Congre state's attorney
Butler, John Davie[3]	1847	Associate	Northfield	
Camp, David M.[4]	1841	Councilor	Derby	Lt. gov., judge, state's attorney
Carter, Able	1841	Associate	Williamstown	Assistant judge
Clarke, DeWitt Clinton.[5]	1841	Associate	Burlington	
Chipman, Daniel[6]	1842	Associate	Middlebury/ Ripton	U.S. senator, Vt. rep., Congre state's attorney
Chipman, Nathaniel	1842	Associate	Tinmouth	Vt. Supreme Co U.S. senator, state's attorney

Sources: Paul Carnahan, librarian, Vermont Historical Society, provided the VHAS membershi roster, the date of a member's election, and the membership status. The career profiles came from various county and town histories, histories of UVM, Norwich University and Middlebury College *The Vermont Encylopedia*, Gene Sessions, "A Political Life in Antebellum Vermont," *Vermont Histc* 81, no. 1 (Winter/Spring 2013), 5–33, and Deming's list of the *Principal Civil Officers of Vermont*.

1. Also U.S. minister to Chile, U.S. marshal, and president of the Burlington branch of the Ban the United States.

2. Also UVM professor of mathematics and natural philosophy, publisher of *The Burlington Fr* *Press*, and founder of the Boston & Vermont Telegraph Co.

3. Also professor of ancient languages and literature, Norwich University.

4. Also U.S. collector of customs at Derby.

5. Also publisher of the *Burlington Free Press*, quartermaster of Vermont, and secretary to Vern Senate.

6. Also member of the Council, three Constitutional Conventions, and biographer.

Member	Election Date	Category/ office	Residence	Positions Held
Colby, Stoddard B.	1849	Vice president	Derby/ Montpelier	Vt. senator
Collamer, Jacob	1847	Vice president	Royalton/ Woodstock	Vt. senator, U.S. senator, state's attorney
Crafts, Samuel C.	1841	Associate	Craftsbury	Governor, assistant judge, Vt. rep., Congress
Davis, Ira	1841	Associate	Norwich	Vt. rep.
Eastman, Charles G.[7]	1841	Associate/ councilor	Montpelier	Vt. senator
Fay, Samuel[8]	1842	Associate	Bennington	Vt. rep.
Goodrich, Chauncey[9]	1841	Associate	Burlington	
Hall, Hiland[10]	1841	Associate/ president	Bennington	Governor, Vt. Supreme Court, Congress
Hall, Samuel Read[11]	1842	Associate	Concord Corners	
Harris, Broughton D.	1849	Councilor	Brattleboro	
Hodges, Silas H.[12]	1848	Associate	Rutland/ Clarendon	
Houghton, George F.[13]	1848	Associate/ councilor		
Howe, Zimri	1842	Associate	Castleton	Vt. Supreme Court, U.S. senator
Hyde, Archibald W.[14]	1842	Associate	Burlington	
Jenison, Silas H.	1841	Councilor/ vice president	Shoreham	Governor, lt. gov.
Kimball, Jothn H.[15]	1842	Associate/ councilor	Barton	

7. Also poet, publisher, and owner of the *Vermont Patriot and State Gazette*.
8. Also member of a Constitutional Convention.
9. Also printer, publisher, and bookseller.
10. Also comptroller of U.S. Treasury, U.S. land commissioner in California, and historian.
11. Also educator, author of the first work on teacher education, and founder of the normal school movement to train teachers.
12. Also state auditor of accounts and member of a Constitutional Convention.
13. Also noted orator.
14. Also U.S. collector of customs.
15. Also Orleans County sheriff.

Member	Election Date	Category/ office	Residence	Positions Held
Lyman, George	1842	Associate	Hartford	Vt. rep.
Mansur, George B.[16]	1841	Recording secretary, VHAS founder	Montpelier	
Mattocks, John	1843	Vice president	Peacham	Governor, Vt. Supreme Court, Vt. rep., Congress
Merrill, Orasmus C.[17]	1842	Associate	Bennington	Judge, Vt. rep., Vt. senator, state's attorney, Congress
Paddock, James A.	1842	Associate	Craftsbury	Vt. Supreme Cour judge, assistant judge
Paine, Charles[18]	1841	Associate	Northfield	Governor
Phelps, James H.	1847	Associate/ vice president	Townsend	Vt. rep., Vt. senat
Prentis, Samuel	1843	Associate	Windham	Vt. Supreme Cour
Redfield, Isaac F.	1841	Vice president/ councilor	Randolph	Vt. Supreme Cour state's attorney
Robinson, Aaron	1842	Associate	Bennington	Vt. rep., state's attorney
Robinson, David Jr.	1842	Associate	Northfield/ West Fairlee	Vt. rep.
Robinson, John S.	1842	Associate	Bennington	Governor, Vt. rep Vt. senator
Russell, David[19]	1842	Associate	Burlington	U.S. collector of customs
Slade, William[20]	1842	Associate	Middlebury	Governor, lt. gov. U.S. senator
Stanbury, E. A.[21]	1841	Corresponding secretary	Burlington	

16. Also Montpelier town clerk, registrar of probate, secretary of civil and military affairs, Verm state treasurer, and editor of the *Vermont Temperance Star.*

17. Also member of the Council and a Constitutional Convention.

18. Also president of the Vermont Central Railroad.

19. Also collector of customs.

20. Also publisher of the *Columbia Patriot* and editor of the *Vermont State Papers.*

21. Also clerk, Chittenden County.

Member	Election Date	Category/ office	Residence	Positions Held
Stevens, Henry[22]	1841	President/ librarian	Barnet	Vt. rep.
Thompson, Daniel P.[23]	1841	Recording secretary/ correspondence secretary	Montpelier	
Thompson, Zadock[24]	1841	Associate	Burlington	
Walton, E. P.[25]	1841	Councilor	Montpelier	
Walton, E. P., Jr.[26]	1841	Associate	Montpelier	U.S. senator, state's attorney
Waterman, Araunah[27]	1842	Associate	Montpelier	Vt. senator, Vt. rep.
Waterman, Joseph	1841	Associate	Johnson	Vt. Supreme Court, Vt. senator
White, Phineas[28]	1842	Associate	Putney	Assistant judge, Vt. rep., Congress, state's attorney
Williams, Norman[29]	1841	Councilor	Woodstock	

22. Also president, Caledonia County Temperance Society, VHAS founder, and keeper of the cabinet.

23. Also, attorney, novelist, compiler of the *Laws of Vermont*, publisher of *Green Mountain Freeman*, secretary of the State Education Society, and founder of VHAS.

24. Also natural and civil historian of Vermont and prolific author.

25. Also publisher of the *Green Mountain Patriot*.

26. Also editor of *Governor & Council* and publisher of the *Vermont Watchman* and *The Vermont Register Almanac*.

27. Also farmer and owner of a woolen factory.

28. Also member of a Constitutional Convention.

29. Also secretary of state and secretary of the Senate and Constitutional Convention.

NOTES

1. Sherman, 1.
2. Halbachs, 43.
3. Assman, "Transformations Between History and Memory," 5.
4. Assman, "Memory, Individual and Collective," 206.
5. By 1870 town school superintendents evaluated new teachers with questions about their knowledge of Ethan Allen. *The Biennial Report of the Vermont Board of Education, with the Report of the Secretary, made to the Board October, 1872* (Montpelier: Freeman Steam Printing House and Bindery, 1872), presents the questionnaires from Windham and Grand Isle Counties, 160 and 170. For school histories composed in a catechetical format, see John J. Anderson, *A Grammar School History of the United States* (1870), 62–67, and from a teacher of prospective teachers, Samuel R. Hall, *Outlines of the Geography, Natural and Civil History and Constitution of Vermont* (1864).
6. Pell's 1930 reprint of *EAN* listed twenty reprints and editions, 133–34.
7. Geary, 12.
8. Schwartz, 93.
9. Einhorn, 34.
10. Taylor, 3.

CHAPTER I. CONFUSED ACCOUNTS OF ETHAN ALLEN'S DEATH: LATER ACCOUNTS COMPOUND THE STORY

1. Levi Allen to Ira Allen, August 2, 1789, *EAHK*, 1:323–24.
2. Ira Allen to Levi Allen, June 5, 1789, *EAHK*, 1:315–16.
3. Ira Allen to Levi Allen, June 5, 1789, *EAHK*, 1:315–16. Ira parted with Levi in Montreal, where Levi unsuccessfully sought passage to England, then headed for Boston, conducting business in Clarendon and several other Vermont towns, Chester, New Hampshire, and Boston. Delayed by winter weather and a serious leak in the first ship he boarded, Levi finally sailed on the brig *Mary Clement* on March 1789 without news of Ethan's death. See Levi Allen to Ethan Allen, January 27, 1789, *EAHK*, 1:290; two subsequent letters in February from Levi Allen to Ira Allen, February 15 and 21, 1789; and two letters from Levi Allen to Ira Allen and Nancy Allen, February 23 and March 19, 1789, *EAHK*, 1:290, 291, 292, and 295. Van de Water, *Reluctant Republic*, 333, and Dwight, 2:284, on March 13; Williamson, 156, and Randall, 527, on March 17.

4. Ethan Allen to Stephen R. Bradley, November 16, 1787, *EAHK*, 1:249–50.

5. Nathan Perkins, 27–28.

6. *RG & C*, 3:181.

7. South Hero's nineteenth-century historian reported that Ebenezer Allen's first house was a traditional 16' x 16' log cabin, "a very comfortable log house"; Hemenway, 2:520. After 1787 a frame addition served as a public house and in the nineteenth century was incorporated into a larger building still standing on the site. Hemenway, 2:262. Nobility in fact once slept at Allen's public house, in the person of the future father of Queen Victoria, Edward Augustus, Duke of Kent, on a journey from Montreal to New York City in 1793 accompanied by his mistress Thérèse Bernadine Montgenêt, also known as Mme de Saint-Laurent. See Mollie Gillen, *The Prince and his Lady: The Love Story of the Duke of Kent and Madame de St Laurent* (St. Martins Press: London, 1970).

8. Stewart H. Holbrook, 249–50.

9. Van de Water, *Reluctant Republic*, 333.

10. Jellison, 330.

11. Charles Miner Thompson, 351.

12. *EAN*, 9, 124.

13. Rees, 251–63.

14. *Burlington Free Press*, March 26, 1943. Jellison relies on the *Free Press* account, notes Stewart H. Holbrook's "entertaining . . . fictionalized" version of Allen's night at Ebenezer's place on South Hero, but then discounts these and all other accounts by noting that Allen became comatose on the sled returning to Burlington on the lake's ice and remained so until his death later in the day (330 and 350). Pell says that Allen never slept during his "Final Frolic," and died on February 17 while crossing the ice on the sled (268, 317). Bellesiles avoids the traditional story of the night before Allen's death and, following Pell, reports him dying on February 17 on the ice. *Revolutionary Outlaws*, 256.

15. Jellison, 330.

16. Hemenway reports Reverend A. Fleming, 1:536, and Reverend A. Witherspoon, 1:546.

17. Nathan Perkins, 32.

18. Hemenway, 1:571.

19. Ira Allen attributed his brother's death to "arperplaxey," a generic term that probably included ischemic stroke. Medical researchers have concluded that "stroke occurrence rises with decreasing temperature, and that even a moderate decrease in temperature can increase the risk of ischemic stroke." See *Epidemiology*, 14:473–78. Other research has reported that cold weather can increase hospital admittances for stroke or heart attack. See Roger Dobson's article in the *British Medical Journal*, 2, 329:760, for a discussion of the association

between temperature and the risk of stroke and acute myocardial infarction. It seems likely that Allen fell victim to a stroke in a frigid mid-February morning crossing the ice to his Burlington home from South Hero Island.

20. Nathan Perkins, 31, and Lossing, *The Pictorial Field Book*, 1:161. Crockett, 2:435, places the burial on February 17, and the *Gazette*'s front page reported on February 23 that it took place on the eighteenth.

21. *Exercises Attending the Unveiling and Presentation of a Statue of Gen. Ethan Allen*, 7.

22. Ira Allen to Levi Allen, June 5, 1789, *EAHK*, 1:315 and 2:444.

23. Nathan Perkins, 31.

24. Pell, 268; Hiland Hall, 453–54; Charles Miner Thompson, 531.

25. Pell, 268–69; Crockett, 2:435.

26. VG, February 23, 1789.

27. Wardner, *The Birthplace of Vermont*, 344.

28. Graham, 141 and 143.

29. Ethan Allen to Benjamin Stiles, November 16, 1785, *EAHK*, 1:185.

30. Nathan Perkins, 30.

31. Jellison, 331.

32. Dwight, 2:283.

33. Lossing, *The Pictorial Field Book*, 1:161.

34. Hiland Hall, 454.

35. Pell, 269, cites John A. Graham's *A Descriptive Sketch of the Present State of Vermont* (1797) for the reincarnation tale.

36. Stewart H. Holbrook, 260; Wallman, 161.

37. Chittenden, 47.

38. Sherman, Potash, and Sessions, 126. Randall, 533.

CHAPTER II. SEEKING THE MAIN CHANCE:
LIMITED EDUCATION, FAILED VENTURES, AND THE
PROMISE OF THE NEW HAMPSHIRE GRANTS

1. Pell, 2; Jellison, 2.

2. Orrin Peer Allen, *The Allen Memorial*, 13–44, and appendix D, 246–50. Gold, 8–9 and 11.

3. Russell, 126–28.

4. Gross, 79–80, 84.

5. In the rural north, the wealthiest 10 percent of the population owned 40 percent of the property. Sellers, 238.

6. Weaver, 106.

7. *VSP*, 2: Charter, Two Heroes, October 22, 1779.

8. Levi Allen to John Simcoe, May 31, 1792, *EAHK*, 2:99.

9. Jones, 39–43.

10. Ellickson, 138. See also Bellesiles, "Autobiography of Levi Allen," 84.

11. Dexter, 458.

12. Orrin Peer Allen, *The Allen Memorial*, 29; *EAHK*, 2:443.

13. IRAAuto, 1:27. In a letter to "our Good Brother Indians of the four tribes" of Canadian Indians, Allen claimed that he learned to hunt and fight from them. "I was Always a Friend to Indians and have Hunted with them many Times and Know how to Shoot and Ambush Like Indians and am a Great Hunter." Winthrop Hoit, who learned to speak Mohawk as a prisoner in the French and Indian War, and Abraham Nimham, a Wappinger from the Stockbridge settlement who was later commissioned in the Continental Army, carried this letter north as Allen's envoys. Nimham was killed in action outside New York City in 1778. Allen's letter to the Indians appears in Ethan Allen to the Connecticut Assembly, May 26, 1775, *EAHK*, 1:29–30. See also his advice to Schuyler and Montgomery to kill more Indians so that they will withdraw their support for the British. Ethan Allen to Schuyler and Montgomery, September 8, 1775, *EAHK*, 1:49.

14. Large stands of hard and soft woods and few cleared fields and "edge growth" supported a declining deer population in northern New England during the mid- and late eighteenth century as human depredations compounded winter's usual heavy toll. Connecticut deer were extirpated by 1750. Vermont's and New Hampshire's were nearly all gone by 1800. See Cronon, who also cites Dwight's *Travels*, 1:33, for his report on the scarcity of deer and beaver in the upper Connecticut River Valley.

15. *CCHS*, 9:247.

16. Jones, 118.

17. Jay Mack Holbrook, Table 4, ix–x, and Table 6, xii.

18. Gipson, 316–20.

19. Pell, 29–33; Jellison, 32–38; and Randall, 220–25 and 228–33.

20. In 1779, when Massachusetts, New Hampshire, and New York were claiming jurisdiction over the region by then known as Vermont, John Adams described James Duane: he "has a sly, surveying eye, a little squint-eyed; . . . very sensible, I think, and very artful," quoted in Flick, *History of the State of New York*, 309.

21. IANPH, 23–25. If Ethan Allen did admonish James Duane and John Tabor Kemp that "the gods of the valleys are not the gods of the hills," no record of the utterance surfaced until Ira Allen quoted it in his history of Vermont twenty-eight years after its purported delivery and nine years after Ethan's death. Had he made the statement, none of those who have regularly quoted it since the 1830s have suggested its possible origin in the story of Socrates taking his own life as punishment for refusing to recognize the gods of the state. This kind

of epic story would have appealed to Ethan, and he could have learned about it from his tutor Reverend Lee or in his conversations with Thomas Young. In that case he could have made the statement. Muller, "Vermont's 'Gods of the Hills,'" 125–33.

22. Sparks, 240–42; Zadock Thompson, *History of Vermont*, part 2, 20–21.

23. Pell, 323.

24. Jellison, 37.

25. Randall, 234–38.

26. Duane, 8–9.

27. Pell, 33; Jellison, 37; and Charles Miner Thompson, 101.

28. *DCHNY*, 4:682–83.

29. Ibid., 4:689.

30. Duane, 9.

31. *EIRA*, 1:4.

32. *DCHNY*, 4:686.

33. Ibid., 4:728.

34. Ibid., 4:763–64.

35. Ibid., 4:764–65.

36. Jellison, 45–46.

37. Morton, 36–37; Pell, 445–46.

38. *EIRA*, 1:27–29.

39. *DCHNY*, 4:847–54.

40. Ibid., 4:860–61.

41. Ibid., 4:868.

42. Ibid., 4:844–45 and 884–88.

43. See *VSP*, 42, for the text of the Bloody Act of March 9, 1774. Ethan Allen to Crean Brush and Samuel Wells, May 19, 1774, *EAHK*, 1:13–15.

44. *EIRA*, 1:28–29.

45. Pell, 68.

46. Smith, 198–235.

47. *EIRA*, 1:21.

48. Ibid., 1:31.

49. Shapiro, 246–47. Arneil, 186–87.

CHAPTER III. CHASING FAME AND GLORY:
SUCCESS AT TICONDEROGA, BLUNDERING AT
ST. JOHN, AND DEFEAT AT MONTREAL

1. *EAN*, 6–7. French, 81.

2. French, 13–17.

3. Ibid., 18–19, citing Force, 243–45. Ezra Heacock of Sheffield, Connecticut,

accompanied Noah Phelps to the fort a few days before the attack to assure conditions had not changed there. They gained entrance under the pretence of Phelps seeking a haircut from the fort's barber. Bascom, 319.

4. French, 54–55.

5. *EAN*, 9.

6. Arnold, 366–67.

7. Ethan Allen to the Massachusetts Congress, May 11, 1775, *EAHK*, 1:20.

8. Allen reports leading one hundred men and Seth Warner to St. John. Ethan Allen to Noah Lee, May 21, 1775, *EAHK*, 1:27–28.

9. *EAN*, 11–12.

10. Ethan Allen to the New York Congress, June 2, 1775, *EAHK*, 1:34. Isaiah 40:31.

11. Graffagnino, "'The Country My Soul Delighted In,'" 33.

12. Ethan Allen to the New York Congress, June 2, 1775, *EAHK*, 1:34, 35.

13. Gabriel, 33–36.

14. Goodrich, 814–15.

15. *EAN*, 12–13. Philip Schuyler to John Hancock, October 5, 1775, EAP.

16. Goodrich, 815. *EAN*, 36. If captured roaming the countryside in the red wool tuque, the uniform cap of the Quebec region's militia many miles from Chambly and St. John, Allen risked hanging as both a notorious rebel and a spy. Probably unknown to Allen, in August 1775 the Crown had declared the thirteen colonies in a state of rebellion and captured rebels subject to hanging. Morrissey, 14.

17. Ethan Allen to Richard Montgomery, September 20, 1775, *EAHK*, 1:51–52.

18. Nash, 175.

19. In John Smith's 1607 *General Historie of Virginia*, reprinted many times during the eighteenth century, "the Captain; who finding himself beset, bound an *Indian*, whom he had for his Guide, to his arm for a Buckler [a shield], and received their Attack so smartly with his Fire-Arms, that he soon laid three dead upon the Spot, and so wounded and galled divers others, that none of them cared to approach him." Stith, 51. Leary, 13–33. *EAN*, 21–22.

20. *EAN*, 5.

21. Ibid., 9.

22. Ethan Allen to the Continental Congress, May 29, 1775, *EAHK*, 1:32.

23. Adlum, 118.

24. Fitch, 131. On Camel's Rump and Camel's Hump, see IANPH, 12, and the editor's footnote, 1.

25. *EAN*, 48, 52.

26. Graydon, 226, 260.

27. *Reason*, preface.

28. John Jay to Gouverneur Morris, quoted in Stahr, 89.

29. *EAN*, 2. "[I] trusted solely to my memory for the whole."

30. Ibid., 5–6.

31. Washington, 11:381.

32. IANPH, 46.

33. Zadock Thompson, "The Allen Family," in Hemenway, 2:566.

34. Captured and imprisoned in Albany by New York militia after the Saratoga battle, Private David Redding of the Queen's Loyal Rangers escaped during transport to Bennington from the overcrowded Albany prison. Recaptured and taken to Bennington, he was tried by a court on June 4, 1778, for "enemical conduct." When a nonlawyer pointed out the error of only a six-man jury, the judge acquitted Redding, angering a lynch mob threatening to hang him. Ethan Allen quelled the mob by promising that if Redding went free, Allen himself would hang. Governor Thomas Chittenden acted in lieu of the unconvened General Assembly and granted Redding's petition for a reprieve, but ordered the young soldier hanged on June 11. He appointed Allen as state's attorney to prosecute Redding, and ordered a militia force to ensure peace at the second trial. No record of the original trial or a retrial has survived. Nor is it certain that Allen actually prosecuted Redding. On June 6, the General Assembly formed a committee of five members to investigate "the petition presented to this House by David Reading [*sic*], . . . ; and that a Committee of five be appointed to prepare a Bill, in consequence of said petition &c." No other record of an investigation into this matter or a bill survives. Benjamin Holmes hanged Redding on the day and time appointed. On the trial of David Redding, see Spargo, 15–32; *VSP*, 269; *RG & C*, 1:261–64; Palsits, 1:92, 97–98. See also Ethan Allen to Henry Laurens, June 17, 1778, *EAHK*, 1:81, wherein Allen impersonally reports how Vermonters "are determined to rid this Country of Tories, and to Confiscate their Estates, one of those Villains [David Redding] was hanged in this place, the 11th Instant."

CHAPTER IV. ETHAN ALLEN AND THE
HISTORIANS: DISCOVERING A HERO

1. Graffagnino, "The Vermont 'Story,'" 77, and Brown, 278–79.

2. Williams's 1809 reprinting discussed events in Vermont to 1806, sixteen years after Ethan Allen's death. See Graffagnino, "The Vermont 'Story,'" 77–83.

3. Leder, 3.

4. Williams, vii and x.

5. Ibid., 219–20.

6. Ibid., 220–23.

7. Ibid., 226.

8. Williamson, 96, and Graffagnino, "Revolution and Empire," 286.

9. Williams, 265–71.

10. Ibid., 271.

11. Muller, "Ira Allen's Vermont," 223–29; James B. Wilbur, 2:395, 422; and Graffagnino, "The Vermont 'Story,'" 77–80. See Francis Parkman to Henry Stevens, Boston, November 14, 1845, HSC, Box 1, Folder 1, and Henry Stevens to his son, Montpelier, August 29, 1841, HSC, Box 2, File 37. Jared Sparks had clearly seen Ira Allen's account before writing his 1833 "Life of Ethan Allen" for the American Biography series, reprinted by Burlington's Chauncey Goodrich without change as *The Life of Ethan Allen* (1858). Sparks repeats Ira Allen's account of Ethan's bold warning about the "gods of the valleys" (24).

12. Graffagnino, "'Twenty Thousand Muskets!'" 409–31. Duffy and Coyle, "Tales of the Olive Branch," 15–20. The first American edition of Allen's *History* appeared in the *Collections of the Vermont Historical Society* (1870), 319–493.

13. IANPH, preface, 10.

14. Graffagnino, "Revolution and Empire," 347–48.

15. Sparks, 241.

16. Graffagnino, "Revolution and Empire," 24; and Muller, "Vermont's 'Gods of the Hills,'" 125–33.

17. IANPH, 25–48; *EAN*, 124, in Pell's edition.

18. Graffagnino, "The Vermont 'Story.'"

19. Hoskins, preface. Graffagnino suggests that Hoskins plagiarized. "The Vermont 'Story,'" 82.

20. Weems, chapter 13.

21. Hoskins, 45–46.

22. Ibid., 48–49.

23. Ibid., 103–4.

24. Ibid., 107–8.

25. Zadock Thompson (1833), 60.

26. Ibid., 154.

27. Moore, 124.

28. Ibid., 242.

29. Ibid., 94 and 124.

30. Russo, 2.

31. Muller, "Smuggling into Canada," 5–21; and Muller, "'A traitorous and Diabolic Traffic,'" 78–96.

32. Potash, *Vermont's Burned-Over District*, 80.

33. Degree, 151–80. Daniel Chipman played a leading role in the creation of the heroes of early Vermont. An early member of the Vermont Historical and

Antiquarian Society, he published a biography of his brother Nathaniel, *The Life of Hon. Nathaniel Chipman, LL.D.* (1846), and accounts of other early Vermont figures who became heroes.

34. Stilwell, 128–29.

35. Hemenway, 3:894.

36. Stilwell, 107, 130, and 177–78.

37. Zadock Thompson, *History of Vermont*, part I (Natural), 20.

38. Stilwell, 153–55; and Harris, "The Road Less Traveled By."

39. Muller and Hand, appendix A, 401, and appendix B, 403; and U.S. Department of Commerce, A-1, 7.

40. Duffy and Muller, *An Anxious Democracy*, 25 and 28.

41. Narrett, 67.

42. Roth, "Why Are We Still Vermonters?" 201.

43. Russo, 2.

44. Cate, 4. Cate found that "Thompson and his family joined the local Congregational church after hearing Burchard. Thompson wrote that Burchard had 'a thorough knowledge of the human heart' and 'catches all classes and particularly the intellectual.'" For the argument that the founding of the Society was part of the reform agendas of its founders, see Roth, "Why Are We Still Vermonters?" 197–211.

45. For the argument that the founding of the Society was part of the reform agendas of its founders, see Roth, "Why Are We Still Vermonters?" 197–211.

46. Narrett, 69.

47. Roth, "Why Are We Still Vermonters?" 205.

48. Henry Stevens to a benefactor, SCBH, Henry Stevens MSS, Box 2, Folder 39.

49. Narrett, 69 and 75. For Sparks, see Adams; "Jared Sparks," 985–96.

50. Narrett, 80.

51. Bayley quoted in Wardner, *The Birthplace of Vermont*, 344.

52. McCorison, 6–7.

53. Ibid., introduction, 3.

54. Peach, 288.

55. Narrett, 66.

56. See Whittier to Roberts, Danvers, Massachusetts, July 29, 1877, in McCorison, 4. *The New York Times* (August 26, 1877) article reprints the *Free Press* story, as well as Whittier and Roberts's correspondence.

57. Shalhope, 334.

58. Ibid., 339.

59. Jared Sparks to Henry Stevens, February 2, 1843, SCBH, Henry Stevens MSS, Box 3, Folder 16.

60. Sparks, 230.

61. Ibid., 241.

62. Ibid.

63. Ibid., 341 and 347.

64. Ibid., 354–55.

65. Hemenway, 1:571.

66. Zadock Thompson, *History of Vermont*, part II, 212. Potash, taking his title from John Davie Butler's 1846 address to the Vermont Historical and Antiquarian Society, discusses the quality of the interpretations of the history of Vermont and recognizes the development "of the Ethan Allen myth" in his "Deficiencies in Our Past," 212–26. Potash posits that a "second dimension of the Ethan Allen myth emerged in the 1850s and 1860s" through making him a frontier leader in the mode of Daniel Boone, "recasting him from a member of the revolutionary generation to founding father and frontier rebel." He asserts that "the glorification of Ethan Allen ushered in a dramatically new definition of what constitutes Vermont history."

67. Graffagnino, "The Vermont 'Story,'" 84–85; and Henry Stevens to Jared Sparks, February 14, 1843, SCBH, Henry Stevens MSS, Box 3, Folder 12.

68. Zadock Thompson, *History of Vermont*, part II, 21.

69. Ibid., part II, 30.

70. Ibid., part II, 61–62.

71. Ibid., part II, note *, 67.

72. Stone, 2: chapter 6.

73. Zadock Thompson, *History of Vermont*, part II, note *, 67.

74. Narrett, 75.

75. DePuy, xi.

76. Beckley, preface.

77. Carpenter and Arthur, 33–34.

78. Ibid., 198 and 205.

79. Ibid., xv.

80. DePuy, 411.

81. Ibid., 211.

82. Ibid., xiv–xv, 181, 197, and 212.

83. Henry W. DePuy's *Ethan Allen and the Green Mountain Heroes of '76*, first published in 1853, has appeared in numerous reprints, including in 1855 as *The Mountain Hero*. See Bassett, #594, 27.

84. Severance and Houghton, 354.

85. BHHall; and Vermont Historical Society, *Constitution and By-laws*, 14–15.

86. BHHall, v–vi.

87. Ibid., vi–vii.
88. Duffy and Coyle, "Crean Brush," 103–10.
89. BHHall, 603–33.
90. For a biographical sketch of Hiland Hall, see Crockett, 5:112–13.
91. BHHall, 451–52 and 451–75.
92. Graffagnino, "The Vermont 'Story,'" 86.
93. BHHall, 119 and 122.
94. Ibid., 202–7.
95. Ibid., 215–16.
96. Ibid., 375.
97. Ibid., 361–63, 376.
98. Ibid., 376–77.

CHAPTER V. THE MANY GUISES OF THE HERO:
ETHAN ALLEN IN FICTION, STONE, UNIFORM, AND
THE POPLAR IMAGINATION

1. Kammen, 15–17. Bolingbroke, 306–12.
2. Rosenbach, 81–82. *History of America, Abridged for the Use of Children*, 80–88.
3. Gabriel, 13, 195.
4. Kammen, 27.
5. Headley; Jenkins; Peterson; Lossing, *The Pictorial Field Book of the Revolution*; Lossing, *Seventeen Hundred and Seventy-Six*; Griswold; Judson.
6. IANPH, 23. For an analysis of Allen's self-creation and its relation to its posthumous transformations, see McWilliams, 271.
7. Weems, chapter 13. For Weems, Washington was "a Christian gentleman" motivated by his religion. Kitman calls Weems's biography of Washington a seminal work of historical fiction in his humorous *The Making of the President 1789*, 156.
8. "Certificate from Esquire Ira Allen," July [10th] 1778. *SPVT*, 6:376–77. Ira Allen, "Autobiography," 53.
9. Van Doren.
10. Daniel P. Thompson, *The Green Mountain Boys* (2000).
11. Graydon, 253.
12. Ward, 153–75.
13. In 1910 Robert Bascom reported that D. P. Thompson modeled his character Pete Jones on a surveyor Daniel Newton (d. 1834) of Shoreham on a suggestion from Vermont Governor Silas Jenison, Newton's neighbor. Bascom, 319.
14. Melville, 241–60.

15. Ibid., 241–45.

16. On his release by prisoner exchange in May 1778, the Continental Congress, on George Washington's recommendation, commissioned him brevet, that is, temporary, lieutenant colonel without command authority and paid him $75 per month for thirty-one months, as compensation for the term of his captivity. Washington, 4:415, 418 note. Two months later Allen reported to General Horatio Gates that he had recovered from the physical deterioration of imprisonment, and half-heartedly offered to accept an active duty assignment with the Continental Army, noting that he had "plenty of business to occupy" him and that Gates probably has "plenty of officers." Ethan Allen to Horatio Gates, July 15, 1778, *EAHK*, 1:184.

17. The June muster days for town militias, a legal requirement for all able men over the age of eighteen, eventually fell into disuse in the 1840s. SSP, 180–81, 215. Also, Benedict, 1:9–12, traces the post–Mexican War decline of the uniform militias in Vermont and Governor Ryland Fletcher's (1856–58) efforts to revive them with the passage of the Militia Act of 1856.

18. "I had no commission from Congress, yet they [Schuyler and other officers] engaged me, that I should be considered as an officer the same as though I had a commission." *EAN*, 12–14. Ethan Allen to Richard Montgomery, September 20, 1775, *EAHK*, 1:51.

19. Nathan Clark, chairman, Dorset Convention, Kent Tavern, Dorset, to Philip Schuyler, July 27, 1775. "Resolved, that when the Green Mountain Boys are raised each of them shall be furnished with a Coat and that Mr. Peter T. Curtenius [former weaver, then military commissary in Albany, and later state auditor] be requested to purchase coarse green Cloth for that purpose and red Cloth sufficient to face those Coats and to have two hundred and twenty-five coats of a large size made of the said Cloth." Quoted in Goodrich, 815.

20. Graydon, 253. On Allen's return voyage to America, the ship's captain permitted the ship's sail maker to tailor a suit of clothes for him from the cloth he received at Cork. *EAN*, 52.

21. Allen called the short-lived faceoff over the West Union "the siege of Walloomcock" and charged the Vermont treasurer for his "attending" the event £1.10 and £9.2 "for my expenses and the militia." EAP, 407–8. Ann Bleecker carried provisions to her husband in the New York Militia and watched this bloodless incident from the New York riverbank. Allen, she later wrote, "was bound up in gold lace, and felt himself grand as the Great Mogul." She thought Vermont's old spiked cannon added a proper military flavor to the event. Bleecker, 150–53. Quoted in Pell, 220.

22. See *EAN*, 36, on his costume, which, when Allen was captured, including "a good pair of shoes."

23. *Collections of the Vermont Historical Society*, 2:78–80.

24. Benedict, 1:36.

25. Charles Phelps (1717–89) opposed Congress's recognition of Vermont, for which he was jailed and his property confiscated in 1782. He petitioned for a pardon and took an oath of allegiance to Vermont in 1784. Remaining to the end of his life opposed to the State of Vermont, he dated his last will "at New Marlborough, in the county of Cumberland, state of New York." Graffagnino, *TVE*, 233. Graffagnino, "Vermonters Unmasked,"133–61.

26. Jerusha Allen to Ira Allen, February 17, 1793, *EAHK*, 2:411. The miniature of Ira Allen can be seen in the Fleming Museum, University of Vermont.

27. The popular portrait artist John Singleton Copley, while in New York City for six months in 1770–71, painted thirty-seven portraits, including those of Captain John Montresor and, later in London, Montresor's wife, Frances Tucker. Richardson, 1–13. Montresor's natural daughter, Frances Montresor, with her aunt Margaret Schoolcraft Brush and her husband Crean Brush left New York City in 1770 to settle in Westminster in the province of New York's recently organized Cumberland County on the west bank of the Connecticut River, otherwise known as the New Hampshire Grants. Benson Lossing in 1850–51 sketched an image of Crean Brush from an unattributed and now lost portrait of him in the possession of his grandson Henry Norman at Caldwell (now Lake George), New York. An engraving from that sketch appears in Lossing, *The Pictorial Field Book of the Revolution*. H. R. Schoolcraft's recollection of Frances Penniman appears in Ellet, 2:211. Practitioners of physiognomy, a popular "science" of the eighteenth and early nineteenth centuries, believed one could deduce an individual's character from empirical observation of his or her physical features. See Hartley.

28. Remember Baker and Zimri Allen to the Connecticut *Courant*, June 1, 1773, *EAHK*, 1:10–11 and note 3.

29. Graydon, 253.

30. *Burlington Free Press*, June 19, 1858.

31. Holbrook, 5. See also above, chapter 1 for the verses on Ethan's death that provided Holbrook's version of Allen's height: "His tall head busting through the pines."

32. Van de Water, *The Reluctant Republic*, 11–12.

33. Pell, 83: "probably was a green coat with yellow or buff breeches and certainly had large gold epaulettes." Randall, 259, 261, 523. The epaulettes joined Allen's wardrobe sometime between his release from captivity in 1778 and his appearance at the West Union standoff of Vermont militia versus New York troops on the banks of the Walloomsac River in 1780. The only Green Mountaineers who wore green military coats were those who volunteered to join Seth Warner in the Green Mountain rangers with the American invasion of Canada in September 1775. See above, note 19.

34. "B. H. Kinney," Worcester Historical Museum (1985), 23, 29. *Burlington Daily Sentinel*, February 8, 1852.

35. Speech of George Perkins Marsh on the Mexican War in the House of Representatives of the U.S., February 10, 1848, 4.

36. *Bell*, 73.

37. Radley, 46–59.

38. Robbins, 124–26.

39. "I stopped in Rutland and called at Mr Henry Baxters house. I cannot tell you all the conversation, but, as I came away he said that when I wanted the marble, to let him know. 'He did not care whether the State of Vermont paid him for it or not, that was not the object.' I inferred from all he said that he would rather give us the marble than have it made of granite." Larkin G. Mead Jr. to John N. Pomeroy and George P. Marsh, April 26, 1858, GPM.

40. *Exercises Attending the Unveiling and Presentation of a Statute of Gen. Ethan Allen*, 14.

41. Lowenthal, 355. *Report of a Committee* . . . Robbins, 126. *Burlington Free Press*, July 7, 1873.

42. On the lost grave of Ethan Allen, see above, chapter 1, "The Death of Ethan Allen." Originally known as "the burying yard" during Burlington's early settlement years, by 1850 the site was called Green Mount Cemetery. In the twentieth century, it became Greenmount Cemetery.

43. Gillies, 84–85.

44. *Exercises Attending* . . . , 46–48.

45. Chittenden's redemptionist rhetoric had been a commonplace of July 4 speeches for nearly one hundred years. See, for example, Ramsay: the American Revolution could move people and nations "till tyranny and oppression are utterly extirpated from the face of the earth" (15).

46. Hemenway, 2:432. Bryan, *TVE*, 231–32. Resistance to the Embargo Acts and disapproval of the trial in the notorious *Black Snake* affair of 1809 were widespread in Vermont.

47. *Exercises Attending* . . . , 46–50.

48. Bort, *Manchester*, 80–83.

49. Larkin Mead to John N. Pomeroy, March 22, 1858, John N. Pomeroy Collection, SCBH.

CHAPTER VI. MAKING IT UP: ANECDOTES,
LEGENDS, AND OTHER DUBIOUS TALES

1. See Bartlett, *Dictionary of Americanism* for numerous examples of "stump" and "stump speech" in the first half of the nineteenth century.

2. See above, chapter 1, "The Death of Ethan Allen."

3. Lindeman. During Ethan Allen's life, relatively untrained barber-surgeons, some of them "outright quacks, or charlatans," pulled teeth. See McCauley, "The First Dental College," 41–45.

4. Stewart H. Holbrook, 49.

5. Casson, 20–33.

6. The vague age "youth" suggests Ethan running down deer at night perhaps between ages fifteen and twenty-five, that is, 1752 and 1762, in Connecticut. In 1803 Timothy Dwight reported of the Upper Connecticut River Valley: ". . . deer are scarce. There are no elks." Dwight, 4:215. In 1842 Zadock Thompson commented on the scarcity of deer in early Vermont: deer were "eagerly hunted, . . . till their numbers have been constantly diminished within the state, till they have become exceedingly scarce." *History of Vermont*, part I, 51. Responding to the over-exploitation of whitetail deer, the Massachusetts Bay Colony prohibited deer hunting for half the year in 1694. New Hampshire passed a similar law in 1741. Unlike archaeologists in western New York and Pennsylvania, who found extensive archaeological evidence of large deer herds having existed in favorable habitat through many previous centuries, Vermont biologist Leonard Foote found extensive reports of few deer in the earliest European settlement of southern Vermont, 1740s to 1780s. Increased settlement after 1777 produced limited "edge" habitat favorable to deer in the 1780s, but also increased human predation, compelling the government to declare the first closed season in 1791. Foote, 7–12.

7. Stewart H. Holbrook, viii. Nineteenth-century slang, the descriptor "a ring-tail peeler" could be applied to any person, animal, sound, or natural event that exceeded all norms of behavior or performance.

8. Kaubler, 1:1249. Stewart H. Holbrook, 268.

9. Haughen and Santella, 94. Stanfield, 79–80.

10. Daniel P. Thompson's short story collection *Shaker Lovers and Other Tales* (1848) includes "Ethan Allen and the Lost Children." In a letter to Daniel P. Thompson dated 1845, Zadock Thompson transcribed *The Lost Children & Ethan Allen* "by Mr. Timothy Meigs Bradley [a relative of the still living Betsy Taylor, the younger lost child] of Williston." Zadock Thompson gives the tale a long title: "Narrative of the remarkable preservation of two small children lost in the woods in Sunderland, Bennington co. Vt, in the year 1780." Zadock Thompson to Daniel P. Thompkin, D. P. Thompson Papers, Vermont Historical Society. See also *Burlington Sentinel*, March 10, 1849.

11. The lost children tale appeared first in Zadock Thompson's *Gazetteer* (1824), and then in his *History of Vermont* (1842). The history of the town of Sunderland in Hemenway, 1:240, contains a brief version of the lost children

story composed in the 1860s. Allen's modern biographers each offer a long paragraph on the lost children story (Pell, 189; Bellesiles, *Revolutionary Outlaws*, 164; Jellison, 192) that very closely follow Daniel P. Thompson's tale and Zadock Thompson's histories. See also *Proceedings of the Vermont Historical Society*, 96–97. Zadock Thompson's original source for his first account of the lost children story could have been *The Affecting History of the Children in the Woods*. A Hartford, Connecticut, edition appeared in 1796. Folklorists trace the lost children theme to at least the sixteenth century. Charles Perreault drew on it for his Thumbelina tale and the brothers Grimm retold it in the Hansel and Gretel story.

12. Randall, 482. Bellesiles, *Revolutionary Outlaws*, 165. Lutz. For the Victorian view of the representational value and significance of tears, see Miss Peake.

13. Riffaterre, 130.

14. Pell (191) and Jellison (192), who relied on Pell.

15. DePuy, 427.

16. McCorison, 225, 327, 355.

17. John Lansing to Philip Schuyler, July 26, 1780, SCBH, Box 5, Folder 30, describes the informers they engaged and their allegiances to Ethan Allen. A second letter the same day, John Lansing to Philip Schuyler, July 26, 1780, SCBH, Box 5, Folder 31, reports Ethan Allen's activities from May to July. Nothing in Lansing's reports suggests Ethan led a search for lost children during the two months Tichenor reported to him.

18. Pell, 191.

19. *Burlington Sentinel*, March 10, 1849.

20. DePuy, 262.

21. Lossing, *The Pictorial Field Book*, 1:50.

22. *The Aethenaeum*, 47.

23. Brown, 216–17, reports them drinking two bottles of Madeira. DePuy, 262. DePuy, Brown, and others who repeat this anecdote ignore its impossibilities, for example, that Allen had his sword taken from him at Montreal. His British captors would not have allowed him to possess a cavalry or other large sword on parole.

24. Robson, 170.

25. Donald, 39–40. See also Stephen Spielberg's 2012 film *Lincoln* and Doris Kearns Goodwin, *Team of Rivals*, 151. Goodwin cites a contemporary source for this anecdote attributed to Lincoln. We suspect General Ethan Allen Hitchcock might have been Lincoln's source. Ethan Allen went to England once in his life as a prisoner in 1776.

26. Jellison, 194.

27. Hemenway, 1:567.

28. Orrin Peer Allen, 44.

29. BHHall, 609.

30. Vail.

31. Nason, 48, identified John Montresor "as a relative of the Haswell family." His mother Mary Haswell was sister to Rowson's father. Rowson, xxxvii.

32. Henderson, 24:1–23.

33. Samuel Hitchcock to Lucy Allen Hitchcock, August 28, 1791, *EAHK*, 1:378.

34. For a full text of the New York law known as the Bloody Act of March 9, 1774, see *VSP*, 42. Loyalist Crean Brush (1725–78), the principal draftsman of the Bloody Act, settled at Westminster on the east side of the Green Mountains and represented Cumberland County in the New York Assembly from 1770 to the outbreak of the Revolutionary War in 1775.

35. John Buchanan joined the King's American Rangers as captain on March 31, 1777, was mortally wounded at the Battle of Brandywine Creek on September 11, 1777, and died on September 27. Kemble, 137 and 529. Frances Montresor married Buchanan at age sixteen and had a child by him who died shortly after Brush's death. Margaret Brush's petition to Roger Morris, Inspector of Claims of Refugees, January 20, 1779, *Royal Institution Transcripts*, 17–18, William Clements Library, University of Michigan.

36. John Montresor's grandfather, James Gabriel Montresor (1667–1723), originally Jacques La Trésor, a Huguenot major in the Scots Fusiliers, commanded Fort William in Scotland at his death. Major La Trésor's son, also James Montresor and a native British subject, was John Montresor's father. He too served in the British army, as chief engineer at Gibraltar and then as chief engineer in America in the French and Indian Wars. John Montresor in 1770 succeeded his father as chief engineer in America. Schoolcraft also reported that Crean Brush served on General Bradstreet's staff in Albany, where he met and married another Schoolcraft sister, mistakenly identified as Elizabeth, not Margaret, in Whitehall, Bradstreet's Albany mansion. Schoolcraft, 2:211. Godfrey, 262–63. Montresor, 29–30.

37. Randall, 526.

38. Mary's parents, Cornelius Brownson Jr. (1692–1772) and Abigail Jackson (1693–1772) of Woodbury, Connecticut, had ten children: Stephen, Elijah, Gideon, Jedidiah, Anna, Abraham, John, Mary, Israel, and Patience. Herbert Bronson Enderton, 245.

39. Allen's land transactions are variously calculated. See Bellesiles for a list of his land sales, *Revolutionary Outlaws*, appendix H, 290–93.

40. Westminster Deed Book B #61, April 6, 1784. Jellison, 314–15; Bellesiles, *Revolutionary Outlaws*, 243–44.

41. DePuy, 425–26, recites the story of Ethan and Fanny marrying in Stephen Bradley's home and adds the footnote: "This anecdote is given on the authority of William C. Bradley, (son of Stephen R. Bradley,) formerly a member of Congress from Vermont who was present with his father at this occasion." BHHall (629–31) also cites a letter from William C. Bradley in 1857 as his source for the story of their marriage. DePuy, Hall, and others leave unexamined the Bradley toddler's questionable cognizance of the moment and the dialogues the adult Bradley later recites.

42. Bellesiles, *Revolutionary Outlaws*, 365, note 89.

43. Weinerman, 8, 56.

44. Beginning May 15, 1957, Canadian television broadcast in English three weekly episodes of "The Ethan Allen Story" written by Mortimer Braus. Only a synopsis of "The Ethan Allen Story" written by Mortimer Braus has survived. www.guide.com/tvshows/hawkeye-and-the-last-of-the-mohicans-1957/episode-7-season-1/the-ethan-allen-story/201900.

45. Soon after D. P. Thompson's death in 1864, his wife Eunice went to Madison, Wisconsin, to live with her daughter Alma, whose descendants became successful land investors in northern Wisconsin and influential figures in state politics well into the twentieth century. Thompson's only biographer, John T. Flitcraft (*The Novelist of Vermont* [1925]), traced several "Western Sketches" to *The Western Journal* (324).

46. The reputation of the Green Mountain Boys as serious, sober men in Daniel Thompson's version is reported to have reached Madison, Wisconsin, in the 1840s. The *Wisconsin Argus* newspaper reported on October 31, 1844, "Cutter's Temperance Play, 'Green Mountain Boys,' a troupe of five men, performed in Madison, Wisconsin, 31 Oct 1844." Younger, 278.

47. www.leg.state.vt.us/docs/2010/bills/Intro/H-491.pdf.

48. McLaughry.

49. *EAHK*, 1:36–37.

CHAPTER VII. SILENCE AND EXCLUSION:
MURDER, SLAVEHOLDING, AND PLAGIARISM

1. Ethan Allen to Guy Carleton, July 16, 1788, *EAHK*, 1:275.

2. Pell relies on Graham, 317.

3. *EAN*, 28.

4. Ibid., 9.

5. Ethan Allen to the Continental Congress, May 29, 1775, *EAHK*, 1:32.

6. Pell, 65.

7. *EAN*, 8.

8. For the complete text of the Bloody Acts, see *VSP*, 42. For Allen's reaction to the Bloody Acts, see Ethan Allen and others to the People . . . , April 26, 1774, and Ethan Allen to Crean Brush and Samuel Wells, May 19, 1774, *EAHK*, 1:13–17.

9. BHHall, 604–5.

10. *The Boston Gazette* reported Brush's death without details. Benjamin Hall accepted without questioning Boston's *Independent and Universal Advertiser* (May 21, 1778), a Whig newspaper's report that Brush shot himself in the head. He rejected as "tradition" and highly improbable that Brush cut his own throat in a New York lawyer's office.

11. Affidavit of Timothy Lovell, Norman File, The Stephen R. Bradley Papers, SCBH.

12. In 1774 Crean Brush invited his cousins John and Richard Hill from Ireland to join him in Cumberland County and sold them a tract of land to farm for $900, a debt they had reduced to $200 by late 1775. Richard Hill was among the posse at the Westminster courthouse in early 1775 who attempted to keep the court open prosecuting debtors. Robert Cochran, a lieutenant of Allen, led a contingent of Green Mountain Boys to join the "rioters" and took Hill to Northampton, Massachusetts, where a Patriot court released him and other posse men. Refusing to join Seth Warner's Green Mountain rangers in the expedition against Canada in late summer 1775, Hill fled Westminster for refuge in Boston, where he joined Brush and his brother. John had fled New York earlier after a mob of two hundred men dragged him and William Cunningham through the green, tore off their clothes, and stole Cunningham's watch for being Tories. General Howe later appointed Cunningham as warden of New York's Provost Jail where the British kept Ethan Allen in 1777–78. See Dandridge, 33.

13. On Levi Allen's arrest and residence in John Hill's brig or jail at Quebec between June and August 1797, see his letters to various recipients in *EAHK*, 2:507–32.

14. *Loyalist Settlement Claims*, Richard Hill, Digby, Nova Scotia, October 26, 1783, PRO, AO, 12/3, 147–52, William S. Clements Library, University of Michigan.

15. *EAN*, 77–78.

16. The only searches Allen mentions in his narrative were conducted several times as his captors looked for letters in a small trunk of clothing. *EAN*, 6. See also *EAN*, 98, on the hole whittled in the floor with a knife.

17. O'Callaghan, *Names of Persons*, 445. Hemenway, 5:587.

18. Lyons analyzes print material created by men for how they perceived women's sexual role in the period 1730–1830. She identifies the permissive,

Revolutionary-era depiction of women as "constitutionally unable to master their own sexuality." Conceptions of virtue and the need to preserve the social hierarchy of patriarchal marriage led to a redefinition of "the proper location for female sexual behavior in the Early Republic [as] marriage, and marriage only." In restrictive, Early National–era depictions, women are "pious, pure, and chaste" and without sexual urges, while men are unable to control their sexual urges and easily exploit women. In both instances, women are the weaker sex, either unable to control their sexuality or unable to fend off male sexual advances. Lyons, 163, 294, and 305.

19. Roth observes that the revolutionary conflict produced dramatic increases in homicide rates in Boston, New York, and Philadelphia (*American Homicide*, 149). On the Vermont frontier after 1775 political homicides were responsible for more than half the increase of homicides (143).

20. DePuy, 425–26, and Randall, 525.

21. "I do therefore give the said Dinah Mattis and Nancy her child their freedom to pass and repass any where through the United States of America with her behaving as becometh, and to trade and to traffic for herself and child as though she was born free, without being molested by any person or persons." *RC & C*, 1:92–93. *Vermont Historical Society Collections*, 1:249.

22. Williams, 347–51. Graham, 17–29.

23. Ethan Allen's black farmhands do not appear in the U.S. Census for 1791. In 1790 Frances Allen had moved to Westminster and resided with her aunt Margaret Brush Wall.

24. Guyette, 3–7. Melish, 3. *Burlington Free Press*, March 26, 1943.

25. Guyette notes that by 1775–76 Connecticut's black free and slave population exceeded that of all other New England colonies combined. The source of a large portion of Vermont's eighteenth-century settlers, Connecticut, was also the last New England state to gradually outlaw slavery in 1784 (25).

26. True, 227–29, and Graffagnino, "Vermont Attitudes Toward Slavery," 31–35.

27. Stearns, 747–49; Cothren, 15–17, describes the Brownsons' iron and silver mining ventures on Mine Hill. Trumbull, 358–56, reports the lead and silver mining effort.

28. The Stiles family owned several slaves. Benjamin Stiles's mother, Mary Stiles, owned Jeffrey Brace, an African-born slave who gained his freedom by serving in the Continental Army. He eventually settled in St. Albans, Vermont. See Brace.

29. Ethan Allen to Benjamin Stiles, November 16, 1785, *EAHK*, 1:184–85.

30. Levi Allen to Jacob Lansingh, December 3, 1784, and subsequent references to Prince in *EAHK*, 1:165, 284, 292–94.

31. John E. Goodrich was a son of Chauncey Goodrich, the Burlington printer-publisher of numerous editions of the *Narrative of Colonel Ethan Allen's Captivity*.

32. J. E. Goodrich, "Remembrance of Grandmother Allen," SCBH, Box 28.

33. After her marriage to Jabez Penniman in 1793, Frances Allen Penniman managed a household that sheltered three of her children by Ethan Allen, a girl and two boys, and three girls and a boy by Jabez Penniman.

34. Guyette, 7. Whitfield, see http://www.cctv.org/watch-tv/programs /persistence-slavery-early-vermont.

35. True, 228–29. Ethan Allen Hitchcock Papers, Library of Congress.

36. Weld, 79. Lewis. Houghton, 590–92.

37. Samuel Hitchcock to Lucy Hitchcock, December 16 and 18, 1801, *EAHK*, 2:717–19.

38. Correspondence between Ira Allen and Jabez and Frances Penniman concerning the costs of educating Ethan and Hannibal Allen in 1802 appears in *EAHK*, 2:726–27 and 730–34. The Pennimans obtained a decree against Ira Allen from the Court of Chancery in Rutland in May 1803 for $7,000 owed to Frances as a widow's right of dower in the estate of Ethan Allen. In June they obtained a writ in Franklin County Court for Franklin County Sheriff Prince B. Hall to execute the Rutland decree on eight rights of land in Swanton. For the case records of the May and June 1803 trials used to support their claims brought in the 1805 December term of Franklin County Court of Chancery, see Jabez Penniman et uxor vs. Silas Hathaway and Heman Allen for Ira Allen, Franklin County Court Records, Vermont State Archives, Middlesex, Vermont.

39. On Nimrod as "a great hunter before God," see Genesis 10:8–9. Nimrod was a descendant of Noah in the line of Ham, the lowest and least important of Noah's three sons and cursed by Noah: "Cursed be Canaan [Ham's son, Nimrod's grandfather], a slave of slaves shall he be unto his brothers" (Genesis 9:25). By 1800, a pseudo-biblical story placed Ham's dark-skinned descendants in Africa, still under Noah's curse, and thus justly enslaved by Divine Will. As the national debate over slavery and abolition drew closer to a civil war in 1861, the bishop of the Episcopal Diocese of Vermont, Burlington's Reverend John Henry Hopkins, published his lengthy defense of slavery, *Scriptural, Ecclesiastical, and Historical View of Slavery*. Hopkins began with a discussion of Genesis 9:25, affirming Noah's curse on Canaan as the legitimating foundation of chattel slavery under Divine Law (7–12). See Chittenden County Court Records, Caitlin & Jasper vs. Justin Warner, Vermont State Archives, Middlesex, Vermont.

40. Duling, 134–40.

41. Ethan Allen, *Reason*, preface, unpaginated.

42. Ibid., 5.

43. Ethan Allen to James Caldwell, February 7, 1785, *EAHK*, 1:168–69.

44. Ethan Allen to Benjamin Stiles, November 16, 1785, *EAHK*, 1:184–85.

45. Ethan Allen to Hector St. John de Crèvecoeur, March 2, 1786, *EAHK*, 1:190–92, 231.

46. *VG*, June 26, 1786, 3.

47. Ira Allen to Samuel Williams, June 6, 1795, *EAHK*, 1:443.

48. Hawke, 9; Pell, 13, 20.

49. Hawke, 8, 9, 11, 12, and 15; Pell, 14–19.

50. Hemenway, 1:568.

51. Ibid.

52. Anderson, 685, 687.

53. Ethan Allen, *Reason*, preface.

54. Anderson, 695.

55. *VG*, March 6 and 13, 1786, 1; June 6, 1786, 3; and May 5, 1788, 3.

56. *VSP*, 8:272–73.

57. Pell, 228. Allen's biographers have been comfortable with oxymoronic characterizations of their hero.

58. Jellison, 316–19.

59. Ibid., 309.

60. Bellesiles, "Works of Historic Faith," 69–83.

61. Bellesiles, *Revolutionary Outlaws*, 217–44.

62. Barr, 6, note 9.

63. The Anglicized "plagiarise" came into use in the seventeenth century. As in the eighteenth century, today taking someone else's work remains unethical and may incur various sanctions according to circumstances. In schools and universities, as well as learned and similar professions, customary sanctions have included suspension, expulsion, denial of privileges in a workplace, such as a hospital, and termination of employment. Enabled by the U.S. Constitution's Copyright Clause, the Copyright Act of 1790 granted copyright "from the time of recording the title thereof" for fourteen years and a right of renewal for an additional fourteen years if the author survived to the end of the first term. Donner, 361–78. Rosenoer, 34–35.

64. http://vermonthistory.org/research/museum-collections/faces-of -vermont/william-czar-bradley.

65. Ethan Allen to Benjamin Stiles, November 16, 1785, *EAHK*, 1:184–85.

66. *Reason the Only Oracle of Man*'s first printing and subsequent reprints: Bennington, Haswell and Russell, 1784 (actually 1785); New York, G. W. & A. J. Matsell, and Philadelphia, W. Sinclair, 1836; Boston, J. P. Mendum, Cornhill, 1854; New York, Scholars' Facsimiles and Reprints, 1940; Burt Franklin, 1972; and Charles Clendenen's "Ethan Allen Modernization," 2008–9.

67. For Allen's prolix version of Propertius's "in great endeavors even to have had the will is enough" or Seneca's "admire those who attempt great things, even though they fail," see Ethan Allen to St. John de Crèvecoeur, March 2, 1786, *EAHK*, 1:191.

68. *EAN*, 42.

69. Pell, 317.

70. Writing while "Near Chambly" gathering intelligence and recruiting Canadians to the American army, Allen advised Schuyler and Montgomery on the Americans' policy toward Britain's Mohawk allies : "the more You Kill of them the Better, Exchange of Life for Toys they find to be unequal." Ethan Allen to Philip Schuyler and Richard Montgomery, September 8, 1775, *EAHK*, 1:49.

CHAPTER VIII. THE HERO KEEPS
HIS REPUTATION

1. IANPH, 106–8.

2. Ibid., 108.

3. Muller, "Appraisal and Appreciation," x.

4. Quoted in Searls, 2, and in SSP, 287.

5. U.S. Department of Commerce, A 17–21 and A 123–80, 17–18.

6. SSP, 289–90.

7. Wilson, 95.

8. Searls, 4, 19; SSP, 287–91; Harris, "The Road Less Traveled By"; Graffagnino, *Vermont in the Victorian Age.*

9. Searls, 4.

10. Muller, "From Ferment to Fatigue, 1870–1900."

11. Searls, 5–6 and chapter 6.

12. The information on professor and librarian Whitney at Norwich comes from Gene Sessions, letter to the author, October 25, 2012. Professor Samuel Franklin Emerson came to UVM in 1881 to teach Greek and modern languages. He became chair of history and sociology in 1889. Dr. Emerson was a member of the American Historical Association and the Vermont Historical Society. The UVM *Catalog* for 1906–7 for the first time listed a course in U.S. history, and the rather spare history curriculum of six courses did not change until the addition of "Recent European History" in 1922. UVM Dean George V. Kidder wrote to Professor Frederick Tupper that as a UVM undergraduate his "work under Professor Emerson consisted of a course for one year in 'Ancient and Medieval History.'" Henry Wells Lawrence, Ph.D., taught Emerson's courses in 1910–11. Clarence Russell Williams, Ph.D. Yale (1922), joined the faculty in

1923. He had taught American history at Rutgers for a year, and at UVM taught the same courses as Emerson. He updated the "United States History" course to include the Spanish-American War and imperialism, the "Roosevelt regime," and the United States and World War I. In 1926 the *Catalog* announced a new course in "Vermont History" taught by Walter Hill Crockett, a special lecturer and full-time director of publications at UVM, who had recently published his uncritical but very useful five-volume *Vermont: The Green Mountain State* that in much greater detail generally followed the version of the state's early history as written by Zadock Thompson and Hiland Hall. On Professor Emerson, see *The Vermont Alumnus*, May 1939, a folder on him in SCBH, and the *University of Vermont and State Agricultural College Catalogs* for 1906–7, 70–71; 1914–15, 142–43; 1919–20, 117; and 1922–23, 133–34. On Professor Henry Wells Lawrence, see the *Catalog* for 1910–11, 79–80. For Clarence Russell Williams, see *Burlington Free Press*, September 18, 1923, Williams MSS, SCBH, and the *Catalogs* for 1923, 44, 138–39 and for 1926–27, 147. On Middlebury College's history faculty and courses, see *Middlebury College Course Catalog, 1909/10* and *Middlebury College Course Catalog, 1920/21*.

13. Carruth, xix–lix. See also Mary Robinson Perkins, 11–18, on Robinson's writing and his blindness.

14. Rowland E. Robinson, *Vermont*.

15. Ibid., 68.

16. Rowland E. Robinson, *Danvis Folks*. On Nathan Beaman, see his letter of 1835 about his role as Allen's guide, judged "an historic fable" in *Historical Magazine*, 3:273.

17. Rowland E. Robinson, *Vermont*, 68–69, 103, 118, 120–23.

18. Rowland E. Robinson, *Danvis Folks*, 218–19, 223–24; *EAHK*, 1:130–31.

19. Rowland E. Robinson, *Danvis Folks*, 222–23, 258–59.

20. Henry Hall, preface.

21. Lafayette Wilbur, 1:243–46, 248–57.

22. Ibid., 1:263, 266, 267, 269.

23. Crockett, chapter 24, 2:313–44.

24. Ibid., 2:216. On Sherwood, see Pemberton, chapters 5 and 6.

25. Crockett, 2:229 and 336.

26. Ibid., 2:337–38.

27. Wardner, "The Haldimand Negotiations," 21–24, and U.S. Congress, *Debates and Proceedings in the Congress of the United States*, 999–1000.

28. Crockett, 2:437.

29. Rife, "Vermont and Great Britain" and "Ethan Allen."

30. Rife, "Vermont and Great Britain," 50–51, 172–73.

31. Ibid., 176; *EAHK*, 1:126–43.

32. Wardner, *The Birthplace of Vermont*, 518.

33. Ibid., 518 and 522.

34. Wilbur.

35. Wardner, *The Birthplace of Vermont*. Graffagnino, "The Vermont 'Story,'" 89.

36. Pell, 223, 238.

37. Wardner, "The Haldimand Negotiations," 3–29.

38. Ibid., 3.

39. Ibid., 4–6, 28.

40. Ibid., 5–9.

41. Ibid., 16–26.

42. Graffagnino, "The Vermont 'Story,'" 91.

43. Jones, 40–41.

44. Wardner, "The Haldimand Negotiations," 27.

45. Mackintosh, 9–30.

46. *Reluctant Rebel* (1948) and *Catch a Falling Star* (1949), also published as *The Green Cockade* (1949).

47. Van de Water, *The Reluctant Republic*, 75. See Muller, "Appraisal and Appreciation," i–xxi.

48. Van de Water, *The Reluctant Republic* (1974 reprint), 256.

49. Graffagnino, "The Vermont 'Story,'" 92.

50. Muller and Hand, 63, 65.

51. Charles Miner Thompson, 75; Graffagnino, "The Vermont 'Story,'" 92.

52. Charles Miner Thompson, 79, 452.

53. Ibid., 427. D. Gregory Sanford, director of the Vermont State Archives, Paul Carnahan, librarian at the VHS, and J. Kevin Graffagnino, former director of the VHS and now director of the William L. Clement Library at the University of Michigan could not locate "Telemachus" in their collections or other references to it.

54. Ibid., 447–49, 456, 471, 473, and 538.

55. Graffagnino, "The Vermont 'Story,'" 93.

56. Williamson, 1.

57. Ibid., 96–97.

58. Ibid., 105.

59. Ibid., 127–44, 251.

60. Muller, "Ira Allen's *Vermont*," 228.

61. Williamson, 251. Several articles that grew out of the dissertation strengthen the case for the importance of the commercial relationship with Canada: Muller, "Smuggling into Canada," 5–21; "'A traitorous and Diabolic Traffic,'" 78–96; "Jay's Treaty," 33–56.

254 } Notes to Pages 188–201

62. Burt, 172.

63. Jellison, 248, 249–51. See chapter XII, "Flirting With Treason," chapter XIII, "The Haldimand Affair," and chapter XIV, "Vermont Stands Alone" for the treatment of the negotiations.

64. Quoted in Graffagnino, "Revolution and Empire," 177.

65. SSP, 115.

66. Bellesiles, *Revolutionary Outlaws*, dust jacket blurb.

67. Ibid., 186, 198, 200.

68. Ibid., 198, 200, 208, 210.

69. Ibid., 5.

70. Shalhope, xii.

71. Ibid., 183.

72. *Wall Street Journal*, August 22, 2011, sec. A, 11, and *The New York Review*, April 5, 2012, 64–65.

73. Hamilton, 10.

74. Randall, 493, and *EAHK*, 1:130–31.

EPILOGUE: THE HERO LIVES

1. By 1803 Timothy Dwight could report that deer and raccoon were scarce even in the northern Connecticut River Valley. Dwight, 4:215.

2. Bellesiles, "Autobiography," 84.

3. At Portsmouth in 1770 on a mission to acquire documents to validate titles to New Hampshire's grants of land that was in litigation at a New York court, Allen also bought 400 acres in Poultney for £4 from Daniel Warner and a similar parcel for £4 from Zenos Person of Springfield, Massachusetts. In 1771 he sold the Castleton right for £24 to Israel Homes of Salisbury, Connecticut.

4. Ethan Allen to William Burling and Benjamin Ferris, May 10, 1773, *EAHK*, 1:9.

5. Graffagnino, "Revolution and Empire," 52.

6. *EAN*, 71–73.

7. Ethan Allen to Horatio Gates, July 15, 1778, *EAHK*, 1:83–84.

8. On Ethan's attempt to get Levi's Vermont land through the Confiscation Court, see Ethan Allen to the Vermont Court of Confiscation, January 9, 1779, *EAHK*, 1:87. Levi Allen to *Connecticut Courant*, March 2, 1779, *EAHK*, 1:89–90. Levi Allen to the *Connecticut Courant*, March 30, 1779, *EAHK*, 1:91.

9. The Two Heroes Charter was granted to Ethan Allen, Samuel Herrick, and 360 associates on October 27, 1779. *VSP*, 2:192–95. The Resolution of the Council directed Governor Thomas Chittenden and Treasurer Ira Allen to collect payment from proprietors named in the Two Heroes grant by December 20.

The Council appointed Benjamin Wait to collect payments for the Two Heroes from proprietors living in upper Cumberland County and return them to the committee of Chittenden and Ira Allen. *RG & C*, October 28, 1779, 14.

10. Ethan Allen to Royall Tyler, August 28, 1787, *EAHK*, 1:245. Ethan Allen to Hector St. John de Crevècoeur, August 29, 1787, Sotheby's Catalog, 2009.

11. "All of it amounts merely to theory . . . inspired by good wine and punch." Ethan Allen to John Wheelock, August 25, 1788, *EAHK*, 1:279.

12. Ethan Allen to Guy Carleton, June 12, 1787, *EAHK*, 1:222–23.

APPENDIX A. VERMONT HISTORIOGRAPHY, 1807–50: CHANGE AND RESPONSE

1. Narrett, 101. For brief biographical information about Henry Stevens, see the work on his son Henry Stevens Jr., to whom he had written to remind him of his Vermont origins. Parker, 19–21.

2. Narrett, 80. In 1859 legislation changed the name of the Vermont Historical and Antiquarian Society to the Vermont Historical Society. The popular usage of the shortened name became the practice well before the legislation confirmed it. See Vermont Historical Society, *Constitution and By-laws*.

3. Duffy and Muller, " 'The Great Wolf Hunt' " and "Jedidiah Burchard."

4. See Stilwell's preface to *Migration from Vermont*. See Gilmore-Lehne, 227–49.

5. Ludlum, "Autumn, 1830–1870," chapters II, III, and IV.

6. Potash, *Vermont's Burned Over District*, part two.

7. Roth, *The Democratic Dilemma*, chapter 4.

8. The authors have a copy of the dissertation with the copious marginal notes and added pages Bassett appended to the manuscript that was accepted by Harvard University.

9. Wilson, chapter III.

10. Harris, "The Road Less Traveled By," 18, quoting from Bell, 450–66.

11. Harris, "The Road Less Traveled By," 24.

12. Ibid., 20 and 23.

13. Ibid., 28.

14. Ibid., 35.

15. See David Lowenthal's biography, *George Perkins Marsh: Versatile Vermonter* (1958).

16. Dublin, 33.

17. Shalhope, 339.

18. SSP, 194.

19. McGrane, *The Panic of 1837*, 107–8.

APPENDIX B. THE VERMONT HISTORICAL
AND ANTIQUARIAN SOCIETY: DOCUMENTING
AND PROMOTING A HERO

1. William Czar Bradley to Stevens, Westminster, Vermont, August 24, 1841, SCBH, Box 2, Folder 37.

2. Vermont Historical Society, *Constitution and By-laws*, 8.

3. Butler, 30–33. The publication included an appendix "containing the charter, constitution and by-laws of the Society." Cate, 13 and 15.

4. See Appendix C for career patterns of VHS members through 1849.

5. Nuquist, chapter 11, "The Courts of Vermont," 218–30.

6. Stevens to son George, Barnet, Vermont, September 20, 1841, HSC, Box 2, Folder 38. In a perceptive article "Why Are We Still Vermonters?" Roth, concentrating on three of the founders of the Society, Henry Stevens, Daniel P. Thompson, and George Mansur, makes a case for the Society's role evoking the spirit of Vermont's founders and the construction of the myths that emerged around Ethan Allen.

7. Stevens to Elisha Paine, Barnet, Vermont, HSC, Box 2, Folder 38.

8. Mansur to Stevens, September 22, 1841, HSC, Box 2, Folder 38. Mansur to Stevens, Montpelier, Vermont, September 29, 1841, HSC, Box 2, Folder 39. Also, J. Elliot to Stevens, West Brattleboro, October 16, 1841, HSC, Box 2, Folder 39.

9. Chipman to Stevens, Tinmouth, Vermont, October 12, 1841, HSC, Box 2, Folder 39.

10. Chipman to Stevens, Ripton, Vermont, August 2, 1841, HSC, Box 2, Folder 37.

11. Thompson to Stevens, Burlington, Vermont, September 30, 1841, HSC, Box 2, Folder 38. See Searls, 15.

12. Bradley to Stevens, Westminster, Vermont, August 24, 1841, HSC, Box 2, Folder 37.

13. Butler, 5.

14. Ibid., 6-8.

15. Ibid., 15–16.

16. Ibid., 26.

17. Ibid., 23.

BIBLIOGRAPHY

ABBREVIATIONS FOR CITATIONS

AAS   *Proceedings of the American Antiquarian Society*
AFP   Allen Family Papers
BHHall Benjamin H. Hall, *History of Eastern Vermont*
CCHS   Collections of the Connecticut Historical Society
DCHNY   *Documents Relative to the Colonial History of the State of New York*
EAHK   *Ethan Allen and His Kin: Selected Correspondence*
EAN   *A Narrative of Colonel Ethan Allen's Captivity*
EAP   Ethan Allen Papers
EIRA   *Ethan and Ira Allen: Collected Works*
GMB   Daniel P. Thompson, *The Green Mountain Boys*
GPM   George Perkins Marsh Collection
HSC   Henry Stevens Collection
IANPH   Ira Allen, *The Natural and Political History of the State of Vermont*
IRAAuto Ira Allen, "Autobiography" in Wilbur's *Ira Allen: Founder of Vermont*
NEQ   *New England Quarterly*
NYH   *New York History*
NYHSQ   *New York Historical Society Quarterly*
RG & C *Records of the Governor and Council*
SCBH   Special Collections, Bailey Howe Library, University of Vermont
SPVT   *State Papers of Vermont*, Mary Greene et al., eds.
SSP   Sherman et al., *Freedom and Unity*
TVE   *The Vermont Encyclopedia*
USDC   U.S. Department of Commerce
UVM   University of Vermont
VA   Vermont Archives, Office of Secretary of State
VG   *Vermont Gazette*
VSP   *Vermont State Papers*, William Slade, ed.

MANUSCRIPTS

Allen Family Papers, Special Collections, Bailey Howe Library, University of Vermont
Daniel P. Thompson Papers, Vermont Historical Society, Barre, Vermont
Ethan Allen Papers, Vermont State Archives, Montpelier, Vermont

Frederic Haldimand Papers, Microfilm, Bailey Howe Library, University of
    Vermont
George Perkins Marsh Collection, Special Collections, University of Vermont
Henry Stevens Collection, Special Collections, University of Vermont
John N. Pomeroy Collection, Special Collections, University of Vermont
Levi Allen Papers, Vermont State Archives, Montpelier, Vermont
Philip Schuyler Papers, New York Public Library
Stephen R. Bradley Papers, Special Collections, Bailey Howe Library,
    University of Vermont
Zadock Thompson Papers, Special Collections, University of Vermont

NEWSPAPERS

Boston Gazette
Burlington Daily Sentinel
Burlington Free Press
Connecticut Courant
Rivingtons Royal Gazette
Vermont Gazette

BOOKS AND PERIODICALS

Adams, Herbert B. *The Life and Writings of Jared Sparks.* 2 vols. Boston, 1893.
Adlum, John. *Memoirs of the Life of John Adlum in the Revolutionary War.*
    Edited by Howard H. Peckham. Chicago: Caxton Club, 1968.
The Aethenaeum, no. 2411 (January 10, 1874), 47.
The Affecting History of the Children in the Woods. First Vermont Edition.
    Windsor, VT: Printed by O. Farnsworth, 1809.
Allen, Ethan. *An Animadversory Address to the Inhabitants of the State of
    Vermont; with remarks on a proclamation, under the hand of His Excellency
    George Clinton, Esq; Governor of the State of New York.* Hartford: Watson
    and Goodwin, 1778.
——. *A Brief Narrative of the Proceedings of the Government of New York,
    Relative to Their Obtaining the Jurisdiction of That Large District of Land,
    to the Westward from Connecticut River.* Hartford: Eben Watson, 1774.
——. *Narrative of the Capture of Ticonderoga and of His Captivity and
    Treatment by the British. Written by Himself.* Fifth Edition, with notes.
    Burlington, VT: C. Goodrich & S. B. Nichols, 1849.
——. *A Narrative of Colonel Ethan Allen's Captivity Containing His Voyages &
    Travels etc. . . .* Philadelphia: Robert Bell, 1779.

[Allen, Ethan]. *The Present State of the Controversy Between the States of New York and New Hampshire, on the One Part, and the State of Vermont on the Other.* Hartford, CT: Hudson & Goodwin, 1782.

———. *Reason the Only Oracle of Man.* Bennington, VT: Russell & Haswell, 1785. Facsimile, Kraus Reprint Company, 1970.

———. *A Vindication of the Opposition of the Inhabitants of Vermont to the Government of New York, and of Their Right to Form an Independent Government.* Dresden, NH: Alden Spooner, 1779.

Allen, Ethan, and Ira Allen. *Ethan and Ira Allen: Collected Works.* 3 vols. Edited by J. Kevin Graffagnino. Benson, VT: Chalidze Publications, 1992.

Allen, Ethan, and Jonas Fay. *A Concise Refutation of the Claims of New Hampshire and Massachusetts Bay to the Territory of Vermont.* Hartford, CT: Hudson & Goodwin, 1780.

Allen, Ethan, et al. *Ethan Allen and His Kin: Correspondence, 1772-1819.* A Selected Edition in Two Volumes. Edited by John J. Duffy, Ralph H. Orth, J. Kevin Graffagnino, and Michael A. Bellesiles. Hanover, NH: University Press of New England, 1998.

Allen, Ira. "Autobiography." In *Ira Allen, Founder of Vermont, 1751-1814*, by James Wilbur, vol. 1:1–59. 2 vols. Boston: Houghton Mifflin Co., 1928.

———. *The Natural and Political History of the State of Vermont.* London, 1798. Reprinted Rutland, VT, 1968.

Allen, Orrin Peer. *The Allen Memorial (Second Series): Descendants of Samuel Allen of Windsor, Connecticut 1640-1907.* Palmer, CT: C. B. Fiske & Co., 1907.

Anderson, George P. "Who Wrote 'Ethan Allen's Bible'?" *NEQ* (1937), 10:685–96.

Arneil, Barbara. *John Locke and America: The Defence of English Colonialism.* Oxford: Clarendon Press, 1996.

Arnold, Benedict. "Benedict Arnold's Memorandum Book." *Pennsylvania Magazine of History and Biography* (1884), 8:363–76.

Assman, Aleida. "Memory, Individual and Collective." In *The Oxford Handbook of Contextual Political Analysis*, edited by Robert E. Goodin and Charles Tilly. Oxford: Oxford University Press, 2006.

———. "Transformations Between History and Memory." *Social Research*, 75:5.

Bancroft, George. *History of the United States of America, from the discovery of the American Continent.* 10 vols. Boston: Little, Brown and Company, 1854–78.

Barr, John L., comp. *The Genealogy of Ethan Allen and His Brothers and Sisters.* Burlington, VT: Ethan Allen Homestead Trust, 1991.

Barron, Hal S. *Those Who Stayed Behind: Rural Society in Nineteenth-Century New England.* Cambridge: Cambridge University Press, 1984.

Bartlett, John Russell. *Dictionary of Americanisms*. New York: Bartlett & Welford, 1848.

Bascom, Robert. "The Men with Ethan Allen at the Capture of Ticonderoga." *Proceedings of the New York State Historical Association*, 9:314.

Bassett, T. D. Seymour, ed. *Vermont: A Bibliography of Its History*. Vol. 4 of *Bibliographies of New England History*. Boston: G. K. Hall & Co., 1981.

Baxter, Katherine B. *A Godchild of George Washington*. New York: F. T. Neely, 1897.

Beckley, Hosea. *The History of Vermont: with Descriptions, Physical and Topographical*. Brattleboro, VT: George H. Salisbury, 1846.

Bell, Duncan S. A. "Mythscapes: Memory, Mythology, and National Identity." *British Journal of Sociology*, 54:73.

Bell, Michael M. "Did New England Go Downhill?" *Geographic Review*, 79:450–66.

Bellesiles, Michael A. "The Autobiography of Levi Allen." *Vermont History*, 60.

——. "The Establishment of Legal Structures on the Frontier: The Case of Revolutionary Vermont." *The Journal of American* History, 73:895–915.

——. *Revolutionary Outlaws: Ethan Allen and the Struggle for Independence on the Early American Frontier*. Charlottesville: University Press of Virginia, 1993.

——. "Works of Historic Faith: Or, Who Wrote *Reason the Only Oracle of Man*." *Vermont History*, 59:69–83.

Benedict, George G. *Vermont in the Civil War: A History of the Part Taken By the Vermont Soldiers and Sailors in the War for the Union, 1861–1865*. 2 vols. Burlington, VT: The Free Press Association, 1886.

Black's Law Dictionary. 4th ed. St. Paul, MN: West Group, 1968.

Bleecker, Ann. *The Posthumous Works of Ann Eliza Bleecker*. New York: T. & J. Swords, 1793.

Bloody Act of 1774. *Vermont State Papers*, 42.

Bolingbroke, Henry St. John. "Letters on the Study and Use of History." In vol. 3, *Works*. London, 1809.

Bort, Mary Hard. *Manchester: Memories of a Mountain Valley*. Manchester, VT: Manchester Historical Society, 2005.

Brace, Jeffrey. *The Blind African Slave: Memoirs of Boyrereau Brinch, Nicknamed Jeffrey Brace*. With Benjamin F. Prentiss. Edited by Kari J. Winter. Madison: University of Wisconsin Press, 2005.

Brown, Charles W. *Ethan Allen: of Green Mountain Fame, a Hero of the Revolution*. New York: M. A. Donohue & Co., 1902.

Browne, G. P. "CARLETON, GUY, 1st Baron DORCHESTER." In *Dictionary of*

Canadian Biography, vol. 5, University of Toronto/Université Laval, 2003, http://www.biographi.ca/en/bio/carleton_guy_5E.html.

Bryan, David. "Frances Montresor Buchanan Allen Penniman (1760–1834)" and "Jabez Penniman (1764–1841)." In *TVE*, 231–32.

"The Burghers of New Amsterdam and the Freemen of New York, 1675–1866." In *Collections of the New-York Historical Society for the Year 1885*. New York, 1886.

Burrows, Edwin G. *Forgotten Patriots: The Untold Story of American Prisoners During the Revolutionary War*. New York: Basic Books, 2008.

Burt, A. L. *The United States, Great Britain, and British North America*. London: Russell and Russell, 1968.

Butler, John Davie. "Deficiencies in Our History." In *An address Delivered Before the Vermont Historical and Antiquarian Society at Montpelier, October 16, 1846*. Montpelier: Eastman and Danforth, 1846. Reprinted 1940.

Caldwell, Renwick K. "The Man Who Named Vermont." *VH*, 26:249–300.

Carlisle, L. Diana. "Champlain Glass Company: Burlington's First Manufacturing Enterprise." *VH*, 68:136.

Carpenter W. H., and T. S. Arthur. *History of Vermont, from its Earliest Settlement to the Present Time*. New York: Lippincott and Grambo, 1853.

Carruth, Hayden. "Introduction: Vermont's Genius of Folk, Rowland E. Robinson." In *Danvis Tales: Selected Stories by Rowland E. Robinson*, edited by David Budbill. Hanover, NH: University Press of New England, 1995.

Casson, Herbert N. *The Romance of Steel: The Story of a Thousand Millionaires*. New York: A. S. Barnes, 1907.

Cate, Weston A. *Up & Doing: The Vermont Historical Society, 1838-1970*. Montpelier: Vermont Historical Society, 1988.

Chernow, Ron. *Washington: A Life*. New York: Penguin, 2010.

Chipman, Daniel. *The Life of Colonel Seth Warner. . . .* Middlebury, VT: L. W. Clark, 1848.

Chittenden, Lucius E. "Oration." In *Exercises attending the Unveiling and Presentation of a Statue of Gen. Ethan Allen at Burlington, Vermont, July 4th, 1873. . . .* Burlington, VT: Free Press, 1874.

Collections of the Connecticut Historical Society. Rolls of Connecticut Men in the French and Indian War, 1775-1762. Hartford: Connecticut Historical Society, 1903–5.

Cornelius, Elias. *Journal of Dr. Elias Cornelius*. Washington, DC, 1903.

Cothren, William. *History of Ancient Woodbury Connecticut, From the First Indian Deed in 1659 to 1854*. Waterbury, CT: Bronson Brothers, 1854.

Crockett, Walter Hill. *Vermont: The Green Mountain State*. 5 vols. New York: The Century House Co, 1921–23.

Cronon, William. *Changes in the Land: Indians, Colonists, and the Ecology of New England*. New York: Hill and Wang, 1983.

Cross, Whitney. *The Burned Over District*. Ithaca, NY: Cornell University Press, 1950.

Dandridge, Danske. *American Prisoners of the Revolution*. Project Gutenberg, 2004, http://www.gutenberg.org.

Degree, Kenneth A. "Impasse! Vermont's 1813 Legislative Session." *VH*, 78:151–80.

DePuy, Henry W. *Ethan Allen and the Green Mountain Heroes of '76*. Buffalo: Phinney & Co, 1853.

Dexter, Franklin Bowditch. *Biographical Sketches of the Graduates of Yale College with Annals of the College History, October, 1701–May, 1745*. New York: Henry Holt & Co., 1885.

Donald, David Herbert. *Lincoln*. New York: Simon and Schuster, 1995.

Donner, Irah. "The Copyright Clause of the U. S. Constitution: Why Did the Framers Include It with Unanimous Approval?" *The American Journal of Legal History*, 36:361–78.

Duane, James. *A Narrative of the Proceedings Subsequent to the Royal Adjudication, Concerning the Lands to the Westward of the Connecticut River*. New York: John Holt, 1773.

Dublin, Thomas. *Farm to Factory: Women's Letters, 1830–1860*. New York: Columbia University Press, 1981.

Duffy, John J., and Eugene A. Coyle. "Crean Brush vs. Ethan Allen: A Winner's Tale." *VH*, 70:103–10.

——. "Ethan Allen's Irish Friends." *VH*, 63:70–79.

——. "Loyalty and Its Rewards in Eighteenth-Century New England and County Down: The Cousins Crane Brush." *Eighteenth-Century Ireland/Iris an dá chultúr*, 16:118–34.

——. "Tales of the Olive Branch." *The American Neptune*, 59:15–20.

Duffy, John J., and H. Nicholas Muller, III. *An Anxious Democracy: Aspects of the 1830s*. Westport, CT: Greenwood Press, 1982.

——. "'The Great Wolf Hunt': The Popular Response in Vermont to the Lower Canadian Rebellion of 1837." [British] *Journal of American Studies*, 8:2, 153–70.

——. "Jedidiah Burchard and Vermont's 'New Measure' Revivals: Social Adjustment and the Quest for Unity." *VH*, 46:5–20.

Duling, Ennis. "Ethan Allen and *The Fall of British Tyranny*: A Question of What Came First." *VH*, 75:134–40.

Dwight, Timothy. *Travels in New England and New York*. 4 vols. Edited by Barbara Miller Solomon. Cambridge, MA: Belknap Press, 1969.

Einhorn, Robin. "On the Make." *The Nation* (February 4, 2010), 34.

Ellet, Elizabeth Fries. *The Women of the American Revolution.* 2 vols. New York: Baker and Scribner, 1848.

Ellickson, Robert C. *Order without Law: How Neighbors Settle Disputes.* Cambridge, MA: Harvard University Press, 1991.

Enderton, Herbert Bronson, comp. *Some Descendants of John, Richard and Mary Brownson of Hartford, Connecticut.* Vol. 1. San Jose, CA: Privately printed, 1969.

Exercises Attending the Unveiling and Presentation of a Statute of Gen. Ethan Allen at Burlington, Vermont, July 4th, 1873, Including an Oration by Hon. L. E. Chittenden. Burlington, VT: Free Press, 1874.

Fitch, Jabez. *The New-York Diary of Lieutenant Jabez Fitch. . . .* New York: Colburn & Tegg, 1954. Facsimile reprint of 1897 edition.

Flick, Alexander. *History of the State of New York.* New York: Columbia University Press, 1933–37.

Foote, Leonard. "The Vermont Deer Herd." Bulletin 13. Montpelier, VT: Vermont Fish and Game Service, 1946.

Force, Peter, ed. *American Archives.* Series 4. Vol. 2. Washington, DC, 1840.

French, Allen. *The Taking of Ticonderoga in 1775: The British Story/A Study of Captors and Captives.* Cambridge, MA: Harvard University Press, 1928.

Fryer, Mary Beacock. *Buckskin Pimpernel: The Exploits of Justus Sherwood.* Toronto: Dundrun Press, 1984.

Gabriel, Michael P. *Major General Richard Montgomery: The Making of an American Hero.* Madison, NJ: Fairleigh Dickinson University Press, 2002.

Geary, Patrick. *Phantoms of Remembrance: Memory and Oblivion at the End of the First Millennium.* Princeton, NJ: Princeton University Press, 1994.

Gillies, Paul. "Lucius Eugene Chittenden (1824–1900)." In *TVE*, 84–85.

Gilmore-Lehne, William J. "Reflections on Three Classics of Vermont History." *VH*, 59:227–49.

Gipson, Lawrence H. *The British Empire Before the American Revolution: The Triumph of Empire.* Vol. 11. New York: Random House, 1956.

Godfrey, William. *Pursuit of Profit and Preferment in Colonial North America.* Waterloo, ON: Wilfrid Laurier University Press, 1982.

Gold, Theodore Sedgewick. *Historical Records of the Town of Cornwall, Litchfield County, Connecticut.* 2nd ed. Hartford, CT: The Case, Lockwood & Brainard Company, 1904.

Goodrich, John E., ed. *The State of Vermont/Rolls of the Soldiers in the Revolutionary War 1775 to 1783.* Rutland, VT: The Tuttle Company, 1904.

Graffagnino, J. Kevin. "'The Country My Soul Delighted In': The Onion River Land Company and the Vermont Frontier." *NEQ*, 65:24–60.

———. "Revolution and Empire on the Northern Frontier: Ira Allen of Vermont, 1751–1814." Ph.D. dissertation, University of Massachusetts, 1993.

———. "'Twenty Thousand Muskets!!!': Ira Allen and the *Olive Branch* Affair." *William and Mary Quarterly*, 48:409–31.

———. "Vermont Attitudes Toward Slavery: The Need for a Close Look." *VH*, 40:31–35.

———. "The Vermont 'Story': Continuity and Change in Vermont Historiography." *VH*, 46:77–99.

———. *Vermont in the Victorian Age: Continuity and Change in the Green Mountain State, 1850-1900.* Bennington: Vermont Heritage Press, 1985.

———. "Vermonters Unmasked: Charles Phelps and the Patterns of Dissent in Revolutionary Vermont." *VH*, 57:133–61.

Graham, John A. *A Descriptive Sketch of the Present State of Vermont.* London: Henry Fry, 1797. Reprinted Bennington: Vermont Heritage Press, 1987.

Graydon, Alexander. Memoirs of a Life, chiefly passed in Pennsylvania, within the Last Sixty Years; with Occasional Remarks upon the General Occurrences, Character, and Spirit of that Eventful Period. Philadelphia: John Wyeth, 1811.

Griswold, Rufus W., ed. *Washington and the Generals of the American Revolution.* 2 vols. in one. Philadelphia: Carey & Hart, 1847.

Gross, Robert. *The Minutemen and Their World.* New York: Hill & Wang, 1976.

Guyette, Elise A. *Discovering Black Vermont: African American Farmers in Hinesburgh, 1790-1890.* Burlington: University of Vermont Press, 2010.

Halbachs, Maurice. *On Collective Memory.* Edited by Lewis A. Coser. Reprinted Chicago: University of Chicago Press, 1992.

Hall, Benjamin H. *History of Eastern Vermont, From Its Earliest Settlement to the Close of the Eighteenth Century.* New York: Appleton, 1858.

Hall, Henry. *Ethan Allen: The Robin Hood of Vermont.* New York: D. Appleton and Company, 1892.

Hall, Hiland. *The History of Vermont: From Its Discovery to Its Admission into the Union in 1791.* Albany, NY: Joel Munsell, 1868.

Hamilton, Edward R. Bookseller, Falls Village, Connecticut, "Catalogue," August 10, 2012, 10.

Harris, Christopher. *Public Lives, Private Virtues: Images of American Revolutionary War Heroes, 1782-1832.* New York: Garland, 2000.

———. "The Road Less Traveled By: Rural Northern New England in Global Perspective, 1815–1960." Ph.D. dissertation, Northeastern University, 2007.

Hartley, Lucy. *Physiognomy and the Meaning of Expression in Nineteenth-Century Culture.* Cambridge: Cambridge University Press, 2006.

Haughen, Brenda, and Andrew Santella. *Ethan Allen: Green Mountain Rebel.* Bloomington, MN: Compass Point Books, 2005.

Hawke, David. F. "Dr. Thomas Young: Eternal Fisher in Troubled Waters: Notes for a Biography." *New York Historical Society Quarterly,* 54:7–29.

Hawks, Francis L., and William Stevens Perry. *Documentary History of the Protestant Episcopal Church in the United States of America.* New York: James Pott, 1864.

Haynes, Stephen R. *Noah's Curse: The Biblical Justification of Slavery.* New York: Oxford University Press, 2002.

Headley, Joel Tyler. *Washington and His Generals.* 2 vols. New York: Baker and Scribner, 1847.

Hemenway, Abby Maria. *Vermont Historical Gazetteer: A Magazine Embracing the History of Each Town, Civil, Ecclesiastical, Biographical and Military.* 5 vols. Burlington, VT, and other locations: Published by Miss A. M. Hemenway, 1867–91.

———. *Poets and Poetry of Vermont.* Rutland, VT: George A. Tuttle, 1858.

Henderson, Desirée. "Illegitimate Children and Bastard Sequels: The Case of Susanna Rowson's *Lucy Temple.*" *Legacy: A Journal of American Women Writers,* 24:1–23.

History of America, Abridged for the Use of Children. Philadelphia: Wrigley and Berriman for Curtis, 1795.

"History of the Town of Clarendon." *History of Rutland County Vermont with Illustrations And Biographical Sketches of Some of Its Prominent Men And Pioneers.* Edited by H. Y. Smith and W. S. Rann. Syracuse, NY: D. Mason & Co., 1886.

Holbrook, Jay Mack. *Vermont 1771 Census.* Oxford, MA: Holbrook Research Institute, 1982.

Holbrook, Stewart H. *Ethan Allen.* 2nd ed. Portland, ME: Binford & Mott, 1988.

Holden, James, ed. "Some Additional Anecdotes and Data Concerning Ethan Allen." *Proceedings of the New York Historical Association,* 8:43.

Hopkins, John Henry. *A Scriptural, Ecclesiastical, and Historical View of Slavery from the Days of the Patriarch Abraham to the Nineteenth Century Addressed to Right Rev. Alonzo Potter, DD.* New York: W. I. Pooley & Co., 1861.

Hoskins, Nathan. *A History of the State of Vermont from Its Discovery and Settlement to the Close of the Year MDCCCXXX.* Vergennes, VT: J. Shedd, 1831.

Houghton, George P. "Henry Hitchcock." *Vermont Historical Magazine,* 11:590–92.

"Jared Sparks." In *Concise Dictionary of American Biography*. Edited by Joseph G. E. Hopkins. New York: Charles Scribner's Sons, 1964.

Jellison, Charles. *Ethan Allen: Frontier Rebel*. Syracuse, NY: Syracuse University Press, 1969.

Jenkins, John S. *The Lives of Patriots and Heroes, Distinguished in the Battles for American Freedom*. Auburn: J. C. Derby, 1847.

Jones, Matt Bushnell. *Vermont in the Making, 1750–1777*. Cambridge, MA: Harvard University Press, 1939.

Judson, L. Carroll. *The Sages and Heroes of the American Revolution*. In Two Parts. Philadelphia: Moss & Bros., 1854.

Kammen, Michael. *A Season of Youth: The American Revolution and the Historical Imagination*. New York: Oxford University Press, 1980.

Kaubler, Laurence Monroe. *Rattlesnakes: Their Habits, Life Histories, and Influence on Mankind*. 2 vols. Berkley: University of California Press, 1997.

Kemble, Stephen. "Return of the Killed and Wounded at Brandywine." In *Journal of Stephen Kemble & British General Orders 1775–1778*. New York: New York Historical Society, 1868.

Kitman, Marvin. *The Making of the President 1789: The Unauthorized Campaign Biography*. New York: Grove Press, 2001.

Klein, Milton M. "From Community to Status: The Development of the Legal Profession in Colonial New York." *New York History*, 60:136.

Leary, Lewis. "The Adventures of Captain John Smith as Heroic Legend." In *Essays in Early Virginia Literature Honoring Richard Beale Davis*, edited by J. A. Leo Lemay. New York: Burt Franklin & Co., 1977.

Leder, Lawrence H. *The Colonial Legacy*, vol. 4, Early Nationalist Historians. New York: Harpers, 1973.

Lewis, Herman. "Henry H. Hitchcock." In *The Encyclopedia of Alabama*, www.encyclopediaofalabama.org.

Lindeman, Micha, comp. "Ethan Allen and the Dentist," told by S. Slosser, http://medinfo.ufl.edu.

Lossing, Benson. *The Pictorial Field Book of the Revolution Or Illustrations By Pen and Pencil, Of the History, Biography, Scenery, Relics, and Traditions of the War for Independence*. 2 vols. New York: Harper & Brothers, 1860.

———. *Seventeen Hundred and Seventy-Six or the War of Independence: A History of the Anglo-Americans*. New York: Edward Walker, 1847.

Lowenthal, David. *George Perkins Marsh: Versatile Vermonter*. Seattle: University of Washington Press, 1958.

Lutz, Tom. *Crying: The Natural and Cultural History of Tears*. New York: Norton, 2001.

Lyons, Clare A. *Sex Among the Rabble: An Intimate History of Gender and Power in the Age of Revolution*. Chapel Hill: University of North Carolina Press, 2006.

MacKenzie, John. *The Empire of Nature: Hunting, Conservation and British Imperialism*. Manchester: University of Manchester Press, 1988.

Mackintosh, W. A. "Canada and Vermont: A Study in Historical Geography." *Canadian Historical Review*, 7:9–30.

Marsh, George Perkins. *Speech of Mr. Marsh of Vermont on the Mexican War, Delivered in the House of Representatives of the U. S., February 10, 1848*. Washington, DC: J. & G. S. Gideon, 1848.

McCauley, H. B. "The First Dental College: Emergence of Dentistry as an Autonomous Profession." *Journal of the History of Dentistry*, 51:41–45.

———. *Vermont Imprints: 1778 to 1820*. Worcester, MA: American Antiquarian Society, 1963.

McCorison, Marcus Allen, ed. *The Song of Vermonters—1779, By John Greenleaf Whittier*. Hanover, NH: The Pine Tree Press, 1956.

McGrane, Reginald C. *The Panic of 1837*. Chicago: University of Chicago Press, 1975.

McLaughry, John. "What Would Ethan Say?" *Burlington Free Press*, January 12, 2010.

McWilliams, John. "The Faces of Ethan Allen, 1760–1860." *NEQ*, 49:257–82.

Melish, Joanne Pope. *Disowning Slavery: Gradual Emancipation and "Race" in New England, 1780-1860*. Ithaca, NY: Cornell University Press, 1998.

Melville, Herman. *Israel Potter, His Fifty Years of Exile*. New York: Library of America, 1984.

Montresor, F. M. "Who Was Ethan Allen's Wife?" *Genealogical and Biographical Quarterly Bulletin*, 75:29–30.

Moore, Hugh. *Memoir of Col. Ethan Allen; Containing the Most Interesting Incidents Connected with his Private and Public Career*. Plattsburg, NY: O. R. Cook, 1834.

Morgan, Edmund S. *The Genuine Article: A Historian Looks at Early America*. New York: Norton, 2004.

Morrissey, Brendan. *Quebec 1775: The American Invasion of Canada*. London: Osprey Books, 2003.

Morton, Doris Begor. *Philip Skene of Skenesborough*. Granville, NY: Grastorf Press, 1959.

Muller, H. Nicholas, III. "Appraisal and Appreciation." In Frederic Van de Water, *Reluctant Republic*. Woodstock, VT: Countryman Press, 1974.

———. "Commercial History of the Lake Champlain-Richelieu River Route: 1760–1815." Ph.D. dissertation, University of Rochester, 1968.

———. "Early Vermont State Government: 1778–1815." *Occasional Papers,* Vermont Academy of Arts and Sciences, no. 5, 5–10.

———. "The East Union" and "The West Union." In *The Vermont Encyclopedia,* edited by John J. Duffy et al. Hanover, NH: University Press of New England, 2003.

———. "From Ferment to Fatigue, 1870–1900: A New Look at the Neglected Winter of Vermont." *Occasional Paper no. 7.* Burlington: Center for Research on Vermont, 1984.

———. "Ira Allen's Vermont." In *The Colonial Legacy,* vol. 4, *Early Nationalist Historians,* edited by Lawrence Leder. New York: Harpers, 1973.

———. "Jay's Treaty: The Transformation of Lake Champlain Commerce." *VH,* 80:33–56.

———. "Smuggling into Canada: How the Champlain Valley Defied Jefferson's Embargo." *VH,* 38:5–21.

———. "'A traitorous and Diabolic Traffic': The Commerce of the Champlain-Richelieu Corridor During the War of 1812." *VH,* 44:78–96.

———. "Vermont's 'Gods of the Hills': Buying Tradition from a Sole Source." *VH,* 75:125–33.

———, and Samuel B. Hand, eds. *In A State of Nature: Readings in Vermont History.* Montpelier: Vermont Historical Society, 1982.

Narrett, David E. "'I must again remind you that you are a Vermonter': Henry Stevens, Historical Tradition, and Green Mountain State Patriotism in the 1840s." *VH,* 66:65–99.

Nash, Gary B. *The Unknown War of Revolution: The Unruly Birth of Democracy and the Struggle to Create America.* New York: Penguin, 2006.

Nason, Elias. *Memoir of Mrs. Susanna Rowson.* Albany, NY: Joel Munsell, 1870.

Norton, Thomas Elliot. *The Fur Trade in Colonial New York, 1686–1776.* Madison: University of Wisconsin Press, 1974.

Nuquist, Andrew E. and Edith W. *Vermont State Government and Administration.* Burlington: Government Research Center, University of Vermont, 1966.

O'Callahan, Edmund Bailey. *The Documentary History of the State of New York.* Vol. 4. Albany, NY: Charles Van Benthuysen, 1851.

———, ed. *Names of Persons for whom Marriage Licenses Were issued by the Secretary of the Province of New York Previous to 1784.* Albany, NY: Weed, Parsons and Company, 1860.

Paltsits, Victor Hugo, ed. *Minutes of the Commissioners for Detecting and Defeating Conspiracies in the State of New York: Albany County Section.* Vol. 1. Albany, NY, 1909.

Parker, Wyman W. *Henry Stevens of Vermont*. Amsterdam: N. Israel, 1968.

Peach, Arthur W. "The Story of 'The Song of Vermonters, 1779.'" *VH* (1954), 22:288.

Peake, Miss. "The Physiology of Tears." In *The Lady's Newspaper* (London, England), Saturday, January 9, 1847, Issue 2, *Nineteenth Century UK Periodicals*, http://galenet.galegroup.com/ukpc.

Pell, John. *Ethan Allen*. Boston: Houghton Mifflin, 1929.

Pemberton, Ian. "Justus Sherwood, Vermont Loyalist, 1747–1798." Ph.D. dissertation, University of Western Ontario, 1973. Public Archives of Canada, Canadian theses on microfilm, no. 14049.

Perkins, Mary Robinson. "Rowland E. Robinson." In *Rowland E. Robinson: Out of Bondage and Other Stories*, edited by Llewellyn R. Perkins. Rutland, VT: Chas. E. Tuttle Company, 1936.

Perkins, Nathan. *A Narrative of a Tour through the State of Vermont, from April 27 to June 12, 1789, by the Revd Nathan Perkins of Hartford*. Woodstock, VT: The Yankee Bookshop, 1937.

Peterson, Charles J. *The Military Heroes of the Revolution: With a Narrative of the War of Independence*. Philadelphia: William A. Leary, 1848.

Potash, P. Jeffrey. "Deficiencies in Our Past." *VH*, 59:221.

——. *Vermont's Burned-Over District: Patterns of Community Development and Religious Activity, 1761–1850*. Brooklyn, NY: Carlson Publishing, Inc., 1991.

Radley, Alan. "Artefacts, Memory and a Sense of the Past." In *Collective Remembering*, edited by D. Middleton and D. Edwards. London: Sage, 1990.

Ramsay, David. *An Oration on the Advantages of American Independence*. Charleston, SC, 1778.

Randall, Willard Sterne. *Ethan Allen: His Life and Times*. New York: W. W. Norton, 2011.

Records of the Governor and Council of the State of Vermont. Edited by E. P. Walton. Vol. 1: July 1775–December 1777. 8 vols. Montpelier, VT: J. & M. Poland Steam Press, 1873.

Rees, Christine. "The Metamorphosis of Daphne in Sixteenth- and Seventeenth-Century English Poetry." *The Modern Language Review*, 66:251–63.

Report of a Committee . . . for the Erection of a Monument over the Grave of Ethan Allen (1858), George Perkins Marsh Collection, University of Vermont.

Richardson, E. P. "Copley's New York Portraits." *Winterthur Portfolio*, 2:1–13.

Rife, Clarence W. "Ethan Allen: An Interpretation." *New England Quarterly*, 2:561–84.

———. "Vermont and Great Britain: A Study in Diplomacy, 1779–1783." Ph.D. dissertation, Yale University, 1922.

Riffaterre, Michael. *Fictional Truth.* Baltimore: Johns Hopkins University Press, 1993.

Robbins, Daniel. *The Vermont Statehouse: A History and Guide.* Montpelier: Vermont Council on the Arts, 1980.

Robinson, Rowland E. *Danvis Folks and A Hero of Ticonderoga.* Edited by Lewellyn R. Perkins. Rutland, VT: The Tuttle Company, 1934.

———. *Vermont: A Study of Independence.* Boston and New York: Houghton Mifflin and Company, 1892.

Robson, Lucia St. Clair. *Shadow Portraits: A Novel of the Revolution.* New York: Forge Books, 2005.

Rosenbach, A. S. W. *Early American Children's Books.* New York: Kraus Reprint Corp., 1966.

Rosenoer, Jonathan. *Cyberlaw: The Law of the Internet.* Heidelberg: Springer, 1997.

Roth, Randolph. *American Homicide.* Cambridge, MA: Belknap Press.

———. "Why Are We Still Vermonters? Vermont's Identity Crisis and the Founding of the Vermont Historical Society." *VH,* 59:197–211.

Rowson, Susanna. *Charlotte Temple.* With an Introduction by Francis W. Halsey. New York: Funk and Wagnalls, 1905.

Russell, Howard S. *A Long Deep Furrow: Three Centuries of Farming in New England.* Hanover, NH: University Press of New England, 1976.

Russo, David J. *Keepers of Our Past: Local History Writing in the United States, 1820s–1930s.* New York: Greenwood Press, 1988.

Schoolcraft, Henry R. "Frances Allen." In vol. 2 of *The Women of the American Revolution,* compiled by Elizabeth Fries Ellet. 2 vols. New York: George W. Jacobs Co., 1900.

Schwartz, Barry. "Collective Memory and Abortive Commemoration: President's Day and the American Holiday Calendar." *Social Research,* 75:93.

Searls, Paul M. *Two Vermonts: Geography and Identity, 1865–1910.* Hanover, NH: University Press of New England, 2006.

Sellers, Charles Grier. *The Market Revolution: Jacksonian America, 1815–1846.* New York: Oxford University Press, 1991.

Severance, Frank Hayward, and Frederick Houghton. *The Story of Phinney's Western Almanack: With Notes on Other Calendars and Weather Forecasters of Buffalo.* Buffalo: Buffalo Historical Society, 1920.

Shalhope, Robert. *Bennington and the Green Mountain Boys: The Emergence of Liberal Democracy in Vermont, 1760–1850.* Baltimore: Johns Hopkins University Press, 1996.

Shapiro, Darline. "Ethan Allen: Philosopher-Theologian to a Generation of American Revolutionaries." *William and Mary Quarterly*, 3rd series, 21:242–43.

Sherman, Michael. "Ethan Allen and the History that Lives in Our Hearts." *Ethan Allen Oracle: Newsletter of the Ethan Allen Homestead*, May 1999.

Sherman, Michael, Gene Sessions, and P. Jeffrey Potash. *Freedom and Unity: A History of Vermont*. Barre: Vermont Historical Society, 2004.

Siebert, Wilbur H. *American Loyalists in the Seigniories and Eastern Townships of the Province of Quebec*. Ottawa: The Royal Society of Canada, 1913.

Smith, Donald. "Green Mountain Insurgency: Transformation of New York's Forty-Year Land War." *VH*, 64:198–235.

Smith, H. P., and W. S. Rann, eds. *History of Rutland County Vermont: With Illustrations and Biographical Sketches of Some of its Most Prominent Men and Pioneers*. Syracuse, NY: D. Mason & Co., 1886.

Spargo, John. *The Story of David Reading Who Was Hanged*. Bennington, VT, 1945.

Sparks, Jared. *Lives of John Stark, Charles Brockden Brown, Richard Montgomery, and Ethan Allen*, vol. 1 of *The Library of American Biography*. 3 vols. Boston and London: Millard Gray & Co. and James Kennett, 1834.

Stahr, Walter. *John Jay: Founding Father*. London: Hambledon and London, 2005.

Stanfield, Charles A., Jr. *Haunted Vermont: Ghosts and Strange Phenomena of the Green Mountain State*. Mechanicsburg, PA: Stackpole Books, 2007.

State Papers of Vermont. *Volume Six. Sequestration, Confiscation and Sale of Estates*. Edited by Mary Greene Nye. Montpelier, VT: Published by the Authority of Rawson C. Myrick, Secretary of State, 1941.

Stearns, Charles. "The First Mining Operations in North America." *Merchant's Magazine* (1852), 27:747–49.

Stilwell, Lewis D. *Migration from Vermont, 1776-1860*. Montpelier: Vermont Historical Society, 1948.

Stith, William. *The History of the First Discovery and Settlement in Virginia*. Williamsburg, 1747.

Stone, William L. *Life of Joseph Brant—Thayendanegea: Including the Border Wars of the American Revolution, and Sketches of the Indian Campaigns of Generals Harmar, St. Clair, and Wayne, and Other Matters Connected with the Indian Relations of the United States and Great Britain, From the Peace of 1783 to the Indian Peace of 1795*. 2 vols. New York: Alexander V. Blake, 1838.

Taylor, Alan. "The Paragon." *The New Republic* (February 3, 2011), 3.

Thompson, Charles Miner. *Independent Vermont.* Boston: Houghton Mifflin Co., 1942.

Thompson, Daniel P, *The Green Mountain Boys.* Edited by Carol E. and Ida H. Washington. Weybridge, VT: Cherry Tree Book, 2000.

———. *The Green Mountain Boys: A Historical Tale of the Early Settlement of Vermont.* Montpelier: E. P. Walton, 1839.

———. *Shaker Lovers and Other Tales.* Burlington, VT: Goodrich & Nichols, 1848.

Thompson, Zadock. "The Allen Family—an unpublished lecture, delivered at Burlington, March 16, 1852," "Compiled chiefly from papers in the collection of our venerable antiquarian friend, Henry Stevens, of Burlington." *Vermont Historical Magazine.*

———. *A Gazetteer of the State of Vermont; Containing a Brief General View of the State, a Historical and Topographical Description of all the Counties, Towns, Rivers, & c. . . .* Montpelier, VT: E. P. Walton, 1824.

———. *History of the State of Vermont, from its Earliest Settlement to the Close of the Year 1832.* Burlington, VT: Edward Smith, 1833.

———. *History of Vermont, Natural, Civil, and Statistical, In Three Parts, With a new Map of the State, and 200 Engravings.* Burlington, VT: Chauncey Goodrich, 1842.

True, Marshall. "Slavery in Burlington? An Historical Note." *VH,* 50:227–31.

Trumbull, James Russell. *History of Northampton, Massachusetts.* Vol. 1. Northampton: Northampton Press, 1898.

U.S. Congress. *Debates and Proceedings in the Congress of the United States.* Washington, DC: U.S. Congress, 1850. Fifth Congress, 1st and 2nd Sessions.

U.S. Department of Commerce. *Historical Statistics,* A 17–21 and A 123–180. 17–18.

Vail, R. W. G. "Susanna Haswell Rowson, the Author of Charlotte Temple; A Biographical Study." *Proceedings of the American Antiquarian Society* (n.s.), 42: part 1.

Van de Water, Frederic F. *Catch a Falling Star.* New York: Duell, Sloan and Pierce, 1944.

———. *Reluctant Rebel.* New York: Duell, Sloan and Pierce, 1948.

———. *The Reluctant Republic: Vermont, 1724-1791.* New York: The John Day Company, 1941.

———. *The Reluctant Republic: Vermont, 1724-1791.* Woodstock, VT: The Countryman Press, 1974.

Van Doren, Carl. *The American Novel.* New York: Macmillan, 1922. Bartleby. com, 2000.

The Vermont Encyclopedia. Edited by John J. Duffy, Ralph H. Orth, and Samuel B. Hand. Hanover, NH: University Press of New England, 2003.

Vermont Historical Society. *Constitution and By-laws of the Vermont Historical Society*. Woodstock, VT: Davis and Greene, Printers, 1860.

——. *Proceedings of the Vermont Historical Society*. Montpelier, VT: Tuttle & Co., 1872.

Vermont State Papers. Edited by William Slade. Middlebury, VT: J. W. Copeland, 1823.

Wallman, Lester J. "Medicine at UVM." In *The First Two Hundred Years*, edited by Robert V. Daniels. Hanover, NH: University of Vermont, 1991.

Ward, John William. *Andrew Jackson: Symbol For An Age*. New York: Oxford University Press, 1962.

Wardner, Henry S. *The Birthplace of Vermont: A History of Windsor to 1781*. New York: Charles Scribner's Sons, 1927.

——. "The Haldimand Negotiations." *VH*, 2:21–24.

Washington, George. *The Writings of George Washington from the Original Manuscript Sources 1745-1799*. Edited by John C. Fitzpatrick. Published by the U.S. Congress, 1931–40.

Weaver, John C. *The Great Land Rush and the Making of the Modern World, 1650-1900*. Montreal and Kingston: McGill-Queen's University Press, 2003.

Weems, Mason Locke. *History of the Life and Death, Virtues and Exploits of General George Washington*. Philadelphia: Mathew Carey, 1800.

Weinerman, Lea. "The Culture of Memory." *Monitor on Psychology*, 36:8, 56.

Weld, Theodore Dwight. *American Slavery As It Is: Testimony of a Thousand Witnesses*. New York: The American Anti-Slavery Society, 1839.

Whitfield, Harvey A. *The Problem of Slavery in Early Vermont, 1777-1806*. Montpelier: Vermont Historical Society, 2014.

Wilbur, James P. *Ira Allen, Founder of Vermont, 1751-1814*. 2 vols. Boston: Houghton Mifflin Co., 1928.

Wilbur, Lafayette. *Early History of Vermont*. 4 vols. Jericho, VT: Roscoe Printing House, 1899, 1900, 1902, and 1903.

Williams, Samuel. *The Natural and Civil History of Vermont*. Walpole, NH: Isaiah Thomas and David Carlisle, Jr., 1794. Second and enlarged two-volume edition published 1809 by Samuel Mills in Burlington.

Williamson, Chilton. *Vermont in Quandary: 1763-1825*. Montpelier: Vermont Historical Society, 1949.

Wilson, Harold. *The Hill Country of Northern New England: Its Social and Economic History, 1790-1930*. New York: Columbia University Press, 1936.

Younger, Henry C. "Theater Buildings in Madison Wisconsin, 1836–1900." *Wisconsin Magazine of History*, 30:278.

INDEX

Notes: Page numbers in *italics* indicate illustrations; page numbers followed by "n" indicate endnotes. EA refers to Ethan Allen.

Chittenden, Lucius E., 20, 111, 175
Chittenden, Martin, 71
Chittenden, Thomas: and Arlington
Junto, 201–2; Crockett on, 177;
DePuy on, 88; and EA's death,
15; and grain embargo, 11–12;
and Haldimand Negotiations, 85,
178, 180–82, 187, 191–93, 221;
historians' views of, 78–79, 81;
Hoskins on, 68; and Redding,
200, 235n34; and Two Heroes,
201, 254n9; as Vermont founding
father, 60; Williamson on, 187
Claghorn, James, 95
Clark, DeWitt Clinton, 219
Clendenen, Charles, 164
Cline, Allen Marshall, 172
Clinton, George, 90, 187, 202
Cochran, Robert, 34, 36, 39, 247n12
Cole, Ebenezer, 33
Cole, Thomas, 67
collective memory, 2–3, 94, 207
Collins, Huldah, 105
"Commercial History of the Lake
Champlain-Richelieu River Route"
(Muller), 188
consumerism, 6, 136, 207
Contrast, The (Tyler), 151
Cooper, James Fennimore, 67, 96, 133
Copley, John Singleton, 105, 241n27
Cornelius, Elias, 145
Crèvecoeur, Hector St. John de, 158
Crockett, Davy, 98, 169
Crockett, Walter Hill, 175–78, 182
Cross, Whitney R., 74
Crown Point, 44, 48, 98, 102
Cunningham, William, 247n12

Dean, Cyrus, 112
Deism, 17, 67, 160–63

Democracy in America (Tocqueville),
83
Democratic Dilemma, The (Randolph), 213
DePuy, Henry, 87–89, 125, 148, 169,
192, 244n23, 246n41
Descriptive Sketch of the Present State
of Vermont, A (Graham), 17
Dewey, Jedidiah, 32–33, 40
Draper, Lyman Copeland, 75
Duane, James, 31–34, 31, 36–37, 49,
56, 139, 232n20
Dublin, Thomas, 215
Duffy, John J., 211–12
Dwight, Timothy, 18

Early History of Vermont (Hall),
90–92
Early History of Vermont (Wilbur),
174–75
Eastman, Charles W., 220
Easton, James, 43–46
Edwards, Jonathan, 26
Einhorn, Robin, 4
Ejectment Trials, 30–33, 35–37, 40,
50, 57, 63–69, 82–83, 139, 186,
195
Embargo, 11, 70–71, 92, 112, 169,
211–12, 216
Emerson, Samuel Franklin, 172,
251–52n12
Enos, Roger, 15
Erie Canal, 72
Ethan Allen (Holbrook), 119–20
Ethan Allen and the Green Mountain
Heroes of '76 (DePuy), 87–88
Ethan Allen Elementary School, 135
Ethan Allen: Frontier Rebel (Jellison),
188–89
Ethan Allen Health, 137

Roberts, Daniel, 80
Robinson, David, Jr., 80
Robinson, John S., 80
Robinson, Moses, 35, 78
Robinson, Rowland E., 172–74, 185, 189
Robinson, Samuel, 29–30, 36, 68, 78
Robinson, Silas, 35
Robson, Lucia St. Clair, 125
Romance of Steel, The (Casson), 119
Roosevelt, Franklin, 3
Roth, Randolph, 213
Rowson, Susannah Haswell, 127, 245n31
Rush, Benjamin, 159
Russell, Howard S., 214

Safford, Samuel, 15
Schoolcraft, Anna, 127, 129
Schoolcraft, Henry Rowe, 105, 131
Schoolcraft, Margaret. *See* Brush, Margaret Schoolcraft
Schuyler, Philip, 48, 50–52, 123, 165, 173, 191, 232n13, 240n18, 251n70
Schwartz, Barry, 3
Scott, Charles, 195
Scott, Olin, 114–15
Searls, Paul M., 170–71
Sessions, Gene, 212
Shadow Portraits (Robson), 125
Shalhope, Robert E., 80, 191–92, 216
Shapiro, Darlene, 42
Sherman, Michael, 212
Sherwood, Justus, 98, 176, 179, 182, 186–87, 189
Skene, Philip, 37–38
Slade, William, 220
slavery, 148–55, 248n21, 248n23, 248n25, 248n28, 249n39
Smith, Oramel, 76, 218

Social Ferment in Vermont (Ludlum), 212
"Song of the Vermonters," 79, 222
Sparks, Jared, 32, 78, 81–83, *81*, 87, 89, 92–93, 95, 169, 183, 192, 236n11
Stansfield, Charles, 120
Stark, John, 75, 81, 169, 191
Steeple Davis, John, 103, 107–8
Stephenson, Peter, 20, 108, 110
Stevens, Henry, 65, 75–84, *76*, 86–88, 91, 93, 136, 169, 207, 211, 218–22, 256n6
Stiles, Benjamin, Jr., 150, 157, 164, 195, 248n28
Stiles, Ezra, 18, 20
Stilwell, Lewis D., 212, 214–17
St. John, 46–48, 51–53, 55, 91, 138, 140, 173, 199
Stone, William L., 86, 92
Sunderland, Peleg, 44
Susquehanna Land Company, 196

Taylor, Betsy, 122
Taylor, Frederick, 118
Telemachus, 186, 253n53
Ten Eyck, Henry, 35
Thompson, Charles Miner, 185–86
Thompson, Daniel P., 77, 87–88, 93, 96–101, 105–7, 136, 141, 206, 243n10, 244n11, 246n46; on EA as hero, 154; and EA lost children story, 120–22, 136; and Vermont Historical Society, 76, 218–20, 256n6
Thompson, Zadock, *84*, 215–16, 220–21; Benjamin Hall on, 90; on EA as hero, 95, 154, 169; and EA lost children story, 120–22, 163, 243–44n11; on early Vermont

REASON

THE ONLY

ORACLE OF MAN,

OR A

Compenduous Syſtem

OF

Natural RELIGION.

Alternately A D O R N E D with Confutations
of a variety of D O C T R I N E S
incompatible to it ;
Deduced from the moſt exalted Ideas which
we are able to form of the

DIVINE and Human

C H A R A C T E R S,

A N D F R O M T H E

Univerſe in General.

By Ethan Allen, *Eſq;*

B E N N I N G T O N :
S T A T E O F V E R M O N T ;
Printed by H A S W E L L & R U S S E L L.
M,DCC,LXXXIV.

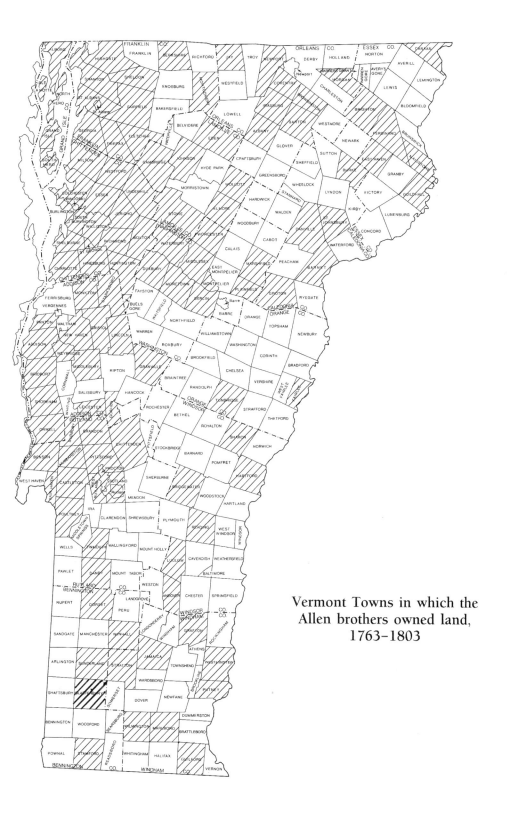

Vermont Towns in which the
Allen brothers owned land,
1763–1803